Jetpack Compose
by Tutorials

First Edition

By Tino Balint & Denis Buketa

Jetpack Compose by Tutorials

Tino Balint & Denis Buketa

Copyright ©2021 Razeware LLC.

ISBN: 978-1-950325-12-2

Dedications

"I would like to thank all the people who were with me while writing this book. To my family which encouraged me and was a shoulder to lean on during the long working hours. To my friends who kept shifting schedules in order to match with mine and were emotional support. To Marko and Ivana, who threw me a surprise party when the book was finished. Lastly, to my raywenderlich.com team. You were always positive, helped me grow and become a better author. All of you are the reason I was able to write my first book and become a book author."

— *Tino Balint*

"To my family and friends. Thank you for supporting me and being patient as I worked on this book. I've told you "no" so many times when you called me to hang out, but you never made me feel guilty about it. Many thanks to the team at raywenderlich.com, my co-author, the editors and everyone involved in this book. You've been a great support and I've enjoyed working with you."

— *Denis Buketa*

About the Authors

Denis Buketa is an author of this book. He's an Android developer who always tries to learn new things and get out of his comfort zone. Besides programming, he's a huge fan of audiobooks and podcasts. He also enjoys hanging out with friends and watching any kind of sport while having a cold beer.

Tino Balint is another author of this book. He's an Android developer with a passion for learning and growth. Likes all geeky things like reading and watching sci-fi and fantasy, playing video and board games. Besides indoor activities, he also likes working out, being in nature, scuba diving, trekking and other outdoorsy action.

About the Editors

Antonio Roa-Valverde is a tech editor of this book. He's a software engineer specialized in Android development. He has a background in Computer Science and R&D, which explains his interest in innovation and shaping new products with potential impact on people. He's also a co-organizer of the GDG Innsbruck and GDG Munich. He can be found close to the mountains, either hiking, riding the mountain-bike or catching some curvy roads by motorcycle.

Dean Djermanović is another tech editor of this book. He's an experienced Android developer from Croatia working at the Five agency where he worked on many interesting apps like the Rosetta Stone app for learning languages which has over 10 million downloads. Previously, he's been a part of two other mobile development agencies in Croatia where he worked on many smaller custom mobile solutions for various industries. He's also a part-time Android lecturer at the Algebra University College in Zagreb. Very passionate about Android, software development, and technology in general. Always trying to learn more, exchange knowledge with others, and improve in every aspect of life. In his free time, Dean likes to work out at the gym, ride a bike, read a good book or watch a good movie.

Sandra Grauschopf is the editor of this book. She is a freelance writer, editor, and content strategist as well as the Editing Team Lead at raywenderlich.com. She loves to untangle tortured sentences and to travel the world with a trusty book in her hand.

Filip Babić is the final pass editor for this book. He's an Android developer & Video Instructor with a huge passion for learning and teaching. He's also a public speaker at conferences, mentor to many people in his spare time and a content creator producing written content on his personal blog and on the raywenderlich.com website and video content for his IT-related podcast. He's also a Google Developer Expert for Android & Kotlin. When he's not talking about coding, writing about coding or coding in general, he plays D&D, Magic The Gathering, video games and does rock climbing.

About the Artist

Vicki Wenderlich is the designer and artist of the cover of this book. She is Ray's wife and business partner. She is a digital artist who creates illustrations, game art and a lot of other art or design work for the tutorials and books on raywenderlich.com. When she's not making art, she loves hiking, a good glass of wine and attempting to create the perfect cheese plate.

Table of Contents

Book License

By purchasing *Jetpack Compose by Tutorials*, you have the following license:

- You are allowed to use and/or modify the source code in *Jetpack Compose by Tutorials* in as many apps as you want, with no attribution required.

- You are allowed to use and/or modify all art, images and designs that are included in *Jetpack Compose by Tutorials* in as many apps as you want, but must include this attribution line somewhere inside your app: "Artwork/images/designs: from *Jetpack Compose by Tutorials*, available at www.raywenderlich.com".

- The source code included in *Jetpack Compose by Tutorials* is for your personal use only. You are NOT allowed to distribute or sell the source code in *Jetpack Compose by Tutorials* without prior authorization.

- This book is for your personal use only. You are NOT allowed to sell this book without prior authorization, or distribute it to friends, coworkers or students; they would need to purchase their own copies.

All materials provided with this book are provided on an "as is" basis, without warranty of any kind, express or implied, including but not limited to the warranties of merchantability, fitness for a particular purpose and noninfringement. In no event shall the authors or copyright holders be liable for any claim, damages or other liability, whether in an action of contract, tort or otherwise, arising from, out of or in connection with the software or the use or other dealings in the software.

All trademarks and registered trademarks appearing in this guide are the properties of their respective owners.

Before You Begin

This section tells you a few things you need to know before you get started, such as what hardware and software you'll need, where to find the project files for this book, and more.

What You Need

To follow along with this book, you'll need the following:

- **Kotlin 1.4**: Since Jetpack Compose relies on a special Kotlin compiler, you need Kotlin 1.4 both to write the code and for the compiler to process special Jetpack Compose annotations.

- **Android Studio Canary**: Jetpack Compose is still in its infancy, in an alpha version, and you need to use bleeding edge versions of Android Studio to use it. Currently, that's an Android Studio Canary build — currently the Arctic Fox release.

- **Android 5.1+**: The `minimumSdkVersion` for the projects targets API 21, so you need a device or an emulator running API 21 or higher.

- **Jetpack Compose Beta04 or greater**: This is the Jetpack Compose version you'll use in the book, and it represents one of the latest versions out there. But because Jetpack Compose is updated every few weeks, there might be a newer version available by the time you read this. We suggest following the book and using the projects with the version we used. You can always explore newer versions of the toolkit, but you might have to apply different migrations to the code. After all, things change frequently in beta versions!

Book Source Code & Forums

Where to download the materials for this book

The materials for this book can be cloned or downloaded from the GitHub book materials repository:

- https://github.com/raywenderlich/jet-materials/tree/editions/1.1

Forums

We've also set up an official forum for the book at forums.raywenderlich.com. This is a great place to ask questions about the book or to submit any errors you may find.

Introduction

If you've been an Android developer even for a few months, you probably thought that the UI toolkit you use every day is not that easy to grasp. Over the years, as Android developed and grew as a platform, the tools for building user interfaces became more powerful and the design system became more beautiful.

Sadly, with all those changes and with newer versions of Android, the process of building interfaces became **more complex**. Additionally, it became increasingly harder to write code that supports all Android versions, as many new APIs and features aren't fully backwards compatible. That means that building components from the standard toolkit doesn't guarantee that those components will work on older versions of the operating system.

Moreover, as you start learning Android development, the first thing you notice is the overwhelming number of different programming and markup languages you need to learn. Not only do you find Android apps written in Kotlin or Java, but you also have to learn Groovy for your build scripts and XML for your UI development.

This **further increases the complexity** of learning Android development, and it makes it harder to follow the code. You have to read through multiple different files, just to learn how a single feature of the project works. If only there was a tool that uses Kotlin, has a clear syntax and lets you develop UI without much sweat…

Well, look no more! **Jetpack Compose** is the one UI toolkit to rule them all. It's a fresh look at building user interfaces, providing:

• A Kotlin-powered API.

• Declarative ways to build the UI so it reacts to state changes.

• A powerful and composable set of components that you can combine, style and animate.

In this book, you'll learn how to build a powerful app using Jetpack Compose, how to style your apps using Material Design, special animations and state transitions, how to use modifiers and much more! This book will serve you as a central point that holds all the information you need to dive deep into Jetpack Compose, then apply it to your personal and production level projects.

How to read this book

The book is aimed at Android developers who aren't familiar with Jetpack Compose and developers who know a little about the toolkit, but haven't had the chance to use it.

If you're **completely new to Jetpack Compose**, we recommend reading it one chapter at a time, in the **order of sections and chapters** shown in the table of contents.

If you're **familiar with the fundamentals** of Jetpack Compose, you can skip to "Section II: Composing User Interfaces" instead. There, you'll continue learning about custom UI components, state management and best practices for styling your UI.

If you're **already using Jetpack Compose** in your projects but want to know about more complex topics and interoperability with legacy UI toolkits, jump to "Section III: Building Complex Apps With Jetpack Compose". You'll build complex use cases on a real-world project and learn about animations and the Compose lifecycle.

At whatever level of knowledge you are, it's useful to check out the book structure and its contents. This book is split into three main sections.

Section I: Getting Started With Jetpack Compose

Android UI Toolkit is **over 10 years old now**! Over the years, it has received numerous updates in terms of functionality, types of UI elements it provides and optimizations. But because of the way the UI team initially developed the toolkit, it also **grew in complexity and the amount of code** for even the simplest of components.

Finally, in 2020, a miracle happened: **Jetpack Compose**. The new UI toolkit was announced and started being seriously developed by Google. Jetpack Compose is a new and fresh toolkit, **built completely in Kotlin**, that offers a clean and **declarative** way to develop custom components and beautiful interfaces.

In this section, you'll learn all about:

- The fundamental components Jetpack Compose provides.

- How to build common user interface components such as containers, navigation controls and lists.

In these four chapters, you'll dive deep into the API and learn so much about this wonderful new UI toolkit.

Section II: Composing User Interfaces

When working on apps and user interfaces, it's not only important to know what each piece of the interface should be, but also how all these pieces **come together** to build a beautiful and fully-functional design that'll wow your users.

Now that you've amassed quite a lot of knowledge about the basics of Jetpack Compose and its fundamental UI elements, you're ready to dive deeper into building custom Compose elements, **managing their state** in a performant way and **styling them** using modifiers and built-in Material Design features.

Over the next four chapters, you'll learn how to:

- Attach `LiveData` structures to your state management.

- Rely on different styling modifiers.

- Combine these topics to create a powerful UI!

Section III: Building Complex Apps With Jetpack Compose

Now that you've built your app's basic UI, it's time to take it to another level. In this section, you'll apply custom, complex designs that help you stand out from thousands of similar apps! This usually involves building **complex custom components** and applying **animations** to represent state changes when your users interact with the UI.

Over the next five chapters, you'll dive deeper into the Jetpack Compose API to learn how to:

• Connect Compose UI to legacy Android code.

• React to Compose UI lifecycles.

• Animate different state changes and user interactions.

In the process, you'll build an awesome app that represents a real-world project and you'll apply some best practices to improve the **user experience**.

We hope you're ready to jump in and enjoy getting to know the power of Jetpack Compose!

Section I: Getting Started with Jetpack Compose

Android UI Toolkit is **over 10 years old now**! Over the years, it has received numerous updates in terms of functionality, types of UI elements it provides and optimizations. But because of the way the UI team initially developed the toolkit, it also **grew in complexity and the amount of code** for even the simplest of components.

Finally, in 2020, a miracle happened: **Jetpack Compose**. The new UI toolkit was announced and started being seriously developed by Google. Jetpack Compose is a new and fresh toolkit, **built completely in Kotlin**, that offers a clean and **declarative** way to develop custom components and beautiful interfaces.

In this section, you'll learn all about:

- The fundamental components Jetpack Compose provides.

- How to build common user interface components such as containers, navigation controls and lists.

In these four chapters, you'll dive deep into the API and learn so much about this wonderful new UI toolkit.

Chapter 1: Developing UI in Android

By Denis Buketa

The **user interface (UI)** is the embodiment of your mobile app. You could say that it's an ever-evolving relationship between a user and the system they interact with. When you look at the big picture, it's easy to understand why UI design is so important: It's the reason products either fail or succeed.

In this chapter, you'll learn about the **design concepts** of the existing **Android UI toolkit**. You'll review the basic building blocks, how to make **custom views**, the process to display the layout on your screen and the **principles** the current toolkit is built upon. You'll learn about the reasoning behind these concepts, their drawbacks, how they evolved and how they influenced the idea behind **Jetpack Compose** — or Compose, for short.

After that, you'll learn about Compose — the awesome new UI toolkit for Android, which is making all the Android kids super hyped! :]

You'll see how Compose approaches each of the concepts of the current Android UI toolkit and why it's the next evolutionary step in Android development.

Unwrapping the Android UI toolkit

In Android, you build your UI as a hierarchy of **layouts** and **widgets**. In code, layouts are represented by ViewGroup objects. They are **containers** that control the **position and behavior of their children** on the screen.

On the other hand, widgets are represented by View objects. They display individual UI components like buttons and text boxes.

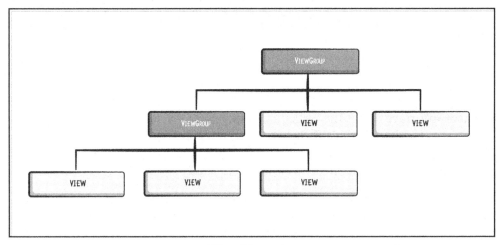

View Hierarchy

As you can see in the image, you define each screen in Android as a tree of ViewGroup and View objects. ViewGroups can contain other ViewGroups and Views. If you're familiar with computer science structures, you'll recognize that ViewGroups are like **nodes** of the **tree structure**, where each View is a **leaf**.

The most important thing to notice here is that your View objects are responsible for the look of your UI. So it makes sense to begin this journey by looking at how you implement and use the View class.

View

As mentioned before, a View represents the *basic building block* for UI components. It occupies a rectangular area on the screen where it **draws** the specific UI component, like a button or a text field.

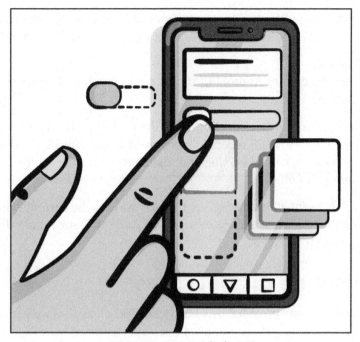

Users Interact with the UI

But user interfaces aren't designed to be static — at least, most of them aren't. Your users want to interact with the UI by clicking, dragging or typing into it.

Fortunately, Views also support this type of interaction and events. Specialized Views often expose a specific set of **listeners** that you use to manage interactive events.

As you know, *with great power comes great responsibility*, and the Android View component is definitely powerful. Every UI component you've ever used is a direct or indirect subclass of View.

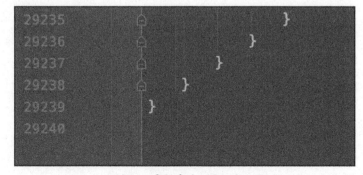

Lines of Code in View.java

As Android grew as a platform, `View` got bigger and bigger. In the current API, the **View.java** file has *over 29,000 lines of code*. Don't believe it? Open it and check it by yourself! :]

This means that the current Android UI toolkit *scales poorly* and is increasingly harder to maintain.

Imagine yourself trying to fix a specific bug in the `View` class file. Every small change you make in the base `View` will reflect in who knows how many ways on the entire Android UI toolkit! You could be fixing one small bug, but at the same time creating dozens or hundreds of others!

`View` is *beyond the point of refactoring*, yet the only way for the current Android UI toolkit to evolve is to make this class even bigger. And this issue is amplified when you try to build **custom** Views.

Implementing custom views

Despite the functionality provided by `View` and the other custom widgets the current API offers, there are cases where you need to create custom views to solve specific problems.

Given how the entire UI toolkit is built on top of the `View`, you'd think it would be very easy to build something custom, that extends the `View` as its parent?

Well, think again! If you wanted to build even the simplest of custom `View`s, you'd have to go through all of these steps:

```
class MyWidget : View {

    // 1 - Overriding constructors
    ...

    // 2 - Inflating layout
    ...

    // 3 - Parsing attributes
    ...

    // 4 - Getters
    ...

    // 5 - Setters
    ...

    // 6 - Measuring and Layout
    ...
```

```
    // 7 - Handling touch events
    ...
  }
```

The first thing you have to do is to create a class that extends from `View`. Writing custom views to solve a particular problem is hard. There are a lot of things that you need to do right:

1. You have to override the `View` constructors. Yes, there are multiple, each with its own use case!

2. To inflate the specific layout, you have to define it as an **XML resource**.

3. To customize your `View` from XML, you have to create special XML attributes and add them to the **attrs.xml** file.

4. To modify your custom widget, you have to add all the necessary **properties** and their respective **getters and setters** to the class.

5. You have to think about **styles** and how your `View` behaves in different display modes, such as **light and dark** theme.

6. If you need **custom measurements** or layouts, you have to override the specific callbacks.

7. Do you need to handle touch events? Then you need **extra code to add touch & gesture support**!

As you can see, there are a lot of things that you need to think about when writing custom views. And as a developer, you probably want a clean and easy API that you can easily expand with your custom implementation. Unfortunately, the current Android UI toolkit is anything but easy.

ViewGroup

After all the work you've put into implementing your custom view, it's time to add it to your UI. But before you do, you have to choose the correct `ViewGroup` for your container. And that might not be such an easy decision. You'll probably end up with more than one. When creating a layout for your screen, you always have to choose which `ViewGroup` to use as your root view.

There are many different types of `ViewGroups` in Android. Some common implementations are `LinearLayout`, `RelativeLayout` and `FrameLayout`. Each of these exposes a different set of parameters you can use to arrange their children:

- **LinearLayout**: Use this when you want to organize children in a row or column.

- **RelativeLayout**: Enables you to specify the location of child objects relative to each other or to the parent.

- **FrameLayout**: One of the simplest containers, usually used to store one widget or `Fragment`.

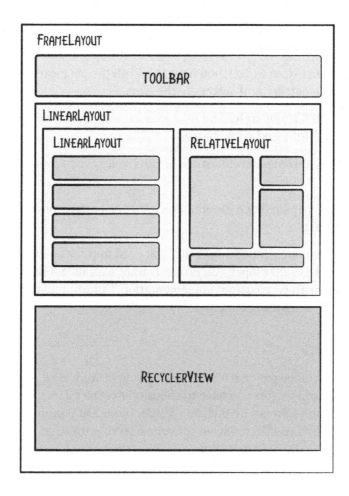

Nested ViewGroups

However, UIs are not always so simple that you can use just one `ViewGroup` in your layouts. When building more complicated UIs, you often define different areas of the screen and use the specific `ViewGroup` that best matches your use case.

Usually, that leads to a lot of **nested** `ViewGroups`, which makes your code hard to read and maintain. Most importantly, it **decreases the performance** of your app.

Recently, the Android UI toolkit received a new `ViewGroup`, to address this issue — `ConstraintLayout`. It allows you to create large and complex layouts with a flat view hierarchy. In short, you use it to create complex **constraints** between views so you don't have to nest so many layouts. Each constraint describes if a `View` is constrainted to the start, end, top or bottom of another `View`.

However this doesn't quite solve the problem of nested layouts. There are times when you can still get better performance by combining simpler `ViewGroups` rather than using `ConstraintLayout`.

Also, you could argue that sometimes in complex UIs, it's easier to understand how the layout is organized when you have some level of nesting. Ironic, right? :]

As you can see, it's not easy to pick a `ViewGroup` when building your UIs. Usually, it becomes easier as you gain experience, but new developers still have a hard time when they start playing with Android.

Displaying views

Now, imagine you've successfully created your layout. You picked just the right `Views`. You created a custom `View` to solve a specific problem. You used the correct `ViewGroups` to organize your `Views`. Now, you want to display your beautiful layout.

But there are *still many more steps* you need to take to achieve this behavior!

As you probably have experience with the Android UI toolkit, you know that most of your UI is defined in XML files. Android provides an XML schema for including `ViewGroup` and `View` classes. So, your layout might look like this:

```xml
<?xml version="1.0" encoding="utf-8"?>
<FrameLayout
    xmlns:android="http://schemas.android.com/apk/res/android"
    android:layout_width="match_parent"
    android:layout_height="match_parent">

    <TextView
        android:layout_width="wrap_content"
        android:layout_height="wrap_content"
        android:text="Hello World"
```

```
        android:layout_gravity="center"/>

  </FrameLayout>
```

This *simple* layout displays a text saying "Hello World".

Cool! But all this work *still isn't enough* to display your UI. To render that layout on the screen, you need to connect it with your Activity or Fragment. If you're working with an Activity, you'd do something like this:

```
class MyActivity : AppCompatActivity() {

  override fun onCreate(savedInstanceState: Bundle?) {
    super.onCreate(savedInstanceState)
    setContentView(R.layout.activity_layout)
  }
}
```

Using setContentView(ViewResource), the Activity takes care of creating a window where you place your UI. This is the simplest way you can display UI elements in Android.

Fragments, on the other hand, represent a piece of behavior or a portion of the UI within an Activity. You can combine multiple Fragments in a single Activity to build a multi-pane UI, and you can also reuse a Fragment in multiple activities. Think of a Fragment as a modular section of an Activity.

```
class MyFragment : Fragment() {

  override fun onCreateView(
    inflater: LayoutInflater,
    container: ViewGroup?,
    savedInstanceState: Bundle?
  ): View {
      return inflater.inflate(R.layout.layout, container, false)
  }
}
```

To provide a layout for a fragment, you must implement onCreateView(). The Android system calls it when it's time for the fragment to draw its UI.

Your implementation of this method must return a View that's the root of your Fragment's layout. To return a layout from onCreateView(), you **inflate** it from a layout resource you define in XML. To help you do so, onCreateView() provides a LayoutInflater — a special component that reads the XML definition, and builds Kotlin and Java objects using the attributes and properties you define, such as the View **width**, **height**, **color**, **constraints** and custom attributes.

This process is also called **layout inflation**, as layouts are similar to baloons — you need to inflate them to take shape and do some work! :]

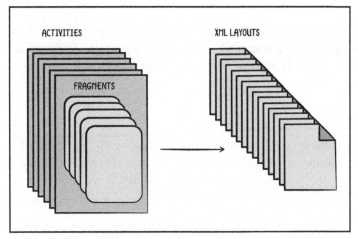

Non-scaleable Layout System

Imagine now, that you you need a screen with an Activity and a Fragment inside it. To create that screen, you'd need the following files: **MyActivity.kt, my_activity.xml, MyFragment.kt, my_fragment.xml**, extra attributes defined in **attrs.xml** and special styling defined in **styles.xml**.

For such a **simple screen**, you have to write **too much code**.

As you see, the current Android UI Toolkit scales *very poorly*. Modern applications usually have dozens, if not hundreds, of features each with its own XML layout, attributes, styles, Kotlin or Java code and much more.

On top of that, it's impossible to organize those files in the resource folder. And if you decide to define list or page items for **dynamic UI components**, things get **even more complicated**.

Separating concerns

It's hard enough to get from a simple layout definition to displaying your UI on the screen, but if you really want to see your UI in action, you have to connect it to your business logic.

You always hear that you should separate your business logic from your UI logic. This concept is known as **separation of concerns (SoC)**. It's a design principle in computer science that says you should separate a program into distinct sections, with each section addressing a distinct **concern**.

A concern is a set of information that affects the code of a computer program. It can be as general as the details of the hardware that runs an app or as specific as the name of the class to instantiate.

SoC includes two main concepts: **coupling** and **cohesion**. You can think of your app as a group of modules. **Each module contains many units.** In general, you want to reduce coupling as much as possible and increase cohesion. But what do these terms mean?

Coupling & Cohesion

Dependencies between different modules represent **coupling**. Parts of one module can influence another. If you make a change to the code in one module, depending on the coupling, you'll have to change other modules as well.

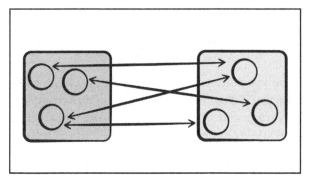

Coupling

On the other hand, cohesion describes how the units inside of a given module belong to one another.

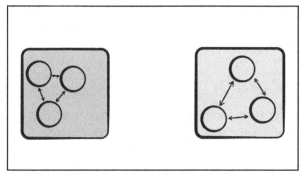

Cohesion

So, the goal is to group as much related code as possible. That way, your code is maintainable over time and scales as your app grows.

With this in mind, think about how you organize code when implementing the Android UI. Note that you have two modules that depend on each other.

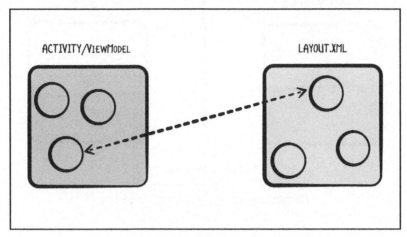

Modules when Implementing Android UI

Why did you define these modules like this? Well, each of the modules is written in another language, and the differences between them cause the framework to require this kind of design.

Your `ViewModel` and layout can be closely related and, therefore, coupled but you don't have a choice of drawing the line of separation, because you write them in different languages, with different semantical properties.

In other words, these units **should be cohesive, but they can't be because of the language difference**. However, they rely on each other in order to work, but the **dependency is implicit**.

Again, this is because of the language difference and the fact that you can't directly communicate to the XML file. You have to inflate it into a Kotlin or Java object, and then communicate with that.

For this reason, as your ViewModel and your layout grow, they become very difficult to maintain.

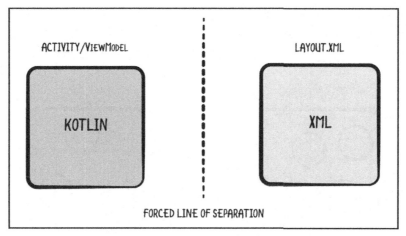

Forced Line of Separation of Concerns

Imperative thinking

Whenever the user performs a specific action in your UI, you have to capture that event, update the **View state** and the UI to represent the newly given state. You do this over and over throughout the lifecycle of your app.

If you want something to animate when your state changes, you need to define how your view changes between different states. This programming style is known as **imperative programming**.

Being imperative means you are commanding or telling the program to do what you want or show the Views you need. It uses statements in the form of functions to change a program's state. Imperative programming focuses on describing *how* a program should operate.

Traditionally, in Android, you use the imperative style to build and manage your UIs. You often create a fully-functional UI and mutate it later using functions, when the state changes.

Imagine a UI for a calendar event. The required properties are a title, an event owner and a link to an online meeting. Other optional properties are a guest list and a room name. If there are more than five guests, the app should collapse the guest list.

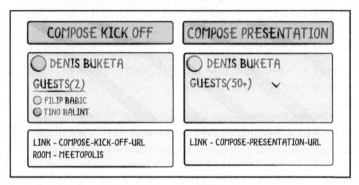

Calendar Event

With imperative thinking, you might use the following code to render the event card:

```kotlin
fun renderEventCard(event: Event) {
  // Handle event title
  setTitle(event.title)

  // Handle event owner
  setOwner(event.owner)

  // Handle event call link
  setCallLink(event.callLink)

  // Handle guest list visibility
  if (event.guests.size > 0 && !hasGuestList()) {
    addGuestList()
  } else if (event.guests.size == 0 && hasGuestList()) {
    removeGuestList()
  }

  // Handle case with more than 5 guests
  if (event.guests.size > 5 && !isGuestListCollapsed()) {
    collapseGuestList()
  } else if (event.guests.size > 0 && isGuestListCollapsed()) {
    expandGuestList()
  }

  // Handle guest count badge
  if (event.guests.size <= 50) {
    setGuestCountText("$count")
  } else {
    setGuestCountText("50+")
  }
}
```

```
// Handle Event Room
if (event.isRoomSelected && !isRoomAdded()) {
  addRoom()
} else if (!event.isRoomSelected && isRoomAdded()) {
  removeRoom()
  }
}
```

The function is just a showcase of how many different states you would need to handle for the given case of a calendar event.

After setting the basic properties like the title, owner and call link, you have to handle four different `if` statements for various states the card might have — like showing the collapsable guest list, guest count or meeting room.

When building the UI for this use case, you need to think about the following:

• Which UI you'd like to display for any given data.

• How to respond to events.

• How your UI changes over time.

Just by the number of `if` checks, there are sixteen different states for your calendar card.

This seemed like a simple use case, but it's actually *very complex*, and lots of bugs can creep in as you develop it. Imagine a more complex example, where you also need to handle the animations between states.

Handling how the UI changes over time is the hardest part of building a UI. But if you can generalize the behavior, you can try to simplify it! :]

Inheritance

One way to make your life easier when it comes to updating your UI is to extract some parts of your UI to custom view classes.

If you have components that you often reuse throughout your app, just create a custom view and keep all that code in one place.

You already saw that making a custom view is hard, but it's useful in situations like this. There's a well-known principle that describes how to organize your code that way — **composition over inheritance**.

This is a principle in object-oriented programming (OOP) that says that classes should achieve polymorphic behavior and code reuse by their composition — that is, by containing instances of other classes that implement the desired functionality — rather than inheriting from a base or parent class.

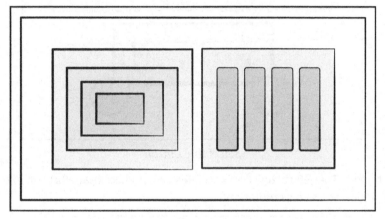

Inheritance vs Composition

In the current Android UI API, inheritance plays a huge part — and that causes problems. For example, Button is one of the most-used widgets in every Android app. When you look at Button's class hierarchy, you'll see something like this:

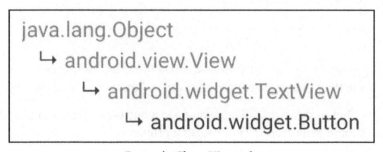

Button's Class Hierarchy

It seems to make sense, as `Buttons` display text. But the issue is that `TextViews` can do a lot of things. For instance, you can make a button selectable, if you want.

Selectable Button

Now, what about `ImageButton`? Can you guess what class `ImageButton` extends? Well, take a look at its class hierarchy:

```
java.lang.Object
    ↳ android.view.View
        ↳ android.widget.ImageView
            ↳ android.widget.ImageButton
```

ImageButton's Class Hierarchy

As you see, you now have two buttons that share the same logic except that one uses an image, while the other uses text for its content. Yet, they extend different classes.

Now, imagine that in some *crazy world* you need a button with an image *and* text. Which class should you extend? That causes a problem.

Inheritance not only introduces a lot of unnecessary logic, but it also limits the classes you can inherit from, as in Kotlin and Java, **you can only inherit from one parent**, there is no multiple inheritance.

Data flow

There's one more important thing to look at in the current Android UI tookit, which has to do with state and the data flow between the UI and the business logic. When talking about state, it's important to consider three main questions:

- What is the source of truth?

- Who owns the state?

- Who updates the state?

It's not simple to answer these questions in Android development, which is why you have so many different architectural patterns.

You have Model-View-Controller (MVC), Model-View-ViewModel (MVVM), Model-View-Presenter (MVP), Model-View-Intent (MVI) and probably many more Model-View-Somethings. These patterns exist to help define and reason about your app's data flow and state management.

Take the Spinner component, for example.

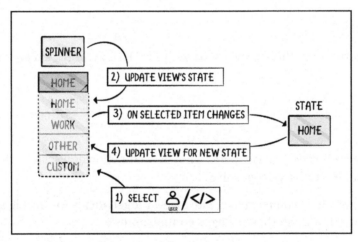

Spinner and State Management

Spinner offers a listener called onSelectedItemChanged that tells you when a user changed the value — but it happens after the value changes. It's hard to build your UI to be a representation of your model if your UI also owns and manages the state.

In this example, Spinner will update its state and notify you about the state change. Your model will update the state and, if you have the logic to update the Spinner when your state changes, you'll update the Spinner once more for that change.

But you cannot know if you are the one changing the `Spinner` state, or if the event came from the user.

It seems you've been reading about a lot of complexity and issues the current UI toolkit provides, so if some of those hit you hard, you'll be glad to hear that there *is* hope — and it's waiting just around the corner! :]

Introduction to Jetpack Compose

In the previous sections, you went through some important concepts and issues regarding the original Android UI toolkit. Now, it's time to say hello to **Jetpack Compose**!

Jetpack Compose is Android's modern toolkit for building native UI. When you learned about how difficult building a UI in Android with the original Android UI toolkit is, you started with the basic, familiar building blocks, `View` and `ViewGroup`. So it makes sense to kick off this introduction with the basic building blocks of Jetpack Compose — **composable functions**.

Composables

Like all great tutorials, this one will start with the "Hello World!" example! :]

```
@Composable
fun GreetingWorld() {

}
```

You can break this code into two parts: First, it's a function and second, that function has an annotation called `@Composable`.

That's pretty much all you need to create a new widget. Ready for the big surprise? In Compose's world, you call these widgets **composables**.

You'll notice that you don't have to extend any class (looking at you, `View`) or overwrite constructors or other functions. All you need to care about is that you write a function and use this new fancy annotation.

Get ready because you'll see that one *a lot*!

In this example, you want to show a message to the user that says "Hello World!". To do that, you can do the following:

```
@Composable
fun GreetingWorld() {
    Text(text = "Hello world!")
}
```

In Compose, calling a function that displays something on the screen is known as **emitting the UI**. So, to emit your message, you need to call a Text function.

Text is also a composable function and it's one of the default composable functions that make up Jetpack Compose. One thing to notice is that composable functions can only be invoked from other composable functions — if you try to remove @Composable, you'll get an error stopping you from using Text().

But what if you want to pass in a specific message or name, or any kind of parameter to the composable? Well, you can do something like this:

```
@Composable
fun Greeting(name: String) {
    Text(text = "Hello $name!")
}
```

Since composables are functions, you can pass data to them as function parameters. In your example, you add a property name to Greeting() and use that data when invoking Text().

The simplest way to think about composables is to understand they're functions that take your data and transform it into your UI. Another way to put it — in Compose, **the UI is a function of the data (state)**.

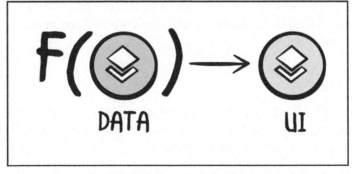

UI as a Function of Data

In the past few years you've probably heard how functional programming, and having pure functions is all the rage. By using Compose you can be a part of the cool group of kids! :]

All jokes aside, this functional paradigm makes it simpler to write and refactor the code. It also makes it easier to visualize it.

Displaying composables

When it comes to displaying your composables, you still use activities or fragments as a starting point. To display the Greeting composable you just saw, you'd do the following:

```
class MainActivity : AppCompatActivity() {

  override fun onCreate(savedInstanceState: Bundle?) {
    super.onCreate(savedInstanceState)
      setContent {
        Greeting("World")
      }
  }
}

@Composable
fun Greeting(name: String) {
  Text (text = "Hello $name!")
}
```

You connect composables with your activities using a **content block**. setContent() defines the Activity's layout. Instead of defining the layout content with an XML file, you just call composable functions.

The magic behind Jetpack Compose transforms these composable functions into the app's UI elements. Chapter 2, "Learning Jetpack Compose Fundamentals", will explore this in more detail!

Using Kotlin

If you haven't noticed so far, Jetpack Compose allows you to write your UI using Kotlin, the amazing language that is so much better than rusty old XML. Not just that — Jetpack Compose is built entirely in Kotlin!

Let's see how using Kotlin features and programming practices that follow OOP can solve the difficulties you read about earlier.

Separation of concerns

You've seen how having different languages to build your business logic and your UI leads to forced separation of concerns. With Jetpack Compose, that line disappears.

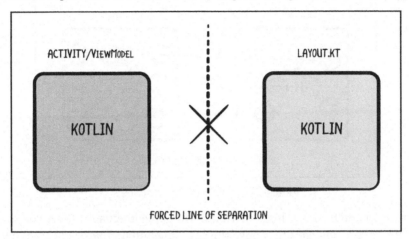

Control of the Line of Separation of Concerns

By using Kotlin to write your UI, you take responsibility for drawing the line of separation. And you can do whatever makes the most sense in your situation. You don't have to conform to the limitations of the operating system.

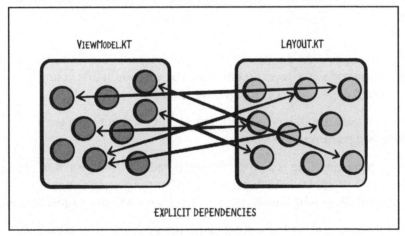

Explicit Dependencies

That means that many of the implicit dependencies that you had between your layout and business logic now become explicit.

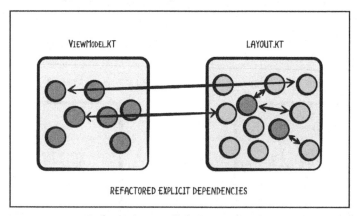

Refactoring Explicit Dependencies

Having your UI and business logic written in the same language allows you to refactor those dependencies to reduce the coupling and increase cohesion in your code.

A framework shouldn't separate your concerns for you. This doesn't mean that you should mix your logic and UI. But by writing everything in Kotlin, you can apply all the good practices to define where you want to draw the line between the two.

Declarative thinking

You've read about how the design of the original Android UI toolkit requires you to write imperative code. Whatever architecture you use, you'll find yourself writing the code that describes *how* your UI changes over time.

In Jetpack Compose, you'll have to shift how you think about UI in terms of **declarative programming**.

Declarative programming is a programming paradigm where you don't focus on describing *how* a program should operate, but *what* the program should accomplish — e.g. **it should show a hidden** Button, rather than **it should hide** a Button.

Remember that example with the event card? You can write that same logic declaratively using Jetpack Compose.

```
@Composable
fun EventCard(event: Event) {
  Title(event.title)
  Owner(event.owner)
```

```
    Call(event.callLink)

    if (event.guests.size > 0) {
      Guests(collapsed = event.guests.size > 5) {
        if (event.guests.size > 50) {
          Badge(text="50+")
        } else {
          Badge(text="$count")
        }
      }
    }

    if (event.isRoomSelected) {
      Room(event.room)
    }
  }
```

Note how you described *what* should happen without saying anything about *how* it should happen. The app will add the guest list and the room name only if they exist. The list collapses when there are more than five guests.

Do you remember those concerns about the UI state? You no longer need to worry about how your UI changes over time. By using this declarative approach, you describe how the UI should look, while the framework controls how you get from one state to the other.

Additionally, the composable function is a function definition, but it describes all possible states of your UI in one place.

Composition

In the example with `Buttons` and `ImageButtons`, you saw how inheritance can lead to specific problems. Jetpack Compose allows you to address those problems by favoring **composition over inheritance**. By examining the same example, you'll see how to approach that problem.

To make a button widget, you do something like this:

```
@Composable
fun TextButton(text: String) {
  Box(modifier = Modifier.clickable(onClick = { ... })) {
    Text(text = text)
  }
}
```

Note how, in this example, you have a Box, which is a composable that lets you **stack multiple composables**. It's also using `Modifier.clickable()`, to make the composable clickable. For now, you don't need to know about modifiers.

You'll learn about the Box component in later chapters. And in Chapter 6, "Using Compose Modifiers" you'll learn about modifiers in greater detail. For now, just know that Box() allows you to wrap your Text() and you use a Modifier to make it clickable.

Now, what if you need a button with an image, as in the previous example? You do something like this:

```
@Composable
fun ImageButton() {
  Box(modifier = Modifier.clickable(onClick = { ... })) {
    Icon(painterResource(id = R.drawable.vector),
contentDescription = "")
  }
}
```

Here, you use Icon() instead of Text(). The next chapter will cover this in more detail. For now, it's enough to say that this composable allows you to display vectors or static images.

To wrap up the example, if you need a button with text and an image, you can now do this:

```
@Composable
fun TextImageButton(text: String) {
  Box(modifier = Modifier.clickable(onClick = { ... })) {
    Row(verticalAlignment = Alignment.CenterVertically) {
      Icon(painterResource(id = R.drawable.vector),
contentDescription = "")
      Text(text = text)
    }
  }
}
```

Here, you combined the Icon and the Text composables in one Row. A Row is similar to a horizontal LinearLayout, where items will be positioned one next to the other, horizontally. By doing so, you successfully created a button with an image and text. So easy! :]

And that's it. With Compose, there's no need to add anything, you simply add the composables you need. You build your widgets from other widgets that you've already created or that Jetpack Compose offers you.

Encapsulation

In the **Data Flow** section, you saw how the data flows between the UI and your business logic. You saw that in the old Android UI toolkit, views also manage state and that they expose callbacks that you use to capture the change in that state.

Compose is designed in a way that your UI is a representation of your data. That means that your UI components — in this case, composables — aren't responsible for *managing* state. They *represent* your state.

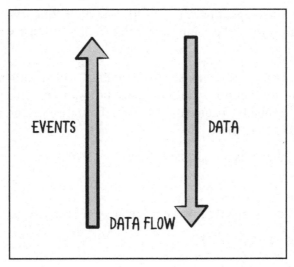

Data Flow

Kotlin allows you to pass down data in the form of function parameters, but you can also pass the callbacks to propagate the events up. This is how you implement the public APIs of your composable functions.

Imagine you want a list of posts that the user can click. You could create a `Post` composable like this:

```
@Composable
fun Post(post: PostData, onClickAction: () -> Unit) {
  Box(modifier = Modifier.clickable(onClick = onClickAction)) {
    Row {
      Icon(bitmap = post.image, contentDescription = "")
      Text(text = post.title)
    }
  }
}
```

You pass the `PostData` down to the function to render a specific `Post` and you also pass a callback to receive the click event when the user clicks the `Post`.

You should strive to have **top-down data flow**, which means that data should flow down to your UI (your composables), and events should flow from your UI to your `ViewModels`.

Recomposition

Recomposition is one of the most important concepts in Jetpack Compose. To put it simply, recomposition allows any composable function to be **re-invoked** at any time.

This is very useful when updating your UI with new state. Whenever state changes, Compose will **re-invoke** all the composables that depend on that state and update your UI.

Chapter 2, "Learning Jetpack Compose Fundamentals" will go into more detail about the recomposition step. For now, you should just be aware that this concept means you don't have to manually update your UI when the state changes, as you had to do with the old Android UI toolkit.

Now, imagine you have a list of posts like this:

```
@Composable
fun Posts(livePosts: LiveData<List<Post>>) {
  val posts by livePosts.observeAsState(initial = emptyList())

  if (posts.isNotEmpty()) {
    PostList(posts)
  } else {
    MessageForEmptyPosts()
  }
}
```

If the number of posts isn't zero, you show a list of posts. If the number of posts is zero, you show a message.

Here, you can see how you can use `LiveData` and observe it as a state. You'll learn more about this in Chapter 7, "Managing State in Compose".

The idea behind this is that you observe the `Posts`' state. Whenever the `livePosts` data changes, Compose re-invokes `Posts()` and **re-evaluates** the logic inside.

If there are no posts, Compose calls `MessageForEmptyPosts()` and your app shows a message for the user. If there are posts, Compose calls `PostList(posts)` and your app shows the list of posts.

Jetpack Compose's tech stack

By now, you should have a better idea of how Compose tries to solve the problems of the old Android UI toolkit. You've seen some examples of what's possible with Jetpack Compose, but how is it all wired under the hood?

Two parts categorize the different components that make up Jetpack Compose: the **development host** and the **device host**.

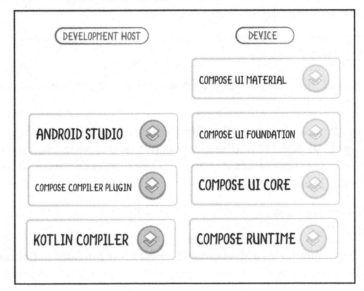

Jetpack Compose Tech Stack

Development host

The development host contains all the tools that help you write your code.

At the bottom, you have a **Kotlin compiler**. Jetpack Compose is written in Kotlin and uses a lot of Kotlin features, which is what makes it so flexible and easy to use. You've seen how Compose uses trailing lambdas to make the code more readable and intuitive.

On top of that, you have a **Compose Compiler Plugin**. Even though you use @Composable as an annotation, Compose doesn't use the annotation processor. This plugin works at the type system level and also at the code generation level to change the types of your composable functions.

If you're not familiar with **annotation processors**, or APTs, they are a special system within the build process that analyze specific annotations and generate code based on them.

This is a great thing because you can use the generated code instead of writing it yourself, but sometimes it's terrible as it **greatly increases the build time** for your project. But because Compose doesn't use APTs, it doesn't slow down your builds!

On top of that, you have **Android Studio**, which includes Compose-specific tools, simplifying the work you do with Compose.

Device host

The second part of this tech stack is your **device**; that is, the environment that runs your Compose code.

At the bottom, there's a **Compose Runtime**. At its core, the Compose logic doesn't know anything about Android or UIs. It only knows how to work with tree structures to emit specific items. That makes it even more interesting because you could use Compose to emit things other than UIs.

On top of that lies **Compose UI Core**. It handles input management, measurement, drawing, layout etc.

These two layers support the widgets that the next layer provides — **Compose UI foundation**. It contains basic building blocks like Text, Row, Column and default interactions.

Finally, there's **Compose UI Material**, an implementation of the Material Design system. It provides Material components out of the box, making it easy to use Material Design in your app.

Key points

- **View.java**'s size makes the old Android UI toolkit hard to maintain and scale.

- Creating custom views is hard and requires too much code.

- Unlike **imperative programming**, **declarative programming** simplifies code and makes it easier to understand.

- In the old Android UI toolkit, it's not clear what the source of truth is, who owns it and who updates it.

- In Jetpack Compose, you use **composables** to build your UI.

- Composables are just functions annotated with @Composable.

- Jetpack Compose is written in Kotlin and allows you to use all the Kotlin features.

- In Jetpack Compose, your UI is a **function of data**.

- You use setContent() as the entry point to display your composables.

- In Compose you control where to draw the line of separation of concerns between your business logic and UI.

- Jetpack Compose favors **composition over inheritance**.

- In Jetpack Compose, you use function parameters to pass down the data and callbacks to propagate events up.

- Jetpack Compose uses **recomposition** to **re-invoke** composables when the state changes.

- Jetpack Compose doesn't use the annotation processor, but rather a **Compose Compiler Plugin** that changes the type of composable functions.

Where to go from here?

That was a *really brief* comparison of the original Android UI toolkit and Jetpack Compose! :]

By now, you should have a feeling of the potential of Jetpack Compose.

Keep the excitement up for the following chapters, where you'll get your hands dirty while learning about some of the existing composables that you can use to build your UI.

In the first section of the book, you'll cover the fundamentals, learn how to use layout and how to create lists — one of the most important UI components! See you there!

Chapter 2: Learning Jetpack Compose Fundamentals

By Tino Balint

In this chapter, you'll cover the basics of Jetpack Compose. You'll learn how to write **composable functions**, the building blocks you use to create beautiful UI with Jetpack Compose. Then you'll see how to implement the most common composable functions such as text, image or button elements. For each composable function, you'll discover how it's used and what its properties are. Finally, you'll implement those composable functions yourself and test them inside the app!

Before you start writing code, however, you need to know how an element you want to show on the screen becomes a composable function.

Composable functions

In the first chapter, you learned how using XML to make a UI differs from using Jetpack Compose. The biggest issues with the former approach are:

- The UI isn't scalable.

- It's hard to make custom views.

- Different sources can manage state.

All of these issues find their root cause in the way the Android `View` builds its state and draws itself and its subclasses. To avoid those issues, you need to use a different basic building block. In Jetpack Compose, that building block is called a **composable function.**

To make a composable function, you'd do something like this:

```
@Composable
fun MyComposableFunction() {
  // TODO
}
```

You need to annotate a function or expression with **@Composable** — a special **annotation class**. Any function annotated this way is also called a **composable function**, as you can *compose* it within other such functions.

Annotation classes simplify the code by attaching metadata to it. **Javac,** the java compiler, uses an **annotation processor** tool to scan and process annotations at compile time.

This creates new source files with the added metadata. In short, by using annotations, you can add behavior to classes and generate useful code, without writing a lot of boilerplate.

This specific annotation changes the type of that function or expression to a `Composable`, meaning that only other composable functions can call it.

The source code for the `Composable` annotation class looks like this:

```
@MustBeDocumented
@Retention(AnnotationRetention.BINARY)
@Target(
    AnnotationTarget.FUNCTION,
    AnnotationTarget.TYPE,
    AnnotationTarget.TYPE_PARAMETER,
    AnnotationTarget.PROPERTY_GETTER
)
annotation class Composable
```

You can see that the Composable annotation class has three annotations of its own:

1. **@MustBeDocumented**: Indicates that the annotation is a part of the public API and should be included in the generated documentation.

2. **@Retention**: Tells the compiler how long the annotation should *live*. By using `AnnotationRetention.BINARY`, the processor will store the code in a binary file during compilation.

3. **@Target**: Describes the contexts where the type applies. `@Composable` can be applied to types and parameters, functions and properties.

In the previous chapter, you learned that to start building the UI, you need to call `setContent()`. That's the Compose way to bind the UI to an Activity or Fragment, similar to how `setContentView()` works.

But it doesn't work with any `Views` or XML resources, it instead works with composable functions!

Setting the content

`setContent()` signature looks like this:

```
fun ComponentActivity.setContent(
    parent: CompositionContext? = null,
    content: @Composable () -> Unit
) { ... }
```

You can see that `setContent()` is an extension function of `ComponentActivity`. Extension functions are functions that add additional functionality to a class without changing its source code. That means you can use `setContent()` on any `ComponentActivity` or its subclasses, like `AppCompatActivity`.

Calling `setContent()` sets the given composable function named `content` as the root view, to which you can add any number of elements. You'll call the rest of your composable functions from within this container.

Notice how `content` is also annotated with `@Composable`. Because of the aforementioned `@Target`, you can apply it to function parameters, as well.

This specific use case marks the lambda function you pass in as a composable function, allowing you to call other composable functions and access things like **resources** and the **context** of Jetpack Compose.

Another parameter inside `setContent()` is the `CompositionContext`, which is a reference to the parent composition. `CompositionContext` is used to coordinate scheduling of composition updates in a composition tree. It ensures that invalidations and data flow logically through the parent and child compositon.

The parent of the root composition is a `Recomposer` which determines the thread where **recomposition** happens — one of the most important features of Jetpack Compose.

In simple terms, recomposition is an event that asks the app to **re-draw** the current UI with new values. Recomposition happens every time a value such as state changes.

You'll learn more about managing states and how recomposition works in Chapter 7, "Managing State in Compose".

Now that you've gone over the basics of Jetpack Compose, you can dive into composable functions! :]

Basic composable functions

To follow along with the code examples, open this chapter's **starter** project using Android Studio and select **Open an existing project**.

Next, navigate to **02-learning-jetpack-compose-fundamentals/projects** and select the **starter** folder as the project root. Once the project opens, let it build and sync and you'll be ready to go!

The starter project consists of three packages and **MainActivity.kt**.

Project Packages

Here's what you should know about the contents:

- **app**: Has only one composable function, which acts as a root layout in your app. You won't need to change it since it only the app navigation, which is already set up for you!

- **router**: Has two helper classes to handle navigation between screens and the **Back** button. You won't need to change anything here, either.

- **screens**: Consists of multiple composable functions for different screens. You'll implement these in this chapter, except for **NavigationScreen.kt**, which contains a layout for navigation that's already made for you.

- **MainActivity.kt**: Contains the setContent() call, setting the first composable function and acting as a root UI component.

Once you're familiar with the file organization, build and run the app. You'll see a screen with basic navigation, as shown below.

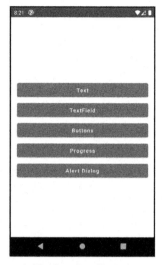

Navigation Screen

The screen contains five buttons, each leading to an empty screen when you click on it. By pressing **Back**, you return to the main screen.

Your goal is to implement a composable function for each of the empty screens. So get to it! :]

Text

When you think about the UI, one of the first things that come to mind is a basic text element, or TextView. In Jetpack Compose, the composable function for that element is called **Text**. Next, you'll see how to add basic text elements to the UI.

Open **TextScreen.kt** and you'll see two composable functions: TextScreen() and MyText():

```
@Composable
fun TextScreen() {
  Column(
    modifier = Modifier.fillMaxSize(), // 1
    horizontalAlignment = Alignment.CenterHorizontally, // 2
    verticalArrangement = Arrangement.Center // 3
  ) {
    MyText()
```

```
    }

    BackButtonHandler {
        JetFundamentalsRouter.navigateTo(Screen.Navigation)
    }
}

@Composable
fun MyText() {
    //TODO add your code here
}
```

TextScreen is already complete. It's a simple composable function that uses a Column component to list out items in a vertical order. In that sense, a Column is just like a vertical LinearLayout!

It's also using **modifiers** and two Column properties to style the Column and align it and its children. Here's more about the properties you're using:

1. By using **modifiers**, you can style each Compose element in multiple different ways. You can change its alignment, size, background, shape and much more. In this case, by using Modifier.fillMaxSize(), you're telling the Column to **match** its parent's width and height.

2. By using horizontalAlignment, you're telling the Column to center its children horizontally.

3. Using verticalArrangement, you place the its items in the Center of its parent.

You'll learn more about **modifiers** in Chapter 6, "Using Compose Modifiers"! Right now, what's important is how to add text elements to your composable functions. Also ignore the BackButtonHandler(), as it's a special composable built to handle back clicks, and you don't need to change it!

Now, change MyText()'s code to the following:

```
@Composable
fun MyText() {
  Text(text = )
}
```

You'll see a variety of choices to import the Text, but make sure to pick the one that comes from **androidx.compose.material**. You'll also get a prompt to provide a text to display. Add the following code as the text parameter:

```
stringResource(id = R.string.jetpack_compose)
```

Compose has a really neat and easy-to-use way to import strings, drawables, colors and other **resources** into your UI elements. Normally, to get a string from resources, you'd call `getString()` on a given `Context`. Since you're working with composable functions, you need a composable function that allows you to do that.

Fortunately, there are many composable functions that let you retrieve different types of resources. In this case, you'll use `stringResource()`, which takes the ID of a string resource you want to load.

Build and run the app. Then on the main screen, click the **Text** button. You should see the following screen:

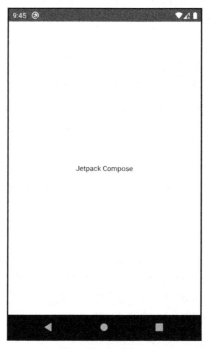

Non-Styled Text

Awesome! There's now a simple text in the middle of the screen that reads **Jetpack Compose**. :]

Now that you've implement the basic `Text()`, it's best to see what other functionality such elements expose. Take a moment to check out what `Text()` has to offer by inspecting the source code:

```
@Composable
fun Text(
    text: String,
```

```
    modifier: Modifier = Modifier,
    color: Color = Color.Unspecified,
    fontSize: TextUnit = TextUnit.Unspecified,
    fontStyle: FontStyle? = null,
    fontWeight: FontWeight? = null,
    fontFamily: FontFamily? = null,
    letterSpacing: TextUnit = TextUnit.Unspecified,
    textDecoration: TextDecoration? = null,
    textAlign: TextAlign? = null,
    lineHeight: TextUnit = TextUnit.Unspecified,
    overflow: TextOverflow = TextOverflow.Clip,
    softWrap: Boolean = true,
    maxLines: Int = Int.MAX_VALUE,
    onTextLayout: (TextLayoutResult) -> Unit = {},
    style: TextStyle = LocalTextStyle.current
)
```

It offers a wide range of parameters for different styles. The first, `text`, lets you set the text you want to display and is the **only required parameter**.

The second, `modifier`, is more complex and offers many different features. In the previous example, you saw that `Column()` used modifiers to fill the parent size, but as mentioned before, you'll learn more about modifiers in Chapter 6, "Using Compose Modifiers".

For now, take a moment to explore some of the parameters the `Text()` element exposes.

Text element parameters

- **color**: Lets you set the text color.

- **fontSize**: Changes the font size. You measure it in **scalable pixels (sp)**.

- **fontStyle**: Lets you choose between normal and italic font.

- **fontWeight**: Sets the weight of the text to **Bold**, **Black**, **Thin** and similar types.

- **textAlign**: Sets the horizontal alignment of the text.

- **overflow**: Determines how the app handles overflow, using either **Clip** or **Ellipsis**.

- **maxLines**: Sets the maximum number of lines.

- **style**: Lets you build a specific style and reuse it, rather than explicitly setting all the other parameters. The current app theme defines the default style, making it easier to support different **themes**.

There are many more parameters, but these are the most important and commonly-used ones.

If you want to know more about Text(), use **Command-Click** on Mac or **Control-Click** on Windows or Linux to click on the Text function call, and preview the source code and documentation.

Now that you've displayed text in your UI, it's time to style it to make it look nicer! :]

Styling your text

Now, you're going to display the text in *italics* with **bold** weight. You'll also change the **color** to use the primary color of the app and change the **text size** to 30 sp.

Change MyText()'s code to the following:

```
@Composable
fun MyText() {
  Text(text = stringResource(id = R.string.jetpack_compose),
      fontStyle = FontStyle.Italic, // 1
      color = colorResource(id = R.color.colorPrimary), // 2
      fontSize = 30.sp, // 3
      fontWeight = FontWeight.Bold // 4
  )
}
```

Once again, there are a few things happening:

1. Using fontStyle, you make the text *italicized.*

2. Passing in a color, you change the color of the text. Also notice how colorResource() lets you easily fetch a color from your resources.

3. The fontSize parameter lets you pass in the size in **scalable pixels**. Notice the .sp property call. Compose has a way to transform Integer values into dp and sp by calling respective properties! These are extension properties, so make sure to add the . operator.

4. And finally, fontWeight makes the text **bold.**

Now build and run the project and open the Text screen to see the new version of your styled text:

Styled Text

You've applied all the styles and the text looks much nicer! Feel free to experiment with other parameters and change the text to your own liking.

Until now, you've had to build and run your app every time you made a change in the Text before you could see the result. This makes it hard to build a complex UI because you have to picture everything in your head. You'll now learn how to avoid that and make your life easier!

Previewing changes

When you work with XML, there's an option to split the screen so you can see both the code and a preview of your UI. You'll be happy to know that Compose offers a similar option!

To use it, you need to annotate your composable function with **@Preview**, like so:

```
@Composable
@Preview
fun MyText() {
  Text(...)
}
```

This allows the Compose compiler to analyze the composable function and generate a preview of it within Android Studio. Now, select the **Split** option on the top-right side of Android Studio. You'll see a preview like this:

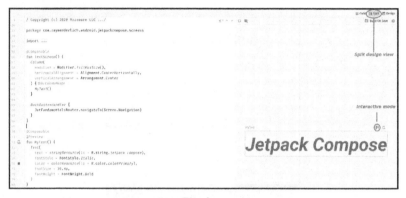

Preview

You can also click the small icon above the preview to enter interactive mode. This lets you perform actions and see how the state changes. You don't need that for the current screen, but it helps when you're building bigger UI components.

One thing to keep in mind is that if you're using preview, your functions need to either:

- Have no parameters

- Have default arguments for all parameters

- Provide a @PreviewParameter as well as a special factory that provides the parameters you want to draw on the UI

But showing static text is a bit dull! Next, you'll see how to implement an input field, so that the user can write something in the app!

TextField

In the legacy Android UI toolkit, you'd use an `EditText` to show input fields to the user. The composable function counterpart is called a `TextField`.

Open **TextFieldScreen.kt** and you'll see two composable functions:

```
@Composable
fun TextFieldScreen() {
  Column(
      modifier = Modifier.fillMaxSize(),
      horizontalAlignment = Alignment.CenterHorizontally,
      verticalArrangement = Arrangement.Center
  ) {
    MyTextField()
  }

  BackButtonHandler {
    JetFundamentalsRouter.navigateTo(Screen.Navigation)
  }
}

@Composable
fun MyTextField() {
  //TODO add your code here
}
```

You'll make your first `TextField` inside `MyTextField()`, similar to what you did in the previous example. Change the code in `MyTextField()` like so:

```
@Composable
fun MyTextField() {
  val textValue = remember { mutableStateOf("") }

  TextField(
    value = textValue.value,
    onValueChange = {
      textValue.value = it
    },
    label = {}
  )
}
```

Make sure you import the `TextField` package from **androidx.compose.material** and the `remember()` and `mutableStateOf()` packages from **androidx.compose.runtime**.

That seems like a lot of code for a simple input field, but it will make sense in a minute! :]

For your TextField to work properly, you must provide a value that **doesn't change during recomposition** — in other words, a **state** value. Using mutableStateOf(), you wrap an empty String into a state holder, which you'll use to store and display the text within the input field.

You also wrapped the state into remember(), which is Compose's way of telling the recomposer that the value should be persisted through recomposition. If you didn't use remember() here, every time you changed the state, it would be **lost and set to the default** value — an empty string.

Next, you connected the value of the textValue holder to the TextField, and within the onValueChange callback, you changed the internal value of the state holder.

What's going to happen now is that every time the user taps on a keyboard button, the internal state will change. This will trigger recomposition and re-drawing the TextField with new text. That's all going to happen really fast, and you won't be able to notice a difference!

Build and run the app to see your changes. Click the **TextField** button from the navigation and you'll see a screen like this:

Non-Styled Text Field

It's a screen with an empty TextField. When you click on that text, a keyboard opens and you can write normally, as you'd expect.

Improving the TextField

If you take a critical look at the screen, you'll see that the current TextField is very basic. It's missing a **hint** and some styling, like a border.

To add the hint and the border, you'll use a special type of TextField called OutlinedTextField. But before you do that, explore the signature of the TextField so you know how you can style the component.

Take a look at the TextField signature, and you'll see something like this:

```
@Composable
fun TextField(
    value: String,
    onValueChange: (String) -> Unit,
    label: @Composable () -> Unit,
    keyboardOptions: KeyboardOptions = KeyboardOptions.Default,
    onImeActionPerformed: (ImeAction,
SoftwareKeyboardController?) -> Unit = { _, _ -> },
    ...
)
```

Like the Text composable function, TexField has many parameters to change its style. Since some of the parameters are the same, this section will only explain the most important new ones.

- **value**: The current text displayed inside the TextField. Note that it's of type TextFieldValue and not String.

- **onValueChange**: A callback that triggers every time the user types something new. The callback provides a new TextFieldValue so you can update the displayed text.

- **label**: The label that's displayed inside the container. When the user focuses on the text, the label will animate above the writing cursor and stay there.

- **keyboardOptions**: Sets the keyboard options such as KeyboardType and ImeAction. Some available KeyboardTypes are: **Email**, **Password** and **Number** while important ImeActions are: **Go**, **Search**, **Previous**, **Next** and **Done**.

- **onImeActionPerformed**: A callback that triggers every time a user makes an input action which performs an ImeAction.

There are many more parameters, but these are some of the core features you'll use in most apps.

Feel free to explore more of these parameters and play around with them, but for now, move onto the OutlinedTextField component, a **material design** inspired input field! :]

Adding an email field with OutlinedTextField

Your next step is to create an email input, one of the most common text fields. Replace the code of MyTextField with the following:

```
@Composable
fun MyTextField() {
  val textValue = remember { mutableStateOf("") }

  val primaryColor = colorResource(id = R.color.colorPrimary)

  OutlinedTextField(
    label = { Text(text = stringResource(id =
R.string.email)) },
    colors = TextFieldDefaults.outlinedTextFieldColors(
        focusedBorderColor = primaryColor,
        focusedLabelColor = primaryColor,
        cursorColor = primaryColor
    ),
    keyboardOptions = KeyboardOptions.Default.copy(keyboardType
= KeyboardType.Email),
    value = textValue.value,
    onValueChange = {
      textValue.value = it
    },
  )
}
```

An OutlinedTextField is just a styling TextField, as it uses a special internal function to draw and animate a border around the field and a description text.

To add a **hint**, or a **label** as it's known in Compose, you used the label property and passed in another composable function. This is the beauty of Compose — whenever you need some functionality, you can use other composable functions to fill that need. In this case, you need to display a text that gives the user a hint about what the input data should be by using a Text().

The second parameter you added is colors. It changes the colors for different parts of the TextField. In this case, you use the primary color from resources to change the border and label colors in focused state and cursor color.

The last change is to change the keyboardType to KeyboardType.Email. To do this you use the KeyboardOptions.Default instance of KeyboardOptions and make a new copy of the object with the desired `keyboardType`. This will open a keyboard that makes it easier to write email domains when `TextField` is in focus.

Build and run your app to test your new email input. The **TextField** screen will look like this:

Styled TextField

The text field has a border and a hint that reads: **Email**. Click it to gain focus.

Focused TextField

The hint **animates** to the top of the border and your text field comes to life with raywenderlich.com's famous green color. Nice! :]

Next, you'll learn how to **button** elements and how to handle click events.

Buttons

With what you've learned so far, you know how to read text from a screen and how to display it. The last thing that you need to make a basic screen is a **button**.

There are many types of buttons in the Android world, but all of them have one thing in common: They can be clicked. Next, you'll see how to implement one, and how to handle the click actions!

Open **ButtonsScreen.kt** and look at the code:

```
@Composable
fun ExploreButtonsScreen() {
  Column(
    modifier = Modifier.fillMaxSize(),
    horizontalAlignment = Alignment.CenterHorizontally,
    verticalArrangement = Arrangement.Center
  ) {

    MyButton()
    MyRadioGroup()
    MyFloatingActionButton()

    BackButtonHandler {
      JetFundamentalsRouter.navigateTo(Screen.Navigation)
    }
  }
}

@Composable
fun MyButton() {
  //TODO add your code here
}

@Composable
fun MyRadioGroup() {
  //TODO add your code here
}

@Composable
fun MyFloatingActionButton() {
  //TODO add your code here
}
```

You can see there are four composable functions in the file.
ExploreButtonsScreen() centers and displays the main layout. You'll use the three empty functions to practice different types of buttons.

Building a login button

First, you'll make the basic button that you'd expect to see while logging in. Start by adding the following code to MyButton():

```
@Composable
fun MyButton() {
  Button(
    onClick = {},
    colors = ButtonDefaults.buttonColors(backgroundColor =
colorResource(id = R.color.colorPrimary)),
    border = BorderStroke(
      1.dp,
      color = colorResource(id = R.color.colorPrimaryDark)
    )
  ) {
    Text(
      text = stringResource(id = R.string.button_text),
      color = Color.White
    )
  }
}
```

In the code above, you aren't performing any actions when the user clicks the button. However, you are using an **empty lambda expression** as onClick to keep it enabled.

To change the background color of the button, you use the ButtonDefaults instance and call buttonColors method on it with the desired background color as a parameter. This method also allows you to change disabledBackgroundColor, contentColor and disabledContentColor if needed.

You also use a BorderStroke to set the background color and add a border with a width of **1 dp** and a dark primary color. Each BorderStroke has to define a color and its width. You can add them to many components, such as buttons, cards and much more.

Finally, you add a Text() as the content of the button, as you learned above, and set the text color to Color.White. The Color component is another part of the Compose framework that defines commonly used colors like White, Black, Gray and so on.

Now, build and run the app and open the **Buttons** screen.

Button

This is how a button with a border looks in Jetpack Compose. It's a pretty simple component following Material Design. You haven't added any specific actions within the onClick handler, but you get the idea! You can set it up to call any functions or other code you want to execute, any time the user taps the button.

Exploring Button

Now, look at the signature of a Button composable function to see what it can do:

```
@Composable
fun Button(
    onClick: () -> Unit,
```

```
    enabled: Boolean = true,
    elevation: Dp = 2.dp,
    shape: Shape = MaterialTheme.shapes.small,
    border: BorderStroke? = null,
    content: @Composable RowScope.() -> Unit,
    ...
)
```

Read about what each of the most important parameters does to get a better understanding:

- **onClick**: The most common property you'll use with buttons, this calls a function when the user clicks the button. If you don't provide `onClick`, the button will be disabled.

- **enabled**: Allows you to control when a button is clickable.

- **elevation**: Sets the elevation of a button. The default elevation is **2 dp**.

- **shape**: Defines the button's shape and shadow. With `MaterialTheme.shapes`, you can choose a shape's size: **small, medium** or **large**.

- **border**: Draws a border around your button.

- **content**: A composable function that displays the content inside the button, usually text.

Again, there are many more parameters, but for the sake of simplicity, only the most important ones are listed.

Now that you know what's possible with `Button`, you can create as many buttons, along with their borders and background colors, as you need!

Next, you'll make a radio button or, more specifically, a group of radio buttons.

RadioButton

As you'd expect, the composable function you use to make radio buttons is named **RadioButton**. A radio button is a small, circular button that the user can select. They're usually used for multiple choice forms or filters, where you can only choose one option at a time. For example, you might have one radio button to opt in to receiving a newsletter and another to opt out, and only one of the two choices can be selected at the same time. This type of component is called a **radio group**.

At this time, Jetpack Compose doesn't have an implementation for a radio group so you'll have to make a custom group yourself! :]

Change the code in MyRadioGroup to the following:

```
@Composable
fun MyRadioGroup() {
  val radioButtons = listOf(0, 1, 2) // 1

  val selectedButton = remember
{ mutableStateOf(radioButtons.first()) } // 2

  Column {
    radioButtons.forEach { index -> // 3
      val isSelected = index == selectedButton.value
      val colors = RadioButtonDefaults.colors( // 4
        selectedColor = colorResource(id =
R.color.colorPrimary),
        unselectedColor = colorResource(id =
R.color.colorPrimaryDark),
        disabledColor = Color.LightGray
      )

      RadioButton( // 5
        colors = colors,
        selected = isSelected,
        onClick = { selectedButton.value = index } // 6
      )
    }
  }
}
```

There are many steps you have to take to build a radio group:

1. You create a list of three different options with values ranging from 0 to 2. These options are indices representing each radio button.

2. You create a selectedButton state that remembers which button is currently selected. It also selects the first button by default.

3. Using a for loop, you add a button to your Column in each iteration of the loop.

4. You can change the color of a RadioButton using the RadioButtonDefaults.colors(). You pass in a color for each of the different states RadioButton can appear in.

5. At the end of each loop iteration, you build a RadioButton and set both the onClick handler and its color when it's selected.

6. Every time a user taps the button, you'll change which button is selected in the state. This triggers a **recomposition** and your UI will update!

Now, build and run your app to try your new creation.

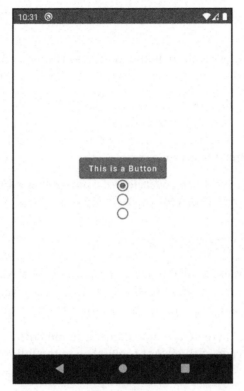

Radio Button

You now see three radio buttons on the screen. The first is selected by default. When you select another radio button, you can see the animation that switches between the buttons.

Exploring RadioButton

To learn more about `RadioButton`, look at its signature:

```
@Composable
fun RadioButton(
    selected: Boolean,
    onClick: () -> Unit,
    modifier: Modifier = Modifier,
    enabled: Boolean = true,
    interactionState: InteractionState = remember
{ InteractionState() },
    colors: RadioButtonColors = RadioButtonDefaults.colors()
)
```

There are fewer parameters than usual, but here are the most important ones:

- **selected**: Toggles the current state of the button between selected and not selected.

- **interactionState**: Allows you to define interactions such as drag gestures and touches.

- **colors**: The color combination for the `RadioButton`. Use the `RadioButtonDefaults` instance to call `colors()` on it to change the default color for different states. The available colors for different states are `selectedColor`, `unselectedColor` and `disabledColor`.

You're almost done with this deep overview of commonly used UI components. There's one more type of buttons for you to complete — `FloatingActionButtons`!

FloatingActionButton

Floating action buttons are named that way because they have a high elevation that positions them above other content on the screen, as if they were floating in the air. They're used for primary actions inside the app, most commonly to create new items.

For your next step, you'll create a simple floating action button that uses an icon. Start by changing the code in the `MyActionButton` to the following:

```
@Composable
fun MyFloatingActionButton() {
  FloatingActionButton(
      onClick = {},
      backgroundColor = colorResource(id =
R.color.colorPrimary),
      contentColor = Color.White,
      content = {
        Icon(Icons.Filled.Favorite, contentDescription = "Test
FAB")
      }
  )
}
```

Here, you add an **empty lambda expression** to keep the button enabled. Next, you set the **background and content color**. Finally, you set the **icon** by using `Icon()` and the predefined, filled, `Favorite` icon and a test `contentDescription` for accessibility.

The `Icons` object contains some predefined and commonly used icons in the Android world. Similar to what the `Color` object does for colors, you can choose between `Filled`, `Default`, `Outlined` and other types of icons as well as predefined vectors, such as the `Favorite`, `Add`, `ArrowBack` and other vector assets.

Exploring FloatingActionButton

To learn more about the `FloatingActionButton`, check out its signature:

```
@Composable
fun FloatingActionButton(
    onClick: () -> Unit,
    modifier: Modifier = Modifier,
    shape: Shape =
MaterialTheme.shapes.small.copy(CornerSize(percent = 50)),
    backgroundColor: Color = MaterialTheme.colors.secondary,
    contentColor: Color = contentColorFor(backgroundColor),
    elevation: FloatingActionButtonElevation =
FloatingActionButtonDefaults.elevation(),
    content: @Composable () -> Unit
)
```

You're already familiar with most, if not all of the, parameters. The most important thing to remember here is that a `FloatingActionButton` has an elevation, is clickable and you add a content to it by using another composable function. In most cases, you'll want to use an `Icon()` for the content. The signature of `Icon()` is very simple:

```
@Composable
fun Icon(
    imageVector: ImageVector,
    contentDescription: String?,
    modifier: Modifier = Modifier,
    tint: Color = LocalContentColor.current.copy(alpha =
LocalContentAlpha.current)
)
```

Icon's main feature is that it allows you to set a vector of the `ImageVector` type, which serves as an icon. There are multiple implementations of `Icon`, which allow you to provide different types of assets, such as `ImageBitmap` and `Painter`!

Now that you've finished the `FloatingActionButton`, build and run the app to see the result.

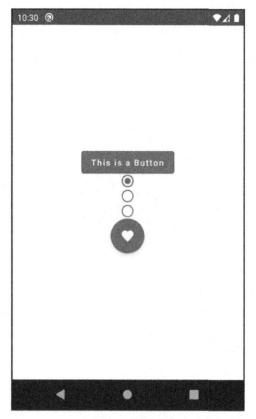

Action Button

Your floating action button now appears with a **favorite** icon in the shape of a heart. When you click it, it produces a **ripple** effect. You can also notice it has a small shadow underneath it, because of its elevation.

The buttons look awesome, and you've learned a top about them! Nice job! :]

More buttons to use

Here's a brief overview of the other types of buttons in Jetpack Compose:

- **IconButton**: Similar to a floating action button but without the floating part — it has no elevation. It's commonly used for navigation.

- **OutlinedButton**: Similar to an `OutlinedTextField`, this offers additional functionality like borders.

- **IconToggleButton**: Has two states for icons that you can toggle on and off.

- **TextButton**: Most commonly found in cards and dialogs, use this button for less pronounced actions.

After learning about all those buttons, you're ready to move on and discover new elements.

Progress Bars

When you perform long operations like fetching data from a server or a database, it's good practice to show a progress bar. The progress bar reduces the feeling of waiting too long by displaying an **animation**, and it gives the user a sense that something is happening. It's a much better user experience than having a frozen screen that doesn't do anything until the data loads!

When you only want the user to know that work is taking place, spinning animated progress bars are a good choice. In cases where you want to track progress and show the user how close they are to finishing the work, you want a progress bar that fills with a color as the progress occurs. This is very common when downloading or uploading files!

Jetpack Compose offers solutions to handle both cases. Open **ProgressIndicatorScreen.kt** and notice there's only one composable function in this file:

```
@Composable
fun ProgressIndicatorScreen() {

  Column(
      modifier = Modifier.fillMaxSize(),
      horizontalAlignment = Alignment.CenterHorizontally,
      verticalArrangement = Arrangement.Center
  ) {
     //TODO add your code here
  }

  BackButtonHandler {
    JetFundamentalsRouter.navigateTo(Screen.Navigation)
  }
}
```

That's because it's so easy to display progress bars with Jetpack Compose that you don't need additional custom composable functions.

Try it out by adding one circular and one linear progress bar inside `Column()` like so:

```
Column(
    modifier = Modifier.fillMaxSize(),
    horizontalAlignment = Alignment.CenterHorizontally,
    verticalArrangement = Arrangement.Center
) {
  CircularProgressIndicator(
      color = colorResource(id = R.color.colorPrimary),
      strokeWidth = 5.dp
  )
  LinearProgressIndicator(progress = 0.5f)
}
```

The column should stay as-is — it's only there to position the elements inside it, and to center them.

You're building both types of progress indicators here. First, you build the `CircularProgressIndicator`, defining an indicator `color` and a `strokeWidth`. These properties serve as styling. You don't have to define the animation yourself, it's already pre-baked into the component!

Then, you build the `LinearProgressIndicator`, and you set its progress to be 50%. Usually, you'd update this progress as your operations are computed within the system, but for the sake of simplicity, you'll make it static for this exercise.

Exploring the progress indicators

Since these are really simple components to implement, they also have very simple definitions. Open the `CircularProgressIndicator` composable function, and you'll see the following:

```
@Composable
fun CircularProgressIndicator(
   modifier: Modifier = Modifier,
   color: Color = MaterialTheme.colors.primary,
   strokeWidth: Dp = ProgressIndicatorDefaults.StrokeWidth
)
```

This function offers a small range of styling. The most important parameter is the progress, which ranges from `0.0` to `1.0` — the number determines the filled ratio of the progress bar. If you don't set the progress, the progress bar will run an infinite spinning animation.

The other styling options change the color and the stroke width. The default stroke width is **4 dp**.

On the other hand, the `LinearProgressIndicator` source code looks like this:

```
@Composable
fun LinearProgressIndicator(
  /*@FloatRange(from = 0.0, to = 1.0)*/
  progress: Float,
  modifier: Modifier = Modifier,
  color: Color = MaterialTheme.colors.primary,
  backgroundColor: Color = color.copy(alpha =
IndicatorBackgroundOpacity)
)
```

The options are almost the same, except it doesn't offer the ability to change the stroke width. Though you usually use a linear progress bar to indicate **static** progress, you can also use it with an infinite animation by not setting the `progress` parameter. The animation will then go from left to right until the operation completes.

Now that you've explored these progress bars, build and run the app, then open the **Progress** screen from the navigation menu:

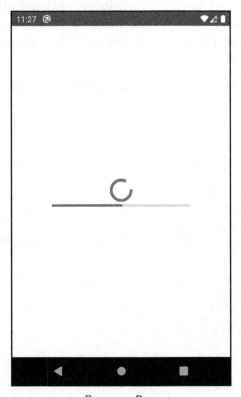

Progress Bars

You can see two progress bars on the screen. The circular one is always spinning in animation while the linear one stays static at the halfway point.

This example shows how simple and easy Jetpack Compose makes it to implement the most common features you use while making apps! :]

Now, it's time to learn about a more complex element, where you'll have to handle states and actions.

AlertDialog

The next composable function you'll implement is an `AlertDialog`. Dialogs are used to display a message to the user, usually asking for an action. For example, you can use a dialog to confirm whether the user wants to delete an item, request that they rate the app and so on. They are very common in apps, and are used across all operating systems — not just Android!

The most important part of working with a dialog is to handle the state that determines when to show or dismiss that dialog. You'll start by adding an alert dialog that has only one button: **Confirm**. The dialog will close when the user clicks the button or clicks outside the dialog.

To implement this behavior, open **AlertDialogScreen.kt** and change code inside `MyAlertDialog` to the following:

```
@Composable
fun MyAlertDialog() {
  val shouldShowDialog = remember { mutableStateOf(true) } // 1

  if (shouldShowDialog.value) { // 2
    AlertDialog( // 3
      onDismissRequest = { // 4
        shouldShowDialog.value = false
        JetFundamentalsRouter.navigateTo(Screen.Navigation)
      },
      // 5
      title = { Text(text = stringResource(id =
R.string.alert_dialog_title)) },
      text = { Text(text = stringResource(id =
R.string.alert_dialog_text)) },
      confirmButton = { // 6
        Button(
          colors = ButtonDefaults.buttonColors(backgroundColor =
colorResource(id = R.color.colorPrimary)),
          onClick = {
            shouldShowDialog.value = false
```

```
            JetFundamentalsRouter.navigateTo(Screen.Navigation)
        }
    ) {
        Text(
            text = stringResource(id = R.string.confirm),
            color = Color.White
        )
    }
}
)
}
}
```

There is a lot of code you had to add, but it's mostly using the components you've previously encountered, such as text and button elements! Go through it step-by-step:

1. You add a state that represents whether to show the dialog or not, and sets the initial state to `true`.

2. Using an `if` statement, you add logic to display the `AlertDialog` only if the state value is `true`. Because Compose renders the UI by calling functions, if the value is `false`, it won't call the function — and in turn, it won't display the dialog!

3. Using `AlertDialog()`, you create your dialog, which has a `title`, a `text` message, a **dismiss request handler**, and a `confirmButton()`.

4. In `onDismissRequest`, you change the state of the dialog to dismiss it, then tell `Navigation` to return to the main navigation screen. `JetFundamentalsRouter` is a pre-baked class used for navigation. You need to call `navigateTo` and add the screen you want to go to as a parameter.

5. You set the `title` and `text` as two `Text()`s and use the provided `stringResources()` to fill it.

6. Finally, you add a `Button()` as the `confirmButton`. Clicking the button dismisses the dialog and navigates to the main navigation screen, just like in `onDismissRequest()`. You add a `Text()` to display the text inside the button with a white color and a predefined string resource.

Now that you've prepared the dialog, build and run the app. On the navigation menu, select the **Alert Dialog** screen.

Alert Dialog

Upon opening the screen, an alert dialog automatically appears. It has a basic title and the text you set. Clicking outside the dialog or inside the confirm button dismisses the dialog and returns you to the previous screen.

Implementing the alert dialog might have looked complicated due to the code size, but most of the code only dealt with styling the alert and handling click events.

Dialogs are easy to create in Jetpack Compose, but keep in mind that you have to handle the state, which requires more effort when you want to reuse dialogs on multiple screens.

Exploring AlertDialog

It's also important to note that Jetpack compose uses **Material Design** dialogs. The most common type is `AlertDialog` you used, so open its signature to see what it can do:

```
@Composable
fun AlertDialog(
  onDismissRequest: () -> Unit,
  confirmButton: @Composable () -> Unit,
  modifier: Modifier = Modifier,
  dismissButton: @Composable (() -> Unit)? = null,
  title: @Composable (() -> Unit)? = null,
  text: @Composable (() -> Unit)? = null,
  shape: Shape = MaterialTheme.shapes.medium,
  backgroundColor: Color = MaterialTheme.colors.surface,
  contentColor: Color = contentColorFor(backgroundColor),
  properties: DialogProperties = DialogProperties()
)
```

There are new parameters to go through here:

- **onDismissRequest**: Executes when a user clicks outside the dialog or presses the **Back** button.

- **confirmButton**: A button that confirms a proposed action. It's usually a `TextButton`.

- **dismissButton**: This button dismisses an action. It's also usually a `TextButton`.

- **title**: Sets the title text with a composable function.

- **text**: Sets the text inside the dialog with a composable function.

- **contentColor**: The color used by elements within the `AlertDialog`.

- **properties**: Platform-specific properties for further customization.

Great job going through all of these components and learning so much about Jetpack Compose! :]

Key points

- Create composable functions with `@Composable`.

- Use `setContent()` inside an `Activity` as the root of your composable functions.

- Use `remember()` to preserve the values of your state through **recompositon**.

- Preview your composable functions by adding `@Preview`.

- `Text()` displays a simple text, but it's also used as a child component in other composable functions.

- `TextField()` allows you to retrieve input from a user. For more styling options, use `OutlinedTextField()`.

- Use `Button()` as the primary element of your app that handles click events.

- Use `RadioButton()` as an element that the user can select. To make a group of radio buttons, you have to write the logic yourself.

- Use `FloatingActionButton()` when you need a button that displays above other elements.

- `CircularProgressIndicator()` and `LinearProgressIndicator()` allow you to either track progress or show a loading animation.

- `AlertDialog()` is easy to use but requires state handling to work.

- **Review all the parameters** that composable functions have to offer to better understand what they can do.

- Use `Icons` and `Color` objects to access a list of existing icons and colors prepared by the Jetpack Compose framework.

Where to go from here?

In this chapter, you learned how to create composable functions and how they work under the hood. You wrote some basic functions that represent UI elements, that almost all apps use.

One thing that's currently missing is something to help you position elements on the screen. If you want to learn more about different Material Design-based components, check out the official reference guide: https://developer.android.com/reference/kotlin/androidx/compose/material/package-summary on the Android developer documentation website.

In the next chapter, you'll learn how to use containers such as the `Column`, `Row`, `Box`, and how to group different elements to create a more complex user interface! :]

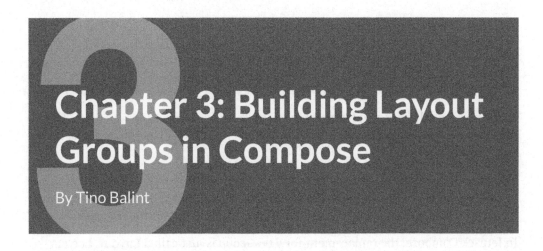

Chapter 3: Building Layout Groups in Compose

By Tino Balint

In this chapter, you'll learn about layouts in Jetpack Compose. Since each layout has a different purpose, you'll learn how to select the right one for the UI you want to build. Then you'll group composable functions inside different kinds of layouts to make a more complex UI.

In the previous chapter, you focused on displaying the elements onscreen; this time, you'll focus on positioning those elements.

As always, it's best to start with the basics. Read on to discover what the Jetpack Compose replacements for the basic layouts in Android are.

Using basic layouts in Jetpack Compose

In the previous chapter, you learned how to write basic composable functions. The next step is to build a more complex UI by positioning those elements in a specific way—arranging them.

When working with XML, you achieve that by using a layout, a class that extends `ViewGroup`. `ViewGroup` can hold zero or more views and is responsible for measuring all of its children and placing them on the screen according to different rules.

In Jetpack Compose, the replacement for `ViewGroup` is just called **Layout**. Look at the source code to understand how `Layout()` works:

```
@Composable inline fun Layout(
  content: @Composable () -> Unit,
  modifier: Modifier = Modifier,
  measurePolicy: MeasurePolicy
)
```

There are two important parameters here:

1. **content**: A composable function that holds children of the `Layout`.

2. **measurePolicy**: Responsible for defining measuring and layout behavior.

Measuring and positioning the elements is a complex job. That's why Jetpack Compose offers predefined layout types that handle this for you.

Every implementation of these predefined layouts has its own logic for positioning the children. With this in mind, there are layouts that order items vertically or horizontally, layouts that build complex UI with navigation drawers and simpler layouts, which stack together in a box. All of those layouts use `measurePolicy` to position items in different ways, so you don't have to do it yourself!

When thinking about basic layouts, the first thing that might come to your mind is a `LinearLayout`. Your next step is to learn about `LinearLayout`'s composable counterpart.

Linear layouts

To follow the code in this chapter, make sure to open this chapter's **starter** project, within the chapter materials.

A LinearLayout characteristically positions its children in a linear flow. This flow is called an **orientation** and can be horizontal or vertical. In Jetpack Compose, there are two different composable functions that replace LinearLayout, one for each orientation. You'll start with the horizontal version—a **Row**.

Using Rows

Open **RowScreen.kt** and look inside. You'll see an empty composable function, MyRow(), where you'll write your code. You'll add a Row, a LinearLayout counterpart, when it comes to horizontal layouts.

Start by replacing MyRow() with the following code:

```
@Composable
fun MyRow() {
  Row(verticalAlignment = Alignment.CenterVertically,
    horizontalArrangement = Arrangement.SpaceEvenly,
    modifier = Modifier.fillMaxSize()) {

    THREE_ELEMENT_LIST.forEach { textResId ->
      Text(
        text = stringResource(id = textResId),
        fontSize = 18.sp
      )
    }
  }
}
```

Here, you added a Row() with several different parameters.

You used Alignment.CenterVertically to center the children vertically, Arrangement.SpaceEvenly for each child to have an equal amount of space and Modifier.fillMaxSize() to make the layout fill the entire screen.

That final step is important because otherwise, a Row would take up only the space it needs to draw its children, since none of its children have weight defined. Without filling the screen size, the arrangement and alignment wouldn't matter and all items would be placed at the top-left of the screen, one after another. You'll learn more about weights in a moment.

Inside the Row(), you placed three Texts using a predefined list that holds string resources. You also increased their font size for readability.

Build and run, then tap on the **Row** button from the navigation menu and take a look at the screen:

Row

You can see three text fields that are centered vertically and arranged so there's equal spacing on all sides.

> **Note**: This is a good time to experiment with different arrangements and observe their result.

Now that you know how to position elements horizontally inside a row, it's time to explore the Row() signature, to see what else you can do.

Exploring Rows

Open the Row() signature, to look at what you can do with it:

```
@Composable
inline fun Row(
```

```
    modifier: Modifier = Modifier,
    horizontalArrangement: Arrangement.Horizontal =
Arrangement.Start,
    verticalAlignment: Alignment.Vertical = Alignment.Top,
    content: @Composable RowScope.() -> Unit
)
```

As you see, there are two new parameters for you to work with: `horizontalArrangement` and `verticalAlignment`.

You use arrangements to position children relative to one another. The possible horizontal arrangements are:

- **SpaceBetween**: The `Row()` places each child with an equal amount of space, without calculating in spacing before the first child, or after the last child.

- **SpaceEvenly**: Similar to `SpaceBetween`, the `Row()` places the children with an equal amount of space, but this time it includes starting or ending spacing.

- **SpaceAround**: The `Row()` places children just like with `SpaceEvenly`, but reduces the space between consecutive children by half.

- **Center**, **Start**, **End**: The `Row()` places children at the center, start or end without space between them.

Using `Alignment` you position the children in a specific way within the parent. Specifically, `verticalAlignment` aligns the children vertically in three different ways:

- **Top**: Aligns the children to the top of the parent.

- **CenterVertically**: Aligns the children in the center of the parent, vertically.

- **Bottom**: Aligns the children to the bottom of the parent.

The final way to position children inside a `Row` is by using **weights**. To add weights, you need to use a special way to access the `weight()` modifier from Compose. In the above example with three `Text` elements, you could use it like so:

```
@Composable
fun RowScope.MyRow() { // This composable is called from inside
the Row
    Text(
        modifier = Modifier.weight(1 / 3f), // here
        ...
    )
}
```

You can set the `weight` of a composable by using a `modifier` parameter. The `weight` can only be set inside a `RowScope` which is a scope for the children of a `Row()`. If you're writing code directly inside the `Row()`, you can use `Modifier.weight()` without extra code.

If you need to make a custom composable that you use inside a `Row`, your composable needs to be an extension function of the `RowScope` like in the example above. Note that in this case, you won't be able to use the composable outside of a `Row()`.

Within `weight()` you define how big of a fraction of the parent the child will take up. In this case, you gave each child a third of the parent! :]

If a child doesn't have a weight, the `Row` will calculate its width using the preferred width first, e.g. using the `size()` modifier. It will then calculate the sizes of the children with weights, proportionally to their weight, based on the remaining available space.

This means that if there is an element taking up `200dp` in width, and you use weights, the weighted children will take up the screen width, minus the `200dp` that's already taken. If none of the children have weight, the `Row()` will be as small as possible to fit all its children without spacing.

Rows represent *horizontal* arrangement of items, and such is its name. Following this logic, a vertical arrangement of items is called a **Column**. Let's see how to use it!

Using Columns

The Compose counterpart for a vertically-oriented `LinearLayout` is a `Column`.

Open **ColumnScreen.kt** and you'll see a similar situation as before—an empty `MyColumn()`, which you'll implement.

Fill in the function, so it looks like this:

```
@Composable
fun MyColumn() {
  Column(
    horizontalAlignment = Alignment.CenterHorizontally,
    verticalArrangement = Arrangement.SpaceEvenly,
    modifier = Modifier.fillMaxSize()
  ) {

    THREE_ELEMENT_LIST.forEach { textResId ->
      Text(
        text = stringResource(id = textResId),
        fontSize = 22.sp
```

```
            )
        }
      }
    }
```

The Column() implementation is the same as the Row(), except you swapped the arrangements and alignments from vertical to horizontal. This is because the items are already placed vertically in a Column, and you need to define how they **behave horizontally** and how to **space them vertically**. With Rows, the situation is the opposite—items are placed horizontally, and the Row needs to know how they **behave vertically** and how to **space them horizontally**.

Build and run and select the **Column** button from the navigation menu.

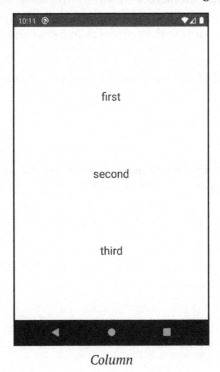

Column

This time, you see that the items are arranged vertically instead of horizontally, with the same spacing.

Now, you've seen how Column and Row are similar to LinearLayouts. They're more powerful, however, because you can arrange the children in several different ways— which the LinearLayout doesn't allow.

Exploring Columns

Now that you've learned how to use Columns, check how they differ from a Row, by opening the Column() signature:

```
@Composable
inline fun Column(
  modifier: Modifier = Modifier,
  verticalArrangement: Arrangement.Vertical = Arrangement.Top,
  horizontalAlignment: Alignment.Horizontal = Alignment.Start,
  content: @Composable ColumnScope.() -> Unit
)
```

As you learned before, the parameters are almost the same, but take a closer look and you'll see that the layout swaps the arrangements and alignments. This means you can do all the same things inside the Column as in a Row, but with different orientations.

Next, you'll learn about a composable counterpart for a FrameLayout, called a **Box**.

Using Boxes

The composable counterpart for a FrameLayout is called a Box. Just like FrameLayout, it's used to display children relative to their parent's edges, and allows you to stack children. This is useful when you have elements that need to be displayed in those specific places or when you want to display elements that overlap, such as dialogs.

Now, open **BoxScreen.kt** and you'll find the usual empty function, MyBox(). Add the following code to complete it:

```
@Composable
fun MyBox(
  modifier: Modifier = Modifier,
  contentModifier: Modifier = Modifier
) {
  Box(modifier = modifier.fillMaxSize()) {
    Text(
      text = stringResource(id = R.string.first),
      fontSize = 22.sp,
      modifier = contentModifier.align(Alignment.TopStart)
    )

    Text(
      text = stringResource(id = R.string.second),
```

Chapter 3: Building Layout Groups in Compose

```
        fontSize = 22.sp,
        modifier = contentModifier.align(Alignment.Center)
    )

    Text(
        text = stringResource(id = R.string.third),
        fontSize = 22.sp,
        modifier = contentModifier.align(Alignment.BottomEnd)
    )
  }
}
```

This time, the function has two parameters—a `modifier` and a `contentModifier`, with default arguments of `Modifier`, the empty modifier implementation. This way, you can pass in custom modifiers that will change how the parent `Box` or each piece of content behaves. After which each element can chain more modifier function calls, to apply additional customization.

This is a good practice, as you can pass in a custom modifier that applies padding or styling to the parent `modifier`, and then reuse custom styles throughout your app, while the end component adds a bit more customization, based on the component. You can do the same for content based modifiers.

Here, the `Box()` has three text fields, as in previous examples, and uses the `align` modifier to position those text fields in three different places.

Build and run, then select the **Box** option from the navigation menu to see the result:

Box

The text fields appear diagonally across the screen, with the first one at the top-left corner, the second one in the center and the last one at the bottom-right corner.

Using a Box is really useful in specific situations, and they make positioning elements incredibly easy.

Exploring Boxes

When you have multiple children inside a Box, they're rendered in the same order as you placed them inside the Box. Here's the implementation:

```
@Composable
fun Box(
    modifier: Modifier = Modifier,
    contentAlignment: Alignment = Alignment.TopStart,
    propagateMinConstraints: Boolean = false,
    content: @Composable BoxScope.() -> Unit
)
```

contentAlignment allows you to set the default Alignment to its children. If you want to have different Alignments between each child, you need to set Alignment by using Modifier.align() on a child.

propagateMinConstraints defines if the minimal constraints should be passed and used for the content too. By default, the constraints of the Box() won't be taken into account when measuring the children.

You can set the Alignment to any edge of the screen as well as in relation to the center, using any of the following types of alignment:

- **TopStart**

- **TopCenter**

- **TopEnd**

- **CenterStart**

- **Center**

- **CenterEnd**

- **BottomStart**

- **BottomCenter**

- **BottomEnd**

Where each of the alignments refers to which part of the screen the Box will attach an item to.

Next, you'll learn about one of the first layouts introduced in Jetpack Compose: the **Surface**.

Using Surfaces

Surface is a new layout that serves as a central metaphor in **Material Design**. What's unique about Surface is it can only hold one child at a time, but it provides many styling options for the content of its children, such as the elevation, border and much more.

It's time to see the Surface in action. Open **SurfaceScreen.kt** and look at the contents:

```
@Composable
fun SurfaceScreen(modifier: Modifier = Modifier) {

  Box(modifier = modifier.fillMaxSize()) {
    MySurface(modifier = modifier.align(Alignment.Center))
  }

  BackButtonHandler {
    JetFundamentalsRouter.navigateTo(Screen.Navigation)
  }
}

@Composable
fun MySurface(modifier: Modifier) {
  //TODO write your code here
}
```

To show all that the Surface can do, the example is set inside a full-screen Box() and an Alignment.Center. All that's left is to implement the empty MySurface(). To do this, add the following code to finish it:

```
@Composable
fun MySurface(modifier: Modifier) {
  Surface(
      modifier = modifier.size(100.dp), // 1
      color = Color.LightGray, // 2
      contentColor = colorResource(id =
R.color.colorPrimary), // 2
      elevation = 1.dp, // 3
      border = BorderStroke(1.dp, Color.Black) // 4
  ) {
    MyColumn() // 5
```

```
    }
  }
```

There are many small steps in this code, so go over them one by one:

1. You first set the size of the surface to 100dp in both height and width using Modifier.size().

2. Then you set the color of the surface to Color.LightGray and the color of its content to colorPrimary. The surface will be gray, and Surface will set the contentColor to all the elements it applies to—such as Text elements.

3. You add an elevation of 1dp to raise the Surface above other elements.

4. You also add a black border to outline the Surface.

5. Finally, you set the child to the Surface to be the MyColumn() you defined earlier.

This is a perfect example of the power of Jetpack Compose. You can **reuse** each of the screens and composable functions you implemented before. This time, you reused MyColumn(), with three vertical Text elements.

Build and run and select **Surface** from the navigation menu.

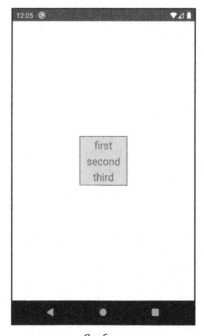

Surface

At the center of the screen is the `Surface` in a light gray color with a black border. Within it is the previously-implemented custom `Column`.

Previously, all the `Text` elements used the default, black color, but using `contentColor` you changed the text color of `Column`'s children to use the green color of raywenderlich.com.

If you're reading the grayscale version of the book, you might not notice the color change as easily, so make sure to build and run the app and preview the changes directly on your phone!

Now let's see what else the `Surface()` allows you to do.

Exploring Surfaces

To see what else a `Surface()` has to offer, open its signature:

```
@Composable
fun Surface(
    modifier: Modifier = Modifier,
    shape: Shape = RectangleShape,
    color: Color = MaterialTheme.colors.surface,
    contentColor: Color = contentColorFor(color),
    border: BorderStroke? = null,
    elevation: Dp = 0.dp,
    content: @Composable () -> Unit
)
```

These parameters define `Surface`'s purpose. There are five purposes in total:

• **Shape**: Clips the children with the defined `shape`.

• **Color**: Fills the shape with a `color` you define.

• **Border**: Draws borders, if they're set.

• **Elevation**: Sets the elevation and draws an appropriate shadow.

• **Content**: Sets the default color for its content with the defined `contentColor`.

The most common way to use a `Surface` is as the root layout of your components. Since it can hold only one child, that child is usually another layout that positions the rest of the elements. The `Surface()` doesn't handle positioning—its child does.

> **Note**: There's a popular custom `Surface` implementation called `Card`. A `Card` has exactly the same five purposes and can only hold one child. The only difference between the `Card` and a `Surface` are its default parameters. A `Card` has a predefined elevation and uses a material theme shape with rounded corners.

Now that you've learned all the basic layouts available in Jetpack Compose, your next step is to learn about a more advanced layout that lets you create a fully-functional UI. That element is called a **Scaffold**.

Scaffold

The `Scaffold` is a new layout that Jetpack Compose introduced. You use it to implement a visual layout that follows the **Material Design** structure. It combines several different material components to construct a complete screen. Because the `Scaffold()` offers multiple ways to build your UI, it's best to jump into the code, and play around with it!

Using Scaffold

Open **ScaffoldScreen.kt** and look inside. You'll see three empty composable functions:

```
@Composable
fun MyScaffold() {
  //todo write your code here
}

@Composable
fun MyTopAppBar(scaffoldState: ScaffoldState) {
  //todo write your code here
}

@Composable
fun MyBottomAppBar() {
  //todo write your code here
}
```

You'll use these empty functions to implement your own `Scaffold` and to add top and bottom app bars.

Start by entering the following code inside `MyScaffold()`. It should look like so:

```
@Composable
fun MyScaffold() {
  val scaffoldState: ScaffoldState = rememberScaffoldState()
  val scope: CoroutineScope = rememberCoroutineScope()

  Scaffold(
      scaffoldState = scaffoldState,
      contentColor = colorResource(id = R.color.colorPrimary),
      content = { MyRow() },
      topBar = { MyTopAppBar(scaffoldState = scaffoldState,
scope = scope) },
      bottomBar = { MyBottomAppBar() },
      drawerContent = { MyColumn() }
  )
}
```

First, you create the scaffold state by calling `rememberScaffoldState()`, then you assign it to the `Scaffold()`. You set `contentColor` to the primary color of the app and `content` to `MyRow()`, which you previously implemented.

Then you create a `scope`, using `rememberCoroutineScope()`. You need to use coroutines to trigger certain `Scaffold()` behavior, such as opening and closing the drawers.

Next, you set the top and bottom bar content to the composables you haven't implemented yet. Here you pass the `scaffoldState` and the scope that'll be used by coroutines.

Finally, you set `MyColumn()` as your drawer. There's a lot going on here, but you'll see how it connects together in a moment.

Make sure to update the `MyTopAppBar` signature to the following:

```
@Composable
fun MyTopAppBar(scaffoldState: ScaffoldState, scope:
CoroutineScope) {}
```

Build and run, then click the **Scaffold** option from the navigation menu.

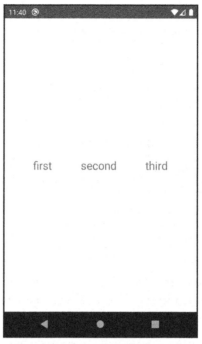

Scaffold

You can see the MyRow() with the three Text elements on the screen, but the top and bottom app bars aren't showing. That's not surprising since you haven't implemented them yet. :]

Additionally, you can open the navigation drawer by swiping from the left to the right side of the screen, to show the MyColumn from before.

Now let's finish the screen by implementing the top and bottom bars.

Completing the screen

To complete the screen, implement the two remaining composables. Add the following code to complete MyTopAppBar():

```
@Composable
fun MyTopAppBar(scaffoldState: ScaffoldState, scope:
CoroutineScope) {
  val drawerState = scaffoldState.drawerState

  TopAppBar(
```

```
    navigationIcon = {
      IconButton(
        content = {
          Icon(
            Icons.Default.Menu,
            tint = Color.White,
            contentDescription = stringResource(R.string.menu)
          )
        },
        onClick = {
          scope.launch { if (drawerState.isClosed)
 drawerState.open() else drawerState.close() }
        }
      )
    },
    title = { Text(text = stringResource(id =
 R.string.app_name), color = Color.White) },
    backgroundColor = colorResource(id = R.color.colorPrimary)
  )
}
```

First, you create a new value called drawerState, using the scaffoldState. You'll use this to access the Scaffold's drawer.

Then, you add an existing predefined implementation of the TopAppBar(). You add an IconButton() with the Menu icon and White content color as the navigationIcon.

For the click action of the IconButton(), you initiate opening the drawer by changing the drawerState inside the scaffoldState.

To change the drawerState, you must do it from a coroutine or another suspend function. In this case you launch a coroutine by using the scope passed from the parent composable. This will open the drawer whenever you click the menu icon.

The navigationIcon is a predefined parameter you can use to define the first element in the TopAppBar, which usually represents a **Home** or **Back** button.

Then you define the title, to represent a simple Text element that shows the app name. Showing a title in the top bar is common behavior for most Android apps.

The TopAppbar is a pretty simple component that lets you define an elevation, a backgroundColor, title and navigationIcon separately, or combined in a single content function, and special actions that define another composable function for menu actions. Play around with other parameters to see how they style the TopAppBar.

Now, implement the `MyBottomAppBar()`:

```
@Composable
fun MyBottomAppBar() {
  BottomAppBar(
    content = {},
    backgroundColor = colorResource(id = R.color.colorPrimary))
}
```

For `MyBottomAppBar()`, you add an existing implementation of the bottom app bar with empty content. You also define `colorPrimary` as the background color.

Build and run again and check the changes to the screen:

Scaffold With App Bars

The screen now shows top and bottom bars as well. The top bar contains the Menu icon, which opens the drawer when the user clicks it.

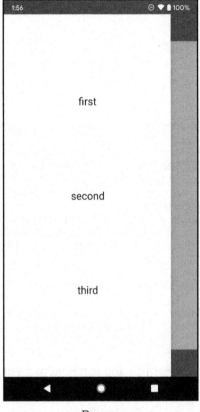

Drawer

The drawer shows the three text fields from MyColumn(). To dismiss the drawer, just click anywhere on the screen, outside of the drawer, or swipe the drawer left.

You've now learned how to group your composables inside layouts, to position them and to give them common properties. You can achieve this by using either multiple basic layouts or one of the advanced layouts.

Aside from Scaffold, advanced layouts also include a ConstraintLayout. ConstraintLayout lets you make constraints between the elements, just like the version you find in XML.

You'll dive deep and learn more about ConstraintLayout in Chapter 9, "Using ConstraintSets in Composables". But before all that, let's explore the Scaffold() signature.

Exploring Scaffold

To learn more about all the parameters the Scaffold() lets you use, open its signature:

```
@Composable
fun Scaffold(
    modifier: Modifier = Modifier,
    scaffoldState: ScaffoldState = rememberScaffoldState(),
    topBar: @Composable () -> Unit = {},
    bottomBar: @Composable () -> Unit = {},
    snackbarHost: @Composable (SnackbarHostState) -> Unit =
{ SnackbarHost(it) },
    floatingActionButton: @Composable () -> Unit = {},
    floatingActionButtonPosition: FabPosition = FabPosition.End,
    isFloatingActionButtonDocked: Boolean = false,
    drawerContent: @Composable (ColumnScope.() -> Unit)? = null,
    drawerGesturesEnabled: Boolean = true,
    drawerShape: Shape = MaterialTheme.shapes.large,
    drawerElevation: Dp = DrawerDefaults.Elevation,
    drawerBackgroundColor: Color = MaterialTheme.colors.surface,
    drawerContentColor: Color =
contentColorFor(drawerBackgroundColor),
    drawerScrimColor: Color = DrawerDefaults.scrimColor,
    backgroundColor: Color = MaterialTheme.colors.background,
    contentColor: Color = contentColorFor(backgroundColor),
    content: @Composable (PaddingValues) -> Unit
)
```

You can see that it has lots of features and components. This breakdown will give you a clear picture of what each does, and how you used them:

- **scaffoldState**: The state of the layout. Unlike the basic layouts, Scaffold requires custom handling of its state. This is important because it can hold several different components that can change its visibility or content. A common example of handling state is changing whether a drawer displays or not.

- **topBar**: A composable that renders the top app bar. While you could create a custom composable, Jetpack Compose offers you a predefined composable to save you the effort.

- **bottomBar**: This composable renders the bottom app bar. As with the previous parameter, you can choose whether to use a custom composable or the predefined BottomAppBar.

- **snackbarHost**: As the name implies, this component hosts a SnackBar. It handles the state when SnackBars should be shown.

- **floatingActionButton**: Lets you set a composable for the main FloatingActionButton on the screen. The default FloatingActionButton is recommended for consistency.

- **drawerContent**: Use this composable for drawers that require a custom implementation.

- **content**: A composable shown inside Scaffold. This is where you put the main content of the screen.

There are also many other parameters which are less important, but you can explore them if you want to play around with your Scaffold.

Now you can move onto building more components in Compose and complex UI, with the knowledge you gained in the first few chapters! :]

Key points

- Use Layouts to position your elements or give them shared properties.

- Row lets you position elements horizontally on the screen.

- Column lets you position elements vertically on the screen.

- Use vertical or horizontal Arrangement to change the position of elements inside the Row or Column.

- Use **weights** to change the **proportion** of the screen your elements will use.

- Box allows you to position the elements in the corners of the screen or stack them on top of each other.

- Within Row, Column, Box, or other functions, you gain access to hidden modifiers from the RowScope, ColumnScope, BoxScope and other scope types, respectively.

- If you want to build components that should only be used within Row, Box or other grouping composables, you can make them an extension function to the appropriate RowScope, BoxScope or other scopes, respectively.

- Making an extension function composable to any Scope gives you access to the Scope's modifiers in the function.

- Group multiple basic layouts to create a more complex screen.

- Use `Surface` to clip the elements inside it with an option to add the border and elevation.

- `Surface` can hold only one child.

- Add another layout inside `Surface` to position the elements.

- `Card` is a just a `Surface` with default parameters.

- `Scaffold` lets you build the entire screen by adding different material components.

- Use `ScaffoldState` to handle states for the components inside the scaffold.

- Use `DrawerState` to handle the drawer state, within a `Scaffold()`.

- `rememberScaffoldState()` will remember the state and preserve it during the recomposition.

- `rememberCoroutineScope()` lets you create a composable-bound `CoroutineScope` to launch coroutines and perform actions like closing or opening drawers.

Where to go from here?

You now know how to use multiple predefined composables to implement different features. You've also learned how to group and position them inside layouts to make a complete screen.

Next, you'll learn about different ways of making lists, how to make adapters and how to get the same result as when you use a `RecyclerView`. Finally, you'll learn how to implement custom grids.

See you in the next chapter!

Chapter 4: Building Lists with Jetpack Compose

By Tino Balint

In previous chapters, you learned about different elements in Compose and how to group and position them inside layouts to build complex UIs. Using that knowledge, you could potentially build any screen.

However, you're missing some functionality that you'll eventually need. What happens when you have to display more elements than you can fit on the screen? In that case, the elements are all composed, but the limited screen size prevents you from seeing all of them. There are even situations where you want to dynamically add an infinite number of new elements on the screen and still be able to see them all.

The solution to this problem is allowing your content to scroll, either vertically or horizontally. The traditional way of implementing this feature is to use `ScrollView`, which allows you to scroll content vertically. For horizontal scrolling, you use `HorizontalScrollView`. Both of them can have only one child view inside them, so to add multiple elements, you need to use a single layout that wraps those elements.

Jetpack Compose gives you a new way to achieve the same result — using scrollable and lazily composed containers.

In this chapter, you'll learn how to make lists and grids in Jetpack Compose to help you fit all your content on the screen. You'll learn how to show content that scrolls vertically or horizontally and how to build an alternative for the traditional `RecyclerView` using composable functions.

Using vertical scrolling modifiers

As you know by now, `Column` is the replacement for `LinearLayout` in the vertical orientation. In Jetpack Compose, you can use the same `Column` composable with extra modifiers that enable scrolling! Let's see how to implement a simple scrolling `Column`.

To follow along with the code examples, open Android Studio and select **Open an Existing Project**. Then, navigate to **04-building-lists-with-jetpack-compose/ projects** and select the **starter** folder.

Once the project builds, you'll see the following structure:

Project Structure

You'll start off by building a vertically scrollable `Column` after which you'll explore its horizontal counterpart. To do that, open **ScrollingScreen.kt** and you'll see two composable functions — `ScrollingScreen()` and `MyScrollingScreen()`:

```
@Composable
fun ScrollingScreen() {
  MyScrollingScreen()

  BackButtonHandler {
    JetFundamentalsRouter.navigateTo(Screen.Navigation)
  }
}

@Composable
fun MyScrollingScreen() {
  //TODO add your code here
}

@Composable
fun BookImage(@DrawableRes imageResId: Int, @StringRes
contentDescriptionResId: Int){
  Image(
    bitmap = ImageBitmap.imageResource(imageResId),
    contentDescription =
stringResource(contentDescriptionResId),
    contentScale = ContentScale.FillBounds,
    modifier = Modifier.size(476.dp, 616.dp)
  )
}
```

As in the previous chapters, `ScrollingScreen()` is already set up to handle the back navigation, so you only need to implement `MyScrollingScreen()`. There is also `BookImage` composable which is predefined. It creates an image of a book in a specific size with the image and content description passed as a parameter.

Change the code of `MyScrollingScreen()` to the following, and include the required imports with the help of Android Studio:

```
@Composable
fun MyScrollingScreen(modifier: Modifier = Modifier) {
  Column(modifier =
modifier.verticalScroll(rememberScrollState())) {
    BookImage(R.drawable.advanced_architecture_android,
R.string.advanced_architecture_android)
    BookImage(R.drawable.kotlin_aprentice,
R.string.kotlin_apprentice)
    BookImage(R.drawable.kotlin_coroutines,
R.string.kotlin_coroutines)
  }
}
```

Here, you added three existing `BookImage` composables to the `Column`. You used existing drawable and string resources for the parameters. To make the `Column` scrollable, you called `verticalScroll()`, and passed in `rememberScrollState()`. This creates a scroll state based on the scroll configuration and handles the scroll behavior during the recomposition so that the position is not lost.

What happens here is that you'll show a `Column`, a vertical list of items. But if the items are too large to show them all at once, it will be scrollable and you'll be able to go through each item respectively.

Build and run the app, then select **Scrolling** from the navigation menu. You'll see the three images, one below the other — but unfortunately, they don't fit on the screen together. Luckily, you made the screen scrollable! :]

Scroll down to see the images that aren't displayed yet.

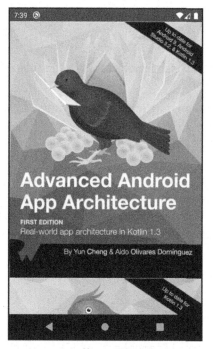

Scrolling Column

Using a scrollable `Column` is very easy, but there is much more you can do with it. Let's explore how it works.

Exploring the scrollable modifier

Look at its source code to see what a verticalScroll can do and how it works when you use it:

```
fun Modifier.verticalScroll(
    state: ScrollState,
    enabled: Boolean = true,
    flingBehavior: FlingBehavior? = null,
    reverseScrolling: Boolean = false
)
```

First, look at the function parameters. Some of them you already know, but there are a few important new ones:

- scrollState is the current state of the scroll. It determines the offset from the top and can also start or stop **smooth scrolling** and **fling animations**.

- enabled enables or disables scrolling. If it's disabled, you can still programmatically scroll to a specific position using the state property. But the user can't use scrolling gestures.

- flingBehavior is used to perform a fling animation with a given velocity.

- reverseScrolling allows you to reverse the direction of the scroll. In other words, setting it to true lets you scroll up. Note that its default value is false.

It's important to understand that verticalScroll() is a **modifier**. This means that you can make your custom composables scrollable as well, by applying it to their modifiers, if that suits your use case.

You applied vertical scrolling to a Column. If you want to apply **horizontal scrolling**, you use a **Row** instead.

Using horizontal scrolling modifiers

Vertical scrolling now works on your screen — but in some cases you need a horizontal scroll, instead.

Just as you had to use a different component for horizontal scrolling called HorizontalScrollView, Jetpack Compose offers its own composable called Row, but you need to set the modifier. To achieve horizontal scroll, you need to apply horizontalScroll(), which works the same as verticalScroll() but in a different direction.

Let's implement a scrollable Row. Inside `MyScrollingScreen()`, replace the `Column` with a `Row` and `verticalScroll` with a `horizontalScroll`:

```
@Composable
fun MyScrollingScreen(modifier: Modifier = Modifier) {
  Row(modifier =
modifier.horizontalScroll(rememberScrollState())) { // here
    ...
  }
}
```

You don't have to do anything else! The scrollable Row is almost identical to the scrollable `Column` in terms of the default behavior. It sets up the horizontal scroll automatically, using `horizontalScroll()`.

Build and run the app and then select **Scrolling** again in the navigation menu. You'll still see the same three images, but now, the scroll works horizontally. And you accomplished this by changing just one line of code!

Scrolling Row

Scrollable columns and rows are great when you have static content, like in the previous examples. However, they aren't a good idea for data collections that change at runtime. That's because scrollable composables compose and render all the elements inside eagerly, which can be a heavy operation when you have a large number of elements to display.

In such cases, as you know from the traditional View system, you'd use a `RecyclerView` to optimize the loading and rendering of the visible elements on the screen. But how does Jetpack Compose deal with this issue? Let's find out! :]

Lists in Compose

To display a large collection of elements in Android, you used the `RecyclerView`. The only elements `RecyclerView` renders are the ones visible on the screen. Only after the user begins to scroll does it render the new elements and display them on screen. It then recycles the elements that go off the screen into a pool of **view holders**.

When you scroll back to see the previous elements, it renders them from the pool. Thanks to this behavior, re-rendering is so quick that it's almost as if the elements were never removed from the screen in the first place. This optimization mechanism gives `RecyclerView` its name.

Loading data only when it's needed is called **lazy loading** and Jetpack Compose doubles down on this method to handle lists. The main two components you use for lazy lists in Compose are the `LazyColumn` and `LazyRow`.

Introducing LazyColumn & LazyRow

`LazyColumn` and `LazyRow` are used for vertical and horizontal scenarios, respectively.

`RecyclerView` uses a `LayoutManager` to set its orientation, but Jetpack Compose doesn't have `LayoutManagers`. Instead, you use two different composable functions to change the orientation. The composables work in almost the same way as `RecyclerView`, but without needing to recycle.

When you use `LazyColumn` or `LazyRow`, the framework composes only the elements that it should show on the screen. When you scroll, new elements are composed and the old ones are disposed of. When you scroll back, the old elements are recomposed. Jetpack Compose doesn't need a recycled `ViewHolder` pool because its recomposition handles caching more efficiently.

Let's implement both vertical and horizontal lists to categorize the books you showed earlier.

Creating lists with LazyColumn & LazyRow

There are many awesome books in our raywenderlich.com library and in different categories. It's best to show them all categorized, so you can easily pick and choose your favorites.

To do this, you'll build a screen with a vertical list, where each composable item inside the list is another horizontal list. You'll split the vertical list into book categories and each book category will have a horizontal list of books that belong there. Look at the image below to get a better understanding:

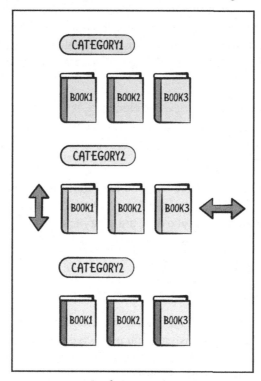

Book Categories

You can see the list of book categories scrolls vertically, while the categories themselves contain books thatscroll horizontally. Your task is to duplicate that implementation, except with a dynamic number of categories and books. That way, as write more books, you can just add them to the list!

Now, open **ListsScreen.kt**. This file contains a predefined property named `items` with a list of book categories. That's the data you'll display on the screen. At the bottom of the file, you'll find the following composable functions:

```
@Composable
fun ListScreen() {
  MyList()
  BackButtonHandler {
    JetFundamentalsRouter.navigateTo(Screen.Navigation)
  }
}

@Composable
fun MyList() {
  //TODO add your code here
}

@Composable
fun ListItem(bookCategory: BookCategory, modifier: Modifier =
Modifier) {
  //TODO add your code here
}
```

`ListsScreen()` is a provided composable that handles the navigation for you, so you don't need to worry about it. Your task is to implement `MyList()` and the `ListItem()`.

Add the following code inside `MyList()` and include the required imports from the `androidx.compose.material` package for `Text` composable and `androidx.compose.foundation` for other composables:

```
@Composable
fun MyList() {
  LazyColumn {
    items(items) { item -> ListItem(item) }
  }
}
```

Here, you added a `LazyColumn()` and set the `items` parameter with the `items` property containing your data. `items` is a list of objects of the `BookCategory` type. Each `BookCategory` contains a `String` with the category name and a list of images showing the books that should appear in that category.

Within the trailing lambda, for each `item` parameter inside the list of `items`, you create a new `ListItem`. This lambda represents the function to transform each of the objects within `items` to a list of composable elements.

This way you can call any number of composable functions to represent your items and you can add special logic depending on the item type, its position and more!

Next, you'll implement `ListItem()`. Replace `ListItem()` with the following code and, once again, don't forget to include the required imports with the help of Android Studio:

```
@Composable
fun ListItem(bookCategory: BookCategory, modifier: Modifier =
Modifier) {
  Column(modifier = Modifier.padding(8.dp)) {
    Text(
      text = stringResource(bookCategory.categoryResourceId),
      fontSize = 22.sp,
      fontWeight = FontWeight.Bold,
      color = colorResource(id = R.color.colorPrimary)
    )
    Spacer(modifier = modifier.height(8.dp))

    // TODO
  }
}
```

This looks like a lot of code, but what it does is quite simple. First, you added a `Column()` as the parent layout of the composable so you can align its children vertically. The `Column()` uses a `padding` modifier to add some space near the borders.

The top child of `Column()` is a `Text()`. You need this to display the title of the category, which is passed as the `text` argument. Note how you styled the text by changing the font size, weight and color.

The next element is a `Spacer`, which adds some space between the category name and the rest of the content. This will let you show the category name on top of the horizontal list of books.

Now add the following code underneath the `Spacer`, to add the horizontal list of books:

```
LazyRow {
  items(bookCategory.bookImageResources) { items ->
    BookImage(items)
  }
}
```

Similar to how you built a vertical list, using a `LazyRow` you create a horizontal list. It receives the list of book images as a parameter and a lambda that builds `BookImages`.

Also add the `BookImage()` in a separate function:

```
@Composable
fun BookImage(imageResource: Int) {
  Image(
    modifier = Modifier.size(170.dp, 200.dp),
    painter = painterResource(id = imageResource),
    contentScale = ContentScale.Fit,
    contentDescription = stringResource(R.string.book_image)
  )
}
```

A `BookImage` is a wrapper for an `Image` composable. `Image()` displays the book image for each element in the list. You used a `size` modifier to set a static size of 170dp width and 200dp height.

Since the list you passed as an argument to `LazyRow()` contains resource IDs instead of the actual images, you need to use `painterResource()` to retrieve the correct asset. Finally, by using `ContentScale.Fit`, you make the image adapt to the size you specified earlier and set the content description with the provided string.

Now, build and run the app. Once the main screen loads, click the **List** button in the navigation menu. Your app will show the following screen:

List

As you see, the books are sorted by category. You can scroll vertically to browse book categories and horizontally to browse books in each category.

By the way, if you're interested in any of the books you see, you can find them in our book library! :]

Lists are very easy to use and understand, especially because their signature requires only a few parameters to make them work. Let's dive a bit deeper into their implementation.

Exploring Lists

Now that you understand the difference and how to implement specific lists, take a look at the signature for LazyColumn and LazyRow:

```
@Composable
fun LazyColumn(
  modifier: Modifier = Modifier,
  state: LazyListState = rememberLazyListState(),
  contentPadding: PaddingValues = PaddingValues(0.dp),
  reverseLayout: Boolean = false,
  verticalArrangement: Arrangement.Vertical =
      if (!reverseLayout) Arrangement.Top else
Arrangement.Bottom,
  horizontalAlignment: Alignment.Horizontal = Alignment.Start,
  flingBehavior: FlingBehavior =
ScrollableDefaults.flingBehavior(),
  content: LazyListScope.() -> Unit
)

@Composable
fun LazyRow(
  modifier: Modifier = Modifier,
  state: LazyListState = rememberLazyListState(),
  contentPadding: PaddingValues = PaddingValues(0.dp),
  reverseLayout: Boolean = false,
  horizontalArrangement: Arrangement.Horizontal =
      if (!reverseLayout) Arrangement.Start else
Arrangement.End,
  verticalAlignment: Alignment.Vertical = Alignment.Top,
  flingBehavior: FlingBehavior =
ScrollableDefaults.flingBehavior(),
  content: LazyListScope.() -> Unit
)
```

The most important parameter to notice here is content which is used for the content inside the list. This content is of a LazyListScope type and not your usual Composable type.

Take a look at the `LazyListScope` interface to learn why is it so important.

```
interface LazyListScope {

    fun item(key: Any? = null, content: @Composable
LazyItemScope.() -> Unit)

    fun items(
        count: Int,
        key: ((index: Int) -> Any)? = null,
        itemContent: @Composable LazyItemScope.(index: Int) ->
Unit
    )

    @ExperimentalFoundationApi
    fun stickyHeader(key: Any? = null, content: @Composable
LazyItemScope.() -> Unit)
}
```

The interface provides a set of functions which help you when building lists:

- `items()` allows you to set a list of item data you would like to use in each of your list items. Once you set the data, you also need to provide an `itemContent` which is a composable used for displaying every item in your list.

- `item()` allows you to add a new composable item to your list. Note that you can use different composable types every time.

- `stickyHeader()` allows you to set the header composable that will remain visible on the top of the list, even after you scroll down to see new items. Note that this function is annotated with `@ExperimentalFoundationApi` which means that it's still in experimental stage and might change or be removed in the future.

Unlike the `RecyclerView`, lists in Jetpack Compose don't require an adapter, view holder layout managers and an RV element in your XML files just to make it work. Using one of the two very simple functions, you can either show a horizontal or a vertical list that is performant and customizable!

There are also extension functions like `itemsIndexed`, which has same features as `items()` but also provides you with an index for each of your items.

That's all for the theory. So far you've implemented simple lists and a list of horizontal lists for your books. The last thing you need to learn how to do is build **grids**.

Grids in Compose

When working with a `RecyclerView`, you can use different types of `LayoutManagers` to place your elements on the screen in different ways. To make grids, for example, you use a `GridLayoutManager` and then set the number of columns inside the grid.

Unfortunately, Jetpack Compose doesn't include a ready-to-use, stable, component to accomplish the same thing. However, thanks to the power of Compose, building your own component isn't hard. You'll see how to do this step-by-step in this section.

The grid you'll implement resembles what you saw in the last list example. This time, however, the elements won't scroll horizontally but will be fixed in place, instead. To better visualize the problem, look at the following image:

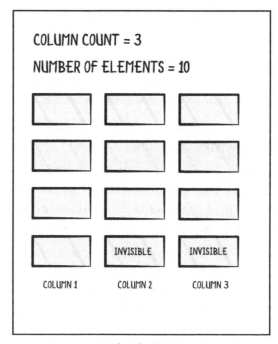

Grid Calculation

As you see, your grid contains ten elements distributed across three columns. The last row shows only one element in the first column, because that's the last element in your list. There are two more elements next to it, but they're marked as invisible in the image. That's a little trick to position the last element properly in the first column — you add invisible elements to occupy the rest of the space. Otherwise, the last element would be in the center of the row.

There are the basic requirements of the grid, but let's dive into the code to make your own grid.

Implementing a grid

Open **GridScreen.kt** and take a moment to look inside. You'll find the usual function to handle the navigation and a list containing the icons that you'll use as the grid's content. At the bottom of the file, you'll find the following composable functions that you need to implement:

```
@Composable
fun GridView(columnCount: Int) {
  //TODO add your code here
}

@Composable
fun RowItem(rowItems: List<IconResource>) {
  //TODO add your code here
}

@Composable
fun RowScope.GridIcon(iconResource: IconResource) {
  //TODO add your code here
}
```

Implementing GridView

First, you'll deal with GridView(). This composable takes a parameter named columnCount, which determines the maximum number of elements you need to place in each row.

Add the following code to the body of GridView:

```
@Composable
fun GridView(columnCount: Int) {
  val itemSize = items.size
  val rowCount = ceil(itemSize.toFloat() / columnCount).toInt()
  val gridItems = mutableListOf<List<IconResource>>()
  var position = 0
}
```

To fill the grid, you use the prepared list of icons called items. First, you store the item size, because you'll use it multiple times.

You then calculate the number of rows you need to display the items. You get this value by dividing the number of items by the column count and using `ceil()` to ensure that you include the last row, even if it isn't full. Now add the next piece of code start building a grid:

```
@Composable
fun GridView(columnCount: Int) {
  ...
  for (i in 0 until rowCount) {
    val rowItem = mutableListOf<IconResource>()
    for (j in 0 until columnCount) {
      if (position.inc() <= itemSize) {
        rowItem.add(IconResource(items[position++], true))
      }
    }
  }
  // TODO
}
```

Next, for each row, you create a list of items that hold an `IconResource`. This is a model class that contains an icon resource and holds a Boolean property to set the icon's visibility.

All items added inside the row this way are set to visible by passing in `true` as the second constructor parameter. Because grids have rows and columns, you need to use a nested for loop to prepare all the items. The next step is to add empty dummy views and finally build the list:

```
@Composable
fun GridView(columnCount: Int) {
  ...
  for (i in 0 until rowCount) {
    val rowItem = mutableListOf<IconResource>()
    for (j in 0 until columnCount) {
      if (position.inc() <= itemSize) {
        rowItem.add(IconResource(items[position++], true))
      }
    }
    // here
    val itemsToFill = columnCount - rowItem.size

    for (j in 0 until itemsToFill) {
      rowItem.add(IconResource(Icons.Filled.Delete, false))
    }
    gridItems.add(rowItem)
  }
  // here
  LazyColumn(modifier = Modifier.fillMaxSize())  {
    items(gridItems) { items ->
      RowItem(items)
```

```
        }
      }
    }
```

You calculate if there's a need to include dummy invisible items by subtracting the current row size from the required `columnCount`. If `columnCount` is larger than `rowItem.size` it means you're in the last row and it isn't full. In that case, you add dummy icons along with the `isVisible` property as `false`, to make them invisible.

Finally, you use a `LazyColumn`, passing the rows that you calculated in `gridItems`.

`RowItem()` is a composable that renders each row inside the column. Implementing this is your next task. :]

Implementing RowItem

Each `RowItem()` will represent a series of `GridIcon`s for that row. Replace the code of the `RowItem()` with the following:

```
@Composable
fun RowItem(rowItems: List<IconResource>) {
  Row {
    for (element in rowItems)
      GridIcon(element)
  }
}
```

Here, you use a Row to lay out the different items within a given row. Each item is then a `GridIcon`, which you'll implement next.

Implementing GridIcon

Each `GridItem()` will show the icon you passed in, or show an invisible icon if you need to add dummy elements to the grid, to fill up the row. Replace the `GridIcon` with the following code to achieve such behavior:

```
@Composable
fun RowScope.GridIcon(iconResource: IconResource) {
  val color = if (iconResource.isVisible)
    colorResource(R.color.colorPrimary)
  else Color.Transparent

  Icon(
    imageVector = iconResource.imageVector,
    tint = color,
    contentDescription = stringResource(R.string.grid_icon),
    modifier = Modifier
```

```
        .size(80.dp, 80.dp)
        .weight(1f)
    )
}
```

Here's a breakdown of the previous code block. First, you calculated the color of the icon using the visibility property. Since Jetpack Compose doesn't have an option to set a composable to invisible, you'll achieve this result by using a transparent color.

Next, you add the calculated color as a `tint` to the `Icon` and set the `size` and `weight` modifiers. To use the `weight` modifier, Compose needs a `Scope`, which you get from the `Row` parent of `GridIcon` by making the `GridIcon` an extension function of the `RowScope`, you get to use all the members from the `RowScope`, such as `weight()`. `weight()` is important to spread the icons evenly between other icons inside a `Row()`.

Build and run the app, then click the **Grid** button in the navigation menu. You'll see the following screen:

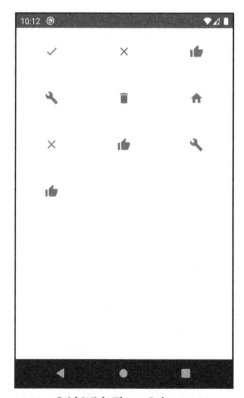

Grid With Three Columns

Awesome! You have a grid of icons on the screen, placed in three columns. You can increase the number of icons inside the `items` list to make the grid scrollable. To experiment with different column counts, replace the value of `columnCount` inside `GridScreen()` with the desired value to see the result. Keep in mind that you're limited to the number of columns that fit the screen.

There is also a built in-composable for grids called `LazyVerticalGrid` which is under `@ExperimentalFoundationApi`. This means that the composable will likely drastically change or be removed in the future. If you are still willing to try it out, replace the code inside the `GridScreen` with the following:

```
@ExperimentalFoundationApi
@Composable
fun GridScreen() {
  LazyVerticalGrid(
    modifier = Modifier.fillMaxSize(),
    cells = GridCells.Fixed(3),
    content = {
      items(items) { item ->
        GridIcon(IconResource(item, true))
      }
    }
  )

  BackButtonHandler {
    JetFundamentalsRouter.navigateTo(Screen.Navigation)
  }
}
```

Also add a `GridIcon()` counterpart, that isn't an extension function:

```
@Composable
fun GridIcon(iconResource: IconResource) {
  val color = if (iconResource.isVisible)
    colorResource(R.color.colorPrimary)
  else Color.Transparent

  Icon(
    imageVector = iconResource.imageVector,
    tint = color,
    contentDescription = stringResource(R.string.grid_icon),
    modifier = Modifier
      .size(80.dp, 80.dp)
  )
}
```

Build and run the app, then click the **Grid** button in the navigation menu. You'll see the same result as with the custom version.

You added a `LazyVerticalGrid` with three parameters: `modifier`, `cells` and `content`. `Cells` describes how columns form. There are two types of `GridCells`:

- **Fixed** sets the fixed amount of cells on the screen.

- **Adaptive** adds as many rows or columns as possible to fit the screen with the provided `minSize` as the minimum size parameter.

The `content` works the same as with `LazyRow` or `LazyColumn`. You provide the collection of data and a composable which is used for every grid cell. `LazyVerticalGrid` then calculates and positions your composable in a grid depending on the `cells` parameter.

Congratulations! You've learned a lot about how to lay out large numbers of elements in Jetpack Compose.

Key points

- Use `Column` with the `verticalScroll` modifier to make the content vertically if it doesn't fit the screen.

- Use `Row` with the `horizontalScroll` modifier to make the content scroll horizontally if it doesn't fit the screen.

- You can make your own composables scrollable by adding the `verticalScroll` or `horizontalScroll` modifiers.

- Use scrollers only for a fixed amount of content.

- For dynamic and larger amounts of content, use lists instead.

- The composable alternatives to `RecyclerView` are called `LazyColumn` and `LazyRow` for the vertical and horizontal scenarios, respectively.

- You can group lists inside each other to make content scrollable in both directions.

- To make grids, use a custom implementation.

- If you use `LazyVerticalGrid`, keep in mind that it might soon be changed or removed.

- Use a transparent color or set an alpha to zero to make an invisible composable.

- Alternatively, you can use `LazyRow` and `LazyColumn` components if you want to manually add items to the list, allowing you to build headers and footers. Learn more about them here: https://developer.android.com/reference/kotlin/androidx/compose/foundation/lazy/package-summary#lazycolumn.

Where to go from here?

In this chapter, you learned how to make scrollable content, scrollable lists for dynamically created elements and custom grids.

You're ready to implement this UI functionality in your own apps. This wrapped up the entire first section! In the next section and the next chapter, you'll learn how to build more complex custom composables using all the knowledge you've gained so far.

See you there! :]

Section II: Composing User Interfaces

When working on apps and user interfaces, it's not only important to know what each piece of the interface should be, but also how all these pieces **come together** to build a beautiful and fully-functional design that'll wow your users.

Now that you've amassed quite a lot of knowledge about the basics of Jetpack Compose and its fundamental UI elements, you're ready to dive deeper into building custom Compose elements, **managing their state** in a performant way and **styling them** using modifiers and built-in Material Design features.

Over the next four chapters, you'll learn how to:

- Attach LiveData structures to your state management.

- Rely on different styling modifiers.

- Combine these topics to create a powerful UI!

You'll build on the knowledge from the previous section of the book by learning new parts of the Jetpack Compose toolkit.

Chapter 5: Combining Composables

by Denis Buketa

Great job on completing the first section of this book! Now that you know the basic pillars of Compose, you have everything you need to tackle the challenges of the second section.

The goal of the second section is to show you Jetpack Compose in action. Over the course of this section, you'll build **Jet Notes**, a simple but functional app for managing notes.

Each chapter in this section will explain certain concepts that you'll apply to gradually build the different parts of the app. **Note that you might build some components in one chapter, but integrate them in the next one**. Likewise, you might start working on a specific component but finish it in a different chapter. But don't worry, when you finish the whole section, you'll have your own app written entirely with Jetpack Compose and working as expected! :]

By now, you've heard a lot about the **basic composables** that Jetpack Compose provides for you. In this chapter:

- You'll learn how to **think** about UI design when building it with Jetpack Compose.

- You'll see how you can **combine** basic composables to create **complex UI**.

- You'll create two components with different **complexity** for **Jet Notes**.

Let's first explore the features you'll build for your app.

Application features

Before you start writing code, have a look at the app concept and its features:

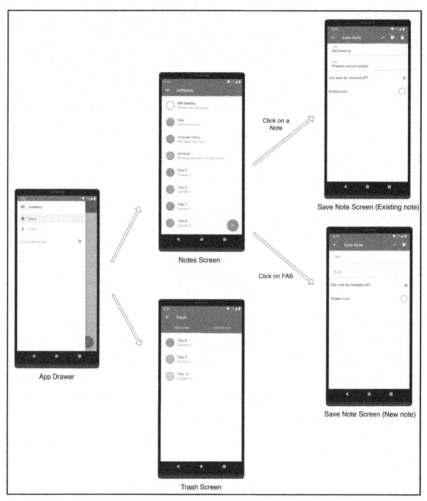

Application Overview

Don't worry about the details on each screen. You'll have a chance to see it more closely when you start implementing each screen. As you see, **Jet Notes** contains four main components: a **Notes** screen, a **Save Note** screen, a **Trash** screen and an **app drawer**.

The **Notes** screen displays the list of created notes. From here, the user can open an existing note, create a new one or open the app drawer.

The **Save Note** screen has two modes: an **edit** mode and a **create a new note** mode. When the user clicks on a note in the **Notes** screen, the **Save Note** screen will open in edit mode. The user can then edit the note or simply move it to the **Trash** screen by clicking a trash icon on the app bar.

To create a new note, the user taps on the Floating Action Button (FAB) available in the **Notes** screen. That opens the **Save Note** screen in the mode for creating a new note.

There are two types of notes: **regular** notes and **checkable** notes. Checkable notes are notes that the user can mark — or check — as **done**. The user can make any note checkable by using a `switch` component in the **Save Note** screen. In the **Notes** screen, checkable notes have a checkbox to mark the note as done.

Tapping the navigation icon on the app bar or swiping from the left border of the screen opens the **app drawer**. The app drawer switches between the **Notes** and the **Trash** screens. Using the drawer, a user can also change the app's theme from light to dark.

In the **Trash** screen, the user can switch between regular and checkable notes using two tabs. The user can select notes and restore them or delete them permanently.

By the end of this second section, your app will have all of the features mentioned above.

Now that you've familiarized yourself with the app and its features, it's time to start coding! :]

Project overview

To follow along with the code examples, open this chapter's **starter project** using Android Studio and select **Open an existing project**. Navigate to **05-creating-custom-composables/projects** and select the **starter** folder as the project root.

Once the project opens, let it build and sync and you'll be ready to go!

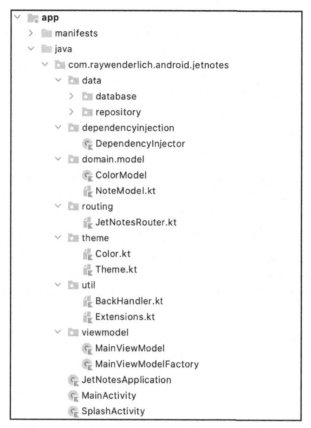

Project Structure

Here are the packages that are already set up for you and what they contain:

• **data**: Contains the code related to the database that stores the notes. It lets you add, remove and update notes.

• **dependencyinjection**: Has one class that's responsible for creating and providing the dependencies you'll need.

• **domain**: Contains two domain models named `NoteModel` and `ColorModel`, which represent **notes** and **colors**, respectively.

• **routing**: Has logic that lets you navigate between screens.

• **theme**: Contains color definitions and a composable function that lets you change the app's theme.

- **util**: Contains a utility composable function to handle the **back press**. It also provides an extension method for creating `Color` instances from `String` color hex definitions.

- **viewmodel**: Contains the `ViewModel` you'll need to implement to manage notes.

- **JetNotesApplication.kt**: An `Application` that initializes the dependency injector.

- **MainActivity.kt**: Contains the `setContent()` call, which sets the first composable function and behaves as the root UI component.

- **SplashActivity.kt**: Responsible for the splash screen that you see when you open the app.

Once you're familiar with the file organization, build and run the app. You'll see an empty screen with no content, as shown below:

Empty Starter Project — App State

Skip ahead to the **final project** and you'll see that you'll build components in this chapter, but you won't fully finish them or integrate them into **Jet Notes** yet. However, you can use the **final project** as a reference to track your progress while you build the composables. In the next chapters, you'll iterate upon them and improve the app.

Thinking in Compose

Before you start coding, look at the **Notes** screen design once more and try to **think in Compose**. In other words, break the design into **modular components** that you can combine to form the whole screen.

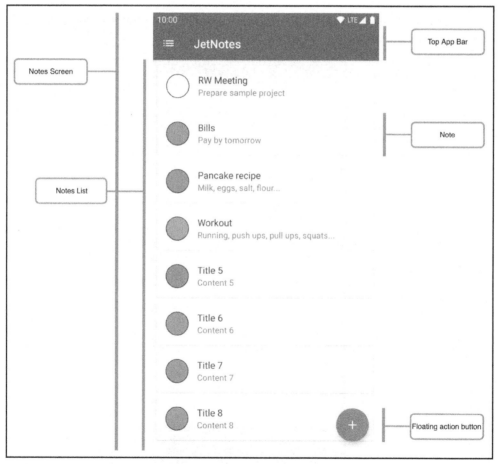

Notes Screen — Components

For example, you can break the **Notes** screen into the following components:

- **Notes Screen**: This component represents the whole **Notes** screen.

- **Top App Bar**: Responsible for displaying the top app bar, which holds the navigation action and the title.

- **Notes List**: Renders the list of created notes.

- **Floating Action Button**: Opens the **Save Note** screen so the user can create a new note.

- **Note**: Represents an individual note.

- **App Drawer**: Contains the drawer that displays when the user swipes from the side or taps on the navigation icon.

In Compose, these components are all represented by **composable functions**. As a developer, you get to decide how deep you want to break down a specific design into its components.

It's also important to consider how you'll use each component. For example, look at the design of the **Notes** and the **Trash** screens. Both screens use the same **Note** component, so creating a reusable **Note** composable makes sense.

This is a great example of **thinking in Compose**.

Bottom-up approach

When building your apps with Jetpack Compose, it's smart to start with smaller composables and build your way up through the design. You call this way of working a **bottom-up** approach.

This is smart because building your app from the smallest components lets you decouple and reuse your code from the very start. By the time you reach the highest-level components, such as the **Notes & Trash Screens**, you'll have built all the fundamental components, so you can easily reuse them in those two screens. This saves time and helps with stability, by reducing the amount of code you need to write!

Now, look at the **Notes** screen again and consider which component is a good candidate to start with.

If you follow the **bottom-up** approach and choose the most fundamental components, you need to start with the **Note** composable. After building the **Note**, you'll be able to use it all over the app.

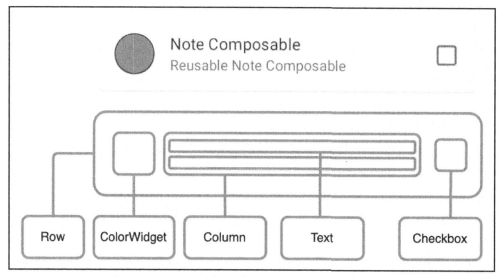

Note Component

When you try to break down the **Note** component, you'll notice that you can build it with the **basic composables** you learned about in the previous section. The color widget, the note's description and the checkbox are organized in a Row. The note's title and its description are organized in a Column.

Now that you have an idea about how to break down your composable, it's time to start coding! :]

Creating the Note composable

Use Android Studio to create a new package called **ui.components**. Then, in that package, create a new Kotlin file named **Note.kt**. Finally, add the following code to **Note.kt**:

```
import androidx.compose.runtime.Composable
import androidx.compose.ui.tooling.preview.Preview

@Composable
fun Note() {

}
```

```
@Preview
@Composable
private fun NotePreview() {
  Note()
}
```

In this code, you simply created a composable function to represent your note. You also added a `NotePreview()` to preview the composable that you're building in Android Studio.

For this to work, make sure you've selected the **Split** option at the top-right corner in Android Studio. This option allows you to preview your composables in the Design panel, while still being able to modify the code.

Build your project now. At this stage, you still won't see anything in the Preview panel because haven't added any composables that emit your UI. Let's do that next!

Android Studio - Preview

Emitting the note's content

Now that you've built the Note composable, your next step is to add the code that will emit the note's content. Add the following code to Note()'s body:

```
Box(
    modifier = Modifier
        .size(40.dp)
        .background(rwGreen)
)
Text(text = "Title", maxLines = 1)
Text(text = "Content", maxLines = 1)
Checkbox(
    checked = false,
    onCheckedChange = { },
    modifier = Modifier.padding(start = 8.dp)
)
```

For this to work, add the following imports to **Note.kt**:

```
import androidx.compose.foundation.background
import androidx.compose.foundation.layout.Box
import androidx.compose.foundation.layout.padding
import androidx.compose.foundation.layout.size
import androidx.compose.material.Checkbox
import androidx.compose.material.Text
import androidx.compose.ui.Modifier
import androidx.compose.ui.unit.dp
import com.raywenderlich.android.jetnotes.theme.rwGreen
```

You've just added composables to represent the color widget, title, content and checkbox. Don't bother with the color widget for now — you won't style it in this chapter. That widget relies heavily on **modifiers**, which you'll learn about in Chapter 6, "Using Compose Modifiers". At this point, if you see modifiers in code, don't spend too much time thinking about them. Just know that they make the UI look a bit nicer. :]

Build your project and you should see something like this in your preview:

Note Composable — Preview

By adding these composables, you've managed to accomplish something: The note's components now appear in the Preview panel. However, as you can see, they're stacked on top of each other. Remember that when you add composable functions, you're **describing the hierarchy** of the elements to render on the screen.

Previously, you read how, at its core, Compose only knows how to work with trees to emit specific items. So, you can represent the hierarchy that you're describing with composable functions by a tree where the nodes are composables.

The four composables inside Note() will produce the following tree with four nodes:

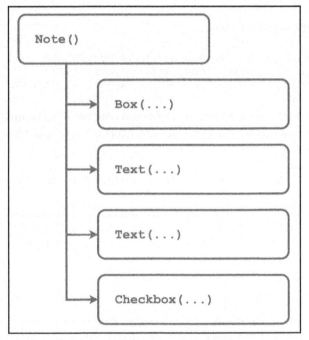

Note Composable - Tree Hierarchy

This is exactly what describing Jetpack Compose as a **declarative** toolkit means. The body of the function *describes* how the UI will look. In this case, the UI will contain four elements. Since no layout policy is described here, the composables will stack upon one other. This is exactly what the preview panel displayed.

It's not, however, what you want. For your next step, you'll add **layout structure** to your composable. Start by replacing the Note() body with the following code:

```
Row(modifier = Modifier.fillMaxWidth()) {
   Box(
     modifier = Modifier
       .size(40.dp)
```

```
        .background(rwGreen)
    )
    Column(modifier = Modifier.weight(1f)) {
        Text(text = "Title", maxLines = 1)
        Text(text = "Content", maxLines = 1)
    }
    Checkbox(
        checked = false,
        onCheckedChange = { },
        modifier = Modifier.padding(start = 8.dp)
    )
}
```

Add the necessary imports as well:

```
import androidx.compose.foundation.layout.Column
import androidx.compose.foundation.layout.Row
import androidx.compose.foundation.layout.fillMaxWidth
```

In the previous code, you organized the title and content in a column. You then aligned the resulting column in a row, along with the Box() and Checkbox() composables.

Build your project again or refresh the Preview panel, and you'll see something like this:

At this point, your Note() doesn't look quite like it did in the initial design. To make them match, you need modifiers. But hey, no worries! You'll continue working on it in Chapter 6, "Using Compose Modifiers".

Right now, you'll focus on building the remaining complex composables that make up your app.

Building the app drawer composable

The next thing you'll do is a little more complex. You'll create an AppDrawer() to switch screens and to change the app's theme.

Once again, before you start coding, look at the design and try to break it into smaller components.

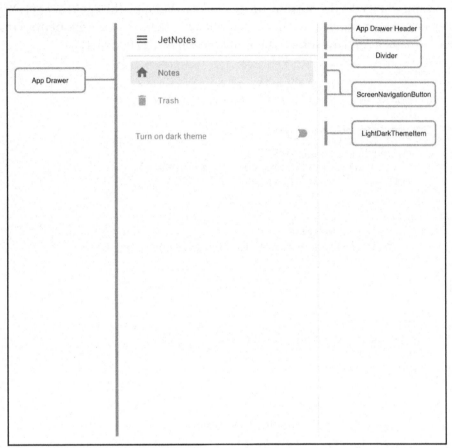

App Drawer — Components

As shown in the figure, you can split this UI component into the following composables:

- **AppDrawer**: Your root composable for the drawer.

- **AppDrawerHeader**: Contains a header with a drawer icon and the app's title.

- **ScreenNavigationButton**: Represents a button that the user can tap to switch between screens.

- **LightDarkThemeItem**: Lets the user change between light and dark themes.

Let's build these components!

Adding a header to the drawer

Once again, you'll take the **bottom-up** approach to building the AppDrawer(). You'll implement smaller components first, then combine them. In **ui.components**, create a new file named **AppDrawer.kt**. Then, add the following code to it:

```
@Composable
private fun AppDrawerHeader() {
  Row(modifier = Modifier.fillMaxWidth()) {
    Image(
      imageVector = Icons.Filled.Menu,
      contentDescription = "Drawer Header Icon",
      colorFilter = ColorFilter
        .tint(MaterialTheme.colors.onSurface),
      modifier = Modifier.padding(16.dp)
    )
    Text(
      text = "JetNotes",
      modifier = Modifier
        .align(alignment = Alignment.CenterVertically)
    )
  }
}

@Preview
@Composable
fun AppDrawerHeaderPreview() {
  JetNotesTheme {
    AppDrawerHeader()
  }
}
```

For this to work, add the following imports as well:

```
import androidx.compose.foundation.Image
import androidx.compose.foundation.layout.Row
import androidx.compose.foundation.layout.fillMaxWidth
import androidx.compose.foundation.layout.padding
import androidx.compose.material.MaterialTheme
import androidx.compose.material.Text
import androidx.compose.material.icons.Icons
import androidx.compose.material.icons.filled.Menu
import androidx.compose.runtime.Composable
import androidx.compose.ui.Alignment
import androidx.compose.ui.Modifier
import androidx.compose.ui.graphics.ColorFilter
import androidx.compose.ui.tooling.preview.Preview
import androidx.compose.ui.unit.dp
import com.raywenderlich.android.jetnotes.theme.JetNotesTheme
```

With this code, you've created a composable for the app drawer header. It's a relatively simple composable, where you use an Image() and a Text() and organize them in a Row().

You also added modifiers to add padding and alignment to these components. Again, don't bother yourself with modifiers as much. You'll learn more about them in the next chapter.

For the Image(), you used a colorFilter to set its color. Specifically, you used MaterialTheme.colors.onSurface for the tint. The MaterialTheme.colors palette is drawn from the system and the root composable functions you use. If you check out the code in AppDrawerHeaderPreview() you'll see the following:

```
@Preview
@Composable
fun AppDrawerHeaderPreview() {
    JetNotesTheme {
        AppDrawerHeader()
    }
}
```

The root composable is JetNotesTheme() in your case. This is a predefined composable function in the **Theme.kt** file. As you use that for the root component, it passed down all its defined colors to the rest of the components, effectively styling them all in the same way. However, that theme doesn't specify the onSurface color yet, so the default value is Color.Black.

For now, that's all you need to know about theming. You'll learn more in Chapter 8, "Applying Material Design to Compose". You could also preview your composable without it, though, if it's confusing.

Build your project and you'll see the following result in your preview panel:

AppDrawerHeader Composable — Preview

Creating the navigation button composable

Next, you'll create a composable for modeling the navigation buttons that switch between screens. To do so, add the following code to **AppDrawer.kt**:

```
@Composable
private fun ScreenNavigationButton(
  icon: ImageVector,
  label: String,
  isSelected: Boolean,
  onClick: () -> Unit
) {
  val colors = MaterialTheme.colors

  // Define alphas for the image for two different states
  // of the button: selected/unselected
  val imageAlpha = if (isSelected) {
    1f
  } else {
    0.6f
  }

  // Define color for the text for two different states
  // of the button: selected/unselected
  val textColor = if (isSelected) {
    colors.primary
  } else {
    colors.onSurface.copy(alpha = 0.6f)
  }

  // Define color for the background for two different states
  // of the button: selected/unselected
  val backgroundColor = if (isSelected) {
    colors.primary.copy(alpha = 0.12f)
  } else {
    colors.surface
  }
}
```

Add the following import as well:

```
import androidx.compose.ui.graphics.vector.ImageVector
```

In the design, the **Screen Navigation** button has an icon and a label. Here, you've added two parameters to your composable to allow that: icon and label.

You've also given the button two states: **selected** and **unselected**. To track which state the button is in, you added the parameter isSelected.

Each state renders differently. The code you added to the body of the function prepares colors for both states. Notice that you used `primary`, `onSurface` and `surface` colors; these colors are defined in your `JetNotesTheme()` from **Theme.kt**. As mentioned previously, if some of these colors aren't specified when you create a color palette for the theme, the default values are used.

Also notice that you've added the `onClick` parameter. Since your button is clickable, it's a good practice to expose that behavior through a lambda function so that the parent composable can take responsibility for it. You'll learn more about how to handle clicks and other events in Chapter 7, "Managing State In Compose".

Next, add the following code to the bottom of `ScreenNavigationButton()`:

```
Surface( // 1
  modifier = Modifier
    .fillMaxWidth()
    .padding(start = 8.dp, end = 8.dp, top = 8.dp),
  color = backgroundColor,
  shape = MaterialTheme.shapes.small
) {
  Row( // 2
    horizontalArrangement = Arrangement.Start,
    verticalAlignment = Alignment.CenterVertically,
    modifier = Modifier
      .clickable(onClick = onClick)
      .fillMaxWidth()
      .padding(4.dp)
  ) {
    Image(
      imageVector = icon,
      contentDescription = "Screen Navigation Button",
      colorFilter = ColorFilter.tint(textColor),
      alpha = imageAlpha
    )
    Spacer(Modifier.width(16.dp)) // 3
    Text(
      text = label,
      style = MaterialTheme.typography.body2,
      color = textColor,
      modifier = Modifier.fillMaxWidth()
    )
  }
}
```

Add the following imports as well:

```
import androidx.compose.foundation.layout.Arrangement
import androidx.compose.material.Surface
import androidx.compose.foundation.clickable
```

```
import androidx.compose.foundation.layout.Spacer
import androidx.compose.foundation.layout.width
```

There's quite a bit of code here, but here's a breakdown:

1. You use Surface() to provide the background color and shape for your button.

2. Inside Surface(), you use a Row() to align the icon and label for the button.

3. Finally, you used Spacer() to add some space between the icon and the label.

Now, you need to create a preview function to visualize your button in the Preview panel. In the same file, add the following function:

```
@Preview
@Composable
fun ScreenNavigationButtonPreview() {
  JetNotesTheme {
    ScreenNavigationButton(
      icon = Icons.Filled.Home,
      label = "Notes",
      isSelected = true,
      onClick = { }
    )
  }
}
```

Don't forget to import the Home icon:

```
import androidx.compose.material.icons.filled.Home
```

As you see, ScreenNavigationButtonPreview() just calls your ScreenNavigationButton(), passing in the parameters it needs. Apart from the icon and label for the button, note how you define its state as **selected** using isSelected = true. In addition, note how onClick() just uses an empty lambda as its argument, since you don't need this behavior for the preview.

Build your project and you should see the following result:

ScreenNavigationButton Composable — Preview

Great! Now, your drawer button is done and you're ready to move on to the next task.

Adding a theme switcher

The theme switcher is a toggle button that lets the user change the app's theme from light to dark.

Add the following code to the end of **AppDrawer.kt**:

```
@Composable
private fun LightDarkThemeItem() {
  Row(
    Modifier
      .padding(8.dp)
  ) {
    Text(
      text = "Turn on dark theme",
      style = MaterialTheme.typography.body2,
      color = MaterialTheme.colors.onSurface.copy(alpha = 0.6f),
      modifier = Modifier
        .weight(1f)
        .padding(start = 8.dp, top = 8.dp, end = 8.dp, bottom =
8.dp)
        .align(alignment = Alignment.CenterVertically)
    )
    Switch(
      checked = JetNotesThemeSettings.isDarkThemeEnabled,
      onCheckedChange =
{ JetNotesThemeSettings.isDarkThemeEnabled = it },
      modifier = Modifier
        .padding(start = 8.dp, end = 8.dp)
        .align(alignment = Alignment.CenterVertically)
    )
  }
}

@Preview
@Composable
fun LightDarkThemeItemPreview() {
  JetNotesTheme {
    LightDarkThemeItem()
  }
}
```

Also include the following imports, to avoid Android Studio's complaints:

```
import androidx.compose.material.Switch
import com.raywenderlich.android.jetnotes.theme.JetNotesThemeSettings
```

The code you just added is quite straightforward. For this composable, you used a Row() to align the content horizontally. As you see, the content is just a Text() and a Switch(). The interesting part is what the Switch() does.

Look at this composable and you'll observe that the checked and onCheckedChange parameters rely on JetNotesThemeSettings.isDarkThemeEnabled to handle the state. There are a few new concepts here, but you'll learn more about them in Chapter 7, "Managing State in Compose". For now, don't worry about them. Just consider that this mechanism allows you to change the app's theme internally.

Build the project and, in the preview, you'll see the following:

LightDarkThemeItem Composable — Preview

Well done! With this, you've completed all the necessary components for the app drawer.

Wrapping up the app drawer

In the previous sections, you created the different building blocks that you need to build the drawer. Now, you need to put them all together. To do so, add the following code to **AppDrawer.kt**:

```
@Composable
fun AppDrawer(
    currentScreen: Screen,
    closeDrawerAction: () -> Unit
) {
    Column(modifier = Modifier.fillMaxSize()) {
        AppDrawerHeader()

        Divider(color = MaterialTheme.colors.onSurface.copy(alpha
= .2f))

        ScreenNavigationButton(
            icon = Icons.Filled.Home,
            label = "Notes",
            isSelected = currentScreen == Screen.Notes,
            onClick = {
                JetNotesRouter.navigateTo(Screen.Notes)
                closeDrawerAction()
            }
        )
```

```
    ScreenNavigationButton(
      icon = Icons.Filled.Delete,
      label = "Trash",
      isSelected = currentScreen == Screen.Trash,
      onClick = {
        JetNotesRouter.navigateTo(Screen.Trash)
        closeDrawerAction()
      }
    )
    LightDarkThemeItem()
  }
}
```

Add the following imports as well:

```
import androidx.compose.material.icons.filled.Delete
import com.raywenderlich.android.jetnotes.routing.JetNotesRouter
import com.raywenderlich.android.jetnotes.routing.Screen
import androidx.compose.material.Divider
import androidx.compose.foundation.layout.Column
import androidx.compose.foundation.layout.fillMaxSize
```

There's not much new in this code, you've just used the composables you created earlier. The important step you've taken here is that you've organized those composables into a `Column()` to give your drawer a proper layout.

In the design, you can see that there's a line between the drawer's header and buttons. To add that line, you used a `Divider()`. Then, for the color, you created a new object with the `onSurface` color, but with a different `alpha` property.

Check `AppDrawer`'s parameters: `currentScreen` and `closeDrawerAction`. With `currentScreen`, you control which screen navigation button is selected. For example, if you want to select the **Notes** button, you'd call the `AppDrawer` composable with `Screen.Notes` as an argument.

Remember how you exposed the click event in the `ScreenNavigationButton()`? Here, you use a similar technique to expose the close drawer event with the `closeDrawerAction` parameter. By doing that, you let the parent composable react to the event.

Notice how this composable passes the lambda argument to `onClick()` of each navigation button. This is used to notify the system that you selected a new screen.

Finally, add the following code to the bottom of **AppDrawer.kt**:

```
@Preview
@Composable
```

```
fun AppDrawerPreview() {
  JetNotesTheme {
    AppDrawer(Screen.Notes, {})
  }
}
```

Here, you passed `Screen.Notes` as the `currentScreen`. By doing that, you selected the **Notes** button.

Since you're calling the `AppDrawer()` within a composable marked with `@Preview`, you don't need to specify any actions for when the app drawer is closed. Therefore, you just passed an empty function as an argument.

Build your project once more and you'll see your completed drawer in your preview:

LightDarkThemeItem Composable — Preview

You already saw how calling composable functions results in a tree. Whenever you call the `AppDrawer()`, Compose will generate a tree where each node is a composable that was used to create it.

Right now, this tree contains only the **UI elements**. Later, you'll see that there are other types of nodes as well. When you compare the `AppDrawer()` and the `Note()`, you'll see that the first one is more complex. However, if you pay attention, you'll notice that both are composed of pretty much the same **basic composables**.

That's the beauty of Jetpack Compose. It's so easy to create complex composables from the most basic ones.

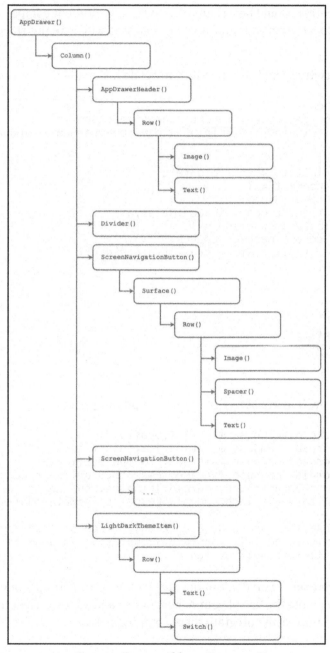

AppDrawer Composable — Compose Tree

Putting all the pieces together

After all this work, it would be a shame not to see the different composables you
built working together in your app. So your final step will be to put the puzzle pieces
together.

Go to **MainActivity.kt** and add the following code inside the `setContent()`:

```
JetNotesTheme {
  val coroutineScope = rememberCoroutineScope()
  val scaffoldState: ScaffoldState = rememberScaffoldState()

  Scaffold(
    scaffoldState = scaffoldState,
    drawerContent = {
      AppDrawer(
        currentScreen = Screen.Notes,
        closeDrawerAction = {
          coroutineScope.launch {
            scaffoldState.drawerState.close()
          }
        }
      )
    },
    content = {
      Note()
    }
  )
}
```

Add the following imports as well, to avoid compilation errors:

```
import androidx.compose.material.Scaffold
import androidx.compose.material.ScaffoldState
import androidx.compose.material.rememberScaffoldState
import androidx.compose.runtime.rememberCoroutineScope
import com.raywenderlich.android.jetnotes.routing.Screen
import com.raywenderlich.android.jetnotes.theme.JetNotesTheme
import
com.raywenderlich.android.jetnotes.ui.components.AppDrawer
import com.raywenderlich.android.jetnotes.ui.components.Note
import kotlinx.coroutines.launch
```

Don't bother yourself if you don't understand some of the concepts or composables
in this code. Just note the use of your `AppDrawer()` and `Note()`. The other code is
here to allow you to easily integrate these composables.

You'll learn more about the `Scaffold()` and theming in Chapter 8, "Applying Material Design to Compose". And you'll get more context about the `ScaffoldState` in Chapter 7, "Managing State in Compose".

Build and run the app. You'll see the **Note** composable on the screen, as shown below. To see your app drawer in action, pull the left edge of the screen toward the right.

Right now, the app isn't that impressive, but don't worry. You'll make it look like the expected design throughout the following chapters.

Note Composable and App Drawer Composable

You can find the final code for this chapter in **05-creating-custom-composables/ projects/final**.

Key points

- Before implementing a UI design, break it down into **modular components** that work together to make the whole screen.

- When implementing a specific UI design, use a **bottom-up** approach. Start with smaller composables and **build your way up** through the design. This will let you decouple and reuse code from the very start.

- Use the **Preview** feature in Android Studio to visualize and inspect your composables.

- Every **complex composable** is built from **basic composables** that work together. It's a small puzzle of simple elements.

- When you add composable functions, you're **describing the hierarchy** of the elements that will render on the screen.

- Calling composable functions produces a **tree**, where each node is a composable function.

Where to go from here?

Congratulations on finishing the chapter! I hope it was a nice ride for you! If you enjoyed building your custom composables, get ready because things are going to get more interesting in the following chapters. :]

In this chapter, you learned how you can use basic composables to create complex ones. You also saw how you should think about your UI design and what approach to take when implementing it.

In the next chapter, you'll learn **how to style** your composables using **modifiers**. You'll also continue adding more composables to improve **Jet Notes**.

Chapter 6: Using Compose Modifiers

by Denis Buketa

A beautiful UI is essential for every app. It doesn't just look nice, it also makes your app *more fun* to use. In the previous chapter, you learned how to create complex composables using basic ones. You also started working on the Note and AppDrawer composables. Now, you'll learn how to make your composables look as beautiful as they are in your ideal design.

In this chapter, you'll:

- Learn **how to style** your composables using **modifiers**.

- Style Note to make it look like it should in the final design.

- Add more composables to **Jet Notes**.

From this point on, every composable you complete will be as beautiful as in your design, by adding those modifiers you've been hearing about for the past few chapters. :]

Modifiers

Modifiers tell a UI element how to **lay out**, **display** or **behave** within its parent layout. You can also say that they **decorate** or **add behavior** to UI elements.

In the previous chapter, you started working on Note().

Note composable - current and final state

In the figure above, you can compare where you left off (above) with how it'll look like by the end of this chapter (below).

To follow along with the code examples, open this chapter's **starter project** in Android Studio and select **Open an existing project**.

Next, navigate to **06-using-compose-modifiers/projects** and select the **starter** folder as the project root. Once the project opens, let it build and sync and you're ready to go!

Note that if you skip ahead to the **final project**, you'll be able to see the completed Note() and some other composables that you'll implement during this chapter.

Whatever you choose, we'll start off by building the NoteColor widget.

Adding NoteColor

The first thing you'll improve in your Note() is the NoteColor. In the **ui.components** package, create a new Kotlin file named **NoteColor.kt**, then add the following code to it:

```
@Composable
fun NoteColor() {
  Box(
    modifier = Modifier
      .size(40.dp)
      .background(Color.Red)
  )
}

@Preview
```

```
@Composable
fun NoteColorPreview() {
  NoteColor()
}
```

To make this work, add the following imports:

```
import androidx.compose.foundation.background
import androidx.compose.foundation.layout.Box
import androidx.compose.foundation.layout.size
import androidx.compose.runtime.Composable
import androidx.compose.ui.Modifier
import androidx.compose.ui.graphics.Color
import androidx.compose.ui.tooling.preview.Preview
import androidx.compose.ui.unit.dp
```

Look at the code now and you can see that you created a Box and passed a modifier to it. In this example, you used two modifier functions: `Modifier.size()` and `Modifier.background()`.

`Modifier.size()` declares the size of the content. You pass the value in **density-independent pixels (dp)** and set the element width and height to the same value.

`Modifier.background()` draws a **shape** with a solid color behind the content. In this case, you passed `Color.Red`.

As you can see, you can easily **chain** several modifiers, one after the other, to **combine** them. In this example, you started the **modifier chain** with `Modifier`, which represents an empty modifier object.

Finally, you used `NoteColorPreview()` to preview your composable in the preview panel.

Build your project and check the preview and you'll see something like this:

NoteColor — Preview

Congratulations, you just created a very simple composable that is 40dp in size and has a red background. Let's see if we can make it even nicer!

Chaining modifiers

Now you have the basic `NoteColor()`, but you still have to add a couple of modifiers to make it match the design.

The next thing you'll do is to make your composable's content round. In the previous example, you saw how to chain multiple modifiers. Here, you'll apply the same principle and change the code so it includes one additional modifier:

```
@Composable
fun NoteColor() {
  Box(
    modifier = Modifier
      .size(40.dp)
      .background(Color.Red)
      .clip(CircleShape) // here
  )
}
```

Don't forget to include these imports as well:

```
import androidx.compose.foundation.shape.CircleShape
import androidx.compose.ui.draw.clip
```

Now, build your project and check the preview. You'll see something like this:

NoteColor - Preview

Surprised? Don't blame yourself if you tried to refresh the preview panel, expecting a different result. :]

The **order of modifiers** in the chain matters. Each modifier not only **prepares** the composable for the next modifier in the chain, but it also **modifies** the composable at the same time.

With this in mind, try to break down the code you wrote. With `Modifier.size()`, you defined the width and the height of the composable.

After that, you have `Modifier.background(Color.Red)`. Since UI elements are represented by rectangular blocks, you end up with a red square.

Then you added `Modifier.clip()`, which clips the content to a specific shape. Since the two modifiers before already modified the composable, your composable didn't change. The content remained the same.

To make this clearer, try adding another `Modifier.background` composable to the chain:

```
@Composable
fun NoteColor() {
  Box(
    modifier = Modifier
      .size(40.dp)
      .background(Color.Red)
      .clip(CircleShape)
      .background(Color.Yellow) // here
  )
}
```

Build the project and check the preview. You'll see something like this:

NoteColor - Preview

Now, you can visualize the effect that `Modifier.clip()` has on your composable. It clipped the **future content** into a circle shape, so when you applied the `Modifier.background(Color.Yellow)`, you ended up with a yellow circle in the red square.

Taking this behavior into consideration, you can now continue working on `NoteColor()` to make it look like the design. Reorder the modifiers to get a circular shape with a specific color:

```
@Composable
fun NoteColor() {
  Box(
    modifier = Modifier
      .size(40.dp)
      .clip(CircleShape)
      .background(Color.Red)
  )
}
```

Here, you moved `Modifier.clip()` to come before the point where you specify the composable background. With that, you clipped the content of your composable to a circle whose width and height are set to the value you specify with `Modifier.size()`.

Build the project and check the preview:

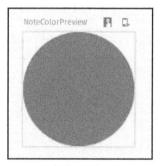

NoteColor - Preview

Excellent! You just created a composable that emits a colored circle of the size you specified.

Rounding out the NoteColor

There are a few more things you need to add before you wrap up this composable. One thing that's missing is the border. To add that, update the code in `NoteColor()` like so:

```
@Composable
fun NoteColor() {
  Box(
    modifier = Modifier
      .size(40.dp)
      .clip(CircleShape)
      .background(Color.Red)
      .border( // new code
        BorderStroke(
          2.dp,
          SolidColor(Color.Black)
        ),
        CircleShape
      )
  )
}
```

To make Android Studio happy, add the following imports as well:

```
import androidx.compose.foundation.BorderStroke
import androidx.compose.foundation.border
import androidx.compose.ui.graphics.SolidColor
```

Here, you added `Modifier.border()`, which gives you a border with the appearance you specified using the `border` and `shape`. For the `border`, you passed `BorderStroke()`, which defined the width of the border and its color. For the `shape`, you used the same shape as you did when clipping the content.

Build the project and you'll see something like this in the preview panel:

NoteColor - Preview

Adding some padding

If you check the design you'll notice that there should be some padding around
NoteColor(). To fix that, update the code like this:

```
@Composable
fun NoteColor() {
  Box(
    modifier = Modifier
      .padding(4.dp) // here
      .size(40.dp)
      .clip(CircleShape)
      .background(Color.Red)
      .border(
        BorderStroke(
          2.dp,
          SolidColor(Color.Black)
        ),
        CircleShape
      )
  )
}
```

Don't forget to add the necessary import:

```
import androidx.compose.foundation.layout.padding
```

Modifier.padding() applies additional space to each edge around the content. In
the code above, you used 4.dp. Note that when you don't specify which edge to pad,
the padding will be applied to all of them. You can also specify to which edge you
want to apply the padding with the following **named arguments**: start, top, end
and bottom.

It's important to pay attention to the order in the chain where you added the
modifier. You want your circle to be the size you specify with the Modifier.size.
You also want your padding to be applied around that circle. So, the best place to put
Modifier.padding is just before Modifier.size.

By doing that, you'll first apply the padding to your composable, then you'll **reserve**
the space of the specified size for your content.

Build the project and check the preview. It will now look like this:

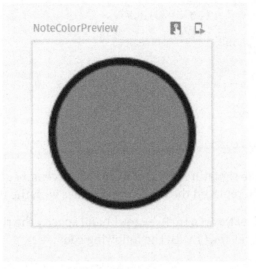

NoteColor - Preview

Improving NoteColor's usability

Regarding NoteColor(), you have all the necessary code to fulfill the design. However, a substantial improvement to making the composable reusable is to allow users to specify different arguments.

Right now, you've hard-coded the values for the size, background color, padding and border width, but your users should be able to change them.

To implement this, just expose those values as parameters by replacing NoteColor() with the following code:

```
@Composable
fun NoteColor(
  color: Color,
  size: Dp,
  padding: Dp = 0.dp,
  border: Dp
) {
  Box(
    modifier = Modifier
      .padding(padding)
      .size(size)
      .clip(CircleShape)
      .background(color)
      .border(
```

```
        BorderStroke(
          border,
          SolidColor(Color.Black)
        ),
        CircleShape
      )
    )
  }
```

Don't forget this import:

```
import androidx.compose.ui.unit.Dp
```

Here, you changed the signature of NoteColor() to accept a color, size, padding and border. You then replaced the hard-coded values with the new parameters.

Now, you need to adapt NoteColorPreview() and specify the right parameters. Replace NoteColorPreview() with the following code:

```
@Preview
@Composable
fun NoteColorPreview() {
  NoteColor(
    color = Color.Red,
    size = 40.dp,
    padding = 4.dp,
    border = 2.dp
  )
}
```

Here, you've used the same values as before, so your preview should remain the same.

Build the project to make sure everything works as expected.

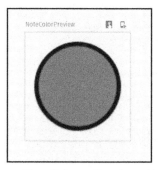

NoteColor — Preview

The next step is to add your new component to the Note.

Adding NoteColor to Note

Great work on completing `NoteColor()`! You can now use it in your `Note` to make it match the design.

In **Note.kt**, replace the `Note()` implementation with the following code:

```
@Composable
fun Note() {
  Row(modifier = Modifier.fillMaxWidth()) {
    NoteColor( // NoteColor instead of Box
      color = rwGreen,
      size = 40.dp,
      padding = 4.dp,
      border = 1.dp
    )
    Column(modifier = Modifier.weight(1f)) {
      Text(text = "Title", maxLines = 1)
      Text(text = "Content", maxLines = 1)
    }
    Checkbox(
      checked = false,
      onCheckedChange = { },
      modifier = Modifier.padding(start = 8.dp)
    )
  }
}
```

In the code above, you removed the `Box` that you used as a placeholder, then added your beautiful `NoteColor`.

Build the project now and you'll see something like this in the preview panel:

Note Composable — Preview With NoteColor

While you're here, check out the modifiers that you added in the previous chapter, when you were working on `Note`.

For `Row()`, you used `Modifier.fillMaxWidth()`. This modifier allows you to specify the fraction of the available width that the composable should use. By default, the fraction is `1f`. So in this case, you specified that the `Row` should take the maximum available width.

For `Column()`, you used `Modifier.weight()`. If you're familiar with the weight property in XML layouts, then you already know what it does. With `weight`, you size the element's width proportional to its weight relative to other weighted sibling elements.

Check the definition of this modifier. It's defined in `RowScope`, which means you can use it on elements in a `Row`. In this case, you used it to make the `Column` take the available width between `NoteColor` and `Checkbox`.

Adding a background to Note

Look at `Note`'s design and notice that it has a white background, its corners are rounded and there's a small shadow around it. Luckily, you can easily use modifiers to add those features!

Update `Note()` code to add the necessary modifiers to `Row()`, as shown below:

```
@Composable
fun Note() {
  val backgroundShape: Shape = RoundedCornerShape(4.dp)
  Row(
    modifier = Modifier
      .padding(8.dp)
      .shadow(1.dp, backgroundShape)
      .fillMaxWidth()
      .heightIn(min = 64.dp)
      .background(Color.White, backgroundShape)
  ) {
    ...
  }
}
```

As usual, don't forget to add the necessary imports:

```
import androidx.compose.foundation.shape.RoundedCornerShape
import androidx.compose.ui.draw.shadow
import androidx.compose.ui.graphics.Color
import androidx.compose.ui.graphics.Shape
import androidx.compose.foundation.layout.heightIn
```

With this code, you introduced four modifiers, two of which are completely new to you:

- **Modifier.padding**: Adds some space between the note and screen edges.

- **Modifier.shadow**: Creates `DrawLayerModifier`, which draws the shadow. The elevation defines the visual depth of a physical object. Furthermore, the physical object has a `shape`. In this case, you defined that the elevation should be `1.dp` and, for the shape, you used `RoundedCornerShape()` to define that the corners should be rounded with a radius of 4dp.

- **Modifier.background**: This is a simple one. As you already learned, it draws a shape with a solid color behind the content.

- **Modifier.heightIn**: Constrains the height of the content between `min` and `max` values. In this case, you don't need a `max` value, but you do need a `min` because you want your composable to be at least `64dp` in height.

Now, build your project and run the app to check how `Note` looks.

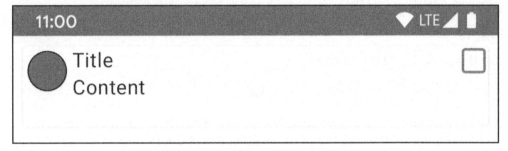

Note Composable With Background

Great! You've successfully added a background to your note. Pay attention to the corners: They're rounded now, and there's a shadow around the note. Also, see how the height of the note matches what you specified.

At this point, however, you've probably noticed that the overall composable looks awkward. That's because its content isn't centered. Fixing the alignment will be your next task.

Centering Text & Checkbox composables

You're getting closer and closer to completing your `Note()`. It now has the correct shape and the right elements, but they aren't positioned properly yet.

Your first step is to fix the position of the `Text` and `Checkbox`. To do this, update the code for `Column` and `Checkbox` in `Note()` so it looks like this:

```
Column(
  modifier = Modifier
    .weight(1f)
    .align(Alignment.CenterVertically)
) {
  Text(text = "Title", maxLines = 1)
  Text(text = "Content", maxLines = 1)
}
Checkbox(
  checked = false,
  onCheckedChange = { },
  modifier = Modifier
    .padding(16.dp)
    .align(Alignment.CenterVertically)
)
```

For this to work, add this import:

```
import androidx.compose.ui.Alignment
```

The key to aligning your composables in this code is `Modifier.align(alignment: Alignment.CenterVertically)`. This modifier allows you to align elements vertically within the Row, so that they are centered.

Just like `Modifier.weight()`, this modifier is defined in a `RowScope`. That means you can only use it in a Row. Notice that you also added `Modifier.padding()` to `CheckBox()` to make it look nicer. This doesn't affect the composable alignment, but it's a good practice to pay attention to the details.

Build and run the app and your note will look like this:

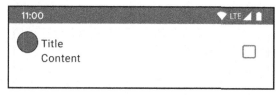

Note Composable Centered Text

Now, both the text and the checkbox are nicely centered in the note.

Centering NoteColor

When you look at NoteColor, you realize that you can't apply a modifier to it like you did for the Column and Checkbox. The NoteColor doesn't expose a modifier as its parameter. It's time to fix that!

In **NoteColor.kt**, update NoteColor() so it looks like this:

```
@Composable
fun NoteColor(
  modifier: Modifier = Modifier, // 1
  color: Color,
  size: Dp,
  padding: Dp = 0.dp,
  border: Dp
) {
  Box(
    modifier = modifier // 2
      .padding(padding)
      .size(size)
      .clip(CircleShape)
      .background(color)
      .border(
        BorderStroke(
          border,
          SolidColor(Color.Black)
        ),
        CircleShape
      )
  )
}
```

There are two things to notice here:

1. You added a **modifier** as a **parameter** to your custom composable and you initialized it with an empty Modifier.

2. You used that modifier as the first in your chain of modifiers in Box(). Remember that, earlier, you used an empty Modifier here instead.

> **Note**: Take the time to digest the difference between using modifier vs Modifier. Only one single character separates the two, but the meaning is completely different. Understanding this can help you avoid quite a few bugs in the future.

What you just did is considered a good practice when creating custom composables with Jetpack Compose. It's always useful to **expose the modifier as a parameter** and to allow users of that composable to add other modifiers, as needed.

Now, go back to **Note.kt** and align the `NoteColor` as well:

```
NoteColor(
    modifier = Modifier.align(Alignment.CenterVertically),
    color = rwGreen,
    size = 40.dp,
    padding = 4.dp,
    border = 1.dp
)
```

As you see, you can now apply the same logic as you did for the `Text` and `Checkbox`, so you add `Modifier.align()` to `NoteColor`.

Build and run the app.

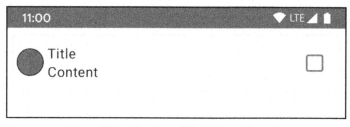

Note Composable Centered

Nice! Every component is now nicely centered in the note. However, the `NoteColor` and the `Text` are a bit cramped on the left side of the note. You'll work on that next.

Taking advantage of the modifier parameter

As mentioned before, when working on custom composables it's a good practice to think about how someone might use that composable.

For `NoteColor` you exposed the `color`, `size`, `padding`, `border` and `modifier` to make it more **flexible**. However, you have to be careful *not* to overdo it. Having a lot of parameters can introduce more complexities than you need.

By exposing the modifier as a parameter, you suddenly allow a lot of customization for your composable. That means that you might be able to remove some parameters because the behavior they provided can now be taken over by the modifier.

For `NoteColor`, notice that you're passing the padding as a parameter. That was useful when you didn't have the modifier as a parameter, but now, you don't need it. You'll do something about that next. :]

Open **NoteColor.kt** and update the code to look like this:

```
@Composable
fun NoteColor(
  modifier: Modifier = Modifier,
  color: Color,
  size: Dp,
  border: Dp
) {
  Box(
    modifier = modifier
      .size(size)
      .clip(CircleShape)
      .background(color)
      .border(
        BorderStroke(
          border,
          SolidColor(Color.Black)
        ),
        CircleShape
      )
  )
}

@Preview
@Composable
fun NoteColorPreview() {
  NoteColor(
    color = Color.Red,
    size = 40.dp,
    border = 2.dp
  )
}
```

In the code above, you removed `padding` from the composable's parameters. You also removed `Modifier.padding()` from the chain of modifiers for the `Box`. You also updated `NoteColorPreview` so it doesn't include padding in the parameters.

Now, you'll get the padding by calling the composable through the `modifier`.

Applying the padding

In **Note.kt**, update `NoteColor` like this:

```
NoteColor(
  modifier = Modifier
    .align(Alignment.CenterVertically)
    .padding(start = 16.dp, end = 16.dp), // here
  color = rwGreen,
  size = 40.dp,
  border = 1.dp
)
```

To add horizontal padding to `NoteColor`, you added `Modifier.padding()` to the `Modifier` that you pass as one of its parameters.

Build and run the app, and you'll see the following result:

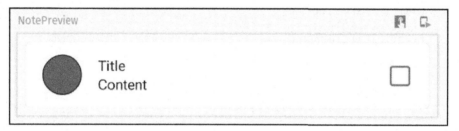

Note Composable With Modifiers

Great job, your note almost matches the design now!

However, the devil is in the details, and there's one thing still missing: the text style. Right now, both the title and the content have the same text style. You'll work on this next.

Styling title and content

Look at the note design once again and you'll see that the title and content have specific text styles. The content text is smaller and has a different color. You won't use modifiers in this case, but it's as good a place as any to wrap up the UI of your `Note`.

In **Note.kt**, edit the code for `Column()` so it looks like this:

```
Column(
  modifier = Modifier
    .weight(1f)
    .align(Alignment.CenterVertically)
) {
  Text(
    text = "Title",
    color = Color.Black,
    maxLines = 1,
    style = TextStyle(
      fontWeight = FontWeight.Normal,
      fontSize = 16.sp,
      letterSpacing = 0.15.sp
    )
  )
  Text(
    text = "Content",
    color = Color.Black.copy(alpha = 0.75f),
    maxLines = 1,
    style = TextStyle( // here
      fontWeight = FontWeight.Normal,
      fontSize = 14.sp,
      letterSpacing = 0.25.sp
    )
  )
}
```

To avoid complaints from Android Studio, add these imports:

```
import androidx.compose.ui.text.TextStyle
import androidx.compose.ui.text.font.FontWeight
import androidx.compose.ui.unit.sp
```

Here, you used the `style` and `color` in your `Text`s to apply **Material Design** to your note.

`TextStyle()` is a styling configuration for the `Text`. It exposes different parameters like `fontWeight`, `fontSize`, `letterSpacing` and more that let you style the text.

In Chapter 8, "Applying Material Design To Compose", you'll see how you can use Material components provided in Jetpack Compose to easily accomplish the same result. But for now, it's good to notice that you can accomplish the same thing using basic components.

Build and run the app. The note now looks like this:

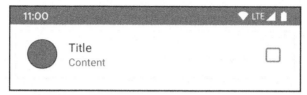

Note Composable

Well done! Your note composable is now as beautiful as it is in the design. :]

Now that you've completed the Note, it would be nice to add some new composables to **Jet Notes**.

Adding the Color composable

No, you're not experiencing *deja vu*. This will be a different composable from the previous NoteColor. :] Since you've completed NoteColor, it makes sense to add a composable that relies on it to build extra functionality.

So now, you'll start working on a color picker composable, like the one shown below:

Color Picker

The color picker allows the user to color code their notes by assigning specific colors to them. The user can open the color picker by clicking on the color palette icon in the app bar or by pulling from the bottom edge of the screen.

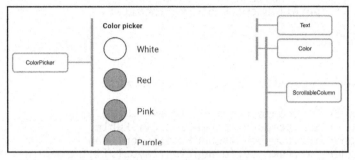

Color Picker — Components

You can break this composable down into smaller ones, as shown in the figure above. By following the **bottom-up** approach, you'll work on ColorItem first.

You'll use this composable in the **Save Note** screen.

Creating the ColorItem

Start by creating a new package called **screens** in the **ui** package. Then, in this package, create a new Kotlin file named **SaveNoteScreen.kt**. Finally, add the following code to **SaveNoteScreen.kt**:

```
@Composable
fun ColorItem(
    color: ColorModel,
    onColorSelect: (ColorModel) -> Unit
) {
  Row(
    modifier = Modifier
      .fillMaxWidth()
      .clickable(
        onClick = {
          onColorSelect(color)
        }
      )
  ) {
    NoteColor(
      modifier = Modifier.padding(10.dp),
      color = Color.fromHex(color.hex),
      size = 80.dp,
      border = 2.dp
    )
    Text(
```

```
        text = color.name,
        fontSize = 22.sp,
        modifier = Modifier
          .padding(horizontal = 16.dp)
          .align(Alignment.CenterVertically)
    )
  }
}
}
```

For this to work, you need to add the necessary imports:

```
import androidx.compose.material.Text
import androidx.compose.foundation.clickable
import androidx.compose.foundation.layout.Row
import androidx.compose.foundation.layout.fillMaxWidth
import androidx.compose.foundation.layout.padding
import androidx.compose.runtime.Composable
import androidx.compose.ui.Alignment
import androidx.compose.ui.Modifier
import androidx.compose.ui.unit.dp
import androidx.compose.ui.unit.sp
import
com.raywenderlich.android.jetnotes.domain.model.ColorModel
import
com.raywenderlich.android.jetnotes.ui.components.NoteColor
import androidx.compose.ui.graphics.Color
import com.raywenderlich.android.jetnotes.util.fromHex
```

OK, it's time to break down the code. In the design, two components work together to make the ColorItem composable: NoteColor and Text. They're aligned next to each other, so you use a Row to position them.

There's one new modifier here that you haven't used so far: Modifier.clickable() in Row. With that modifier, you made the whole ColorItem clickable. As mentioned before, it's a good practice to expose click events to parent composables.

To accomplish that, you passed the onColorSelect(color) call for the onClick. onColorSelect is of type (ColorModel) -> Unit, which is known as a function type. This specific function type says that the function that will be passed to it should take ColorModel as an argument.

To execute it, you used the default call operator: onColorSelect(color), using the function name. This means that when the user clicks on a note, the function that was passed for the onColorSelect parameter will execute.

`ColorItem` has two parameters:

- A `color` parameter of type `ColorModel`, which represents a model class for the color.

- The `onColorSelect` parameter of type `(ColorModel) -> Unit`. This is a lambda that takes `ColorModel` as an argument. That way, you allow the parent composable to know which color the user selected.

Previewing the ColorItem

Finally, add the following preview function to the bottom of **SaveNoteScreen.kt** so you can preview your `ColorItem`:

```
@Preview
@Composable
fun ColorItemPreview() {
  ColorItem(ColorModel.DEFAULT) {}
}
```

Don't forget to add the `Preview` import:

```
import androidx.compose.ui.tooling.preview.Preview
```

Here, you just invoked `Color` with the default color defined in **ColorModel.kt**. For `onColorSelect`, you passed an empty lambda since you don't need it for the preview to work. Thanks to Kotlin, you're able to pass the second argument as a trailing lambda.

Now, build the project. In the preview panel, you'll see this:

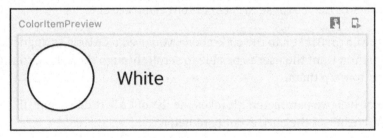

ColorItem — Preview

Great work! You've completed another composable! :]

Now, you can use this composable to complete the color picker.

Wrapping up the ColorPicker composable

With `ColorItem` in place, it's a piece of cake to build `ColorPicker()`.

Add the following code to the top of **SaveNoteScreen.kt**, just above `ColorItem`:

```
@Composable
private fun ColorPicker(
  colors: List<ColorModel>,
  onColorSelect: (ColorModel) -> Unit
) {
  Column(modifier = Modifier.fillMaxWidth()) {
    Text(
      text = "Color picker",
      fontSize = 18.sp,
      fontWeight = FontWeight.Bold,
      modifier = Modifier.padding(8.dp)
    )
    LazyColumn(modifier = Modifier.fillMaxWidth()) {
      items(colors.size) { itemIndex ->
        val color = colors[itemIndex]
        ColorItem(
          color = color,
          onColorSelect = onColorSelect
        )
      }
    }
  }
}
```

As usual, there are a few imports that you need to add as well:

```
import androidx.compose.foundation.lazy.LazyColumn
import androidx.compose.foundation.layout.Column
import androidx.compose.ui.text.font.FontWeight
```

To create the `ColorPicker` in the code above, you used a `Column` to align its title and list of colors. You want the user to be able to scroll through the colors, so you used a `LazyColumn` to wrap them.

`ColorPicker` has two parameters: It takes the list of `ColorModel`s and, like the `ColorItem`, it exposes the click event parameter.

To visualize what you've built so far, add the preview composable to the bottom of **SaveNoteScreen.kt**:

```
@Preview
@Composable
fun ColorPickerPreview() {
```

```
ColorPicker(
    colors = listOf(
        ColorModel.DEFAULT,
        ColorModel.DEFAULT,
        ColorModel.DEFAULT
    )
) { }
}
```

Here, you invoked `ColorPicker()` and passed it a list of default colors. For `onColorSelect`, you passed an empty lambda, since you're not interested in interacting with the composable at this stage.

Build the project and check the preview panel to see this:

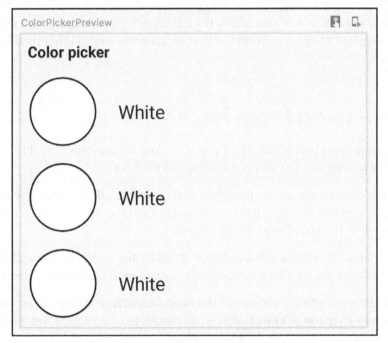

ColorPicker — Preview

Well done! Yet another composable under your belt. :]

You'll see the color picker in action in Chapter 7, "Managing State in Compose".

This is where this chapter ends. Hopefully, you now have a feeling for how powerful modifiers are. You can find the final code for this chapter by navigating to **06-using-compose-modifiers/projects/final**.

Key points

- **Modifiers** tell a UI element how to lay out, display or behave within its parent layout. You can also say that they **decorate** or **add behavior** to UI elements.

- You can **chain** several modifiers, one after the other, to **compose** them.

- The **order of modifiers** in the chain matters. Each modifier **prepares** the composable for the next modifier in the chain, but it also **modifies** the composable at the same time.

- Avoid **hard-coding** the values in your composables. Instead, **expose those values as properties** of the composable function.

- When creating custom composables, it's a good practice to **expose the modifier as a parameter** to allow the users of that composable to add other modifiers, as necessary.

Where to go from here?

Modifiers are a great tool to use when you style your composables. By this point, you should have a sense of what you can accomplish with them.

This chapter didn't cover all the modifiers that Compose offers since there are a lot of them. The good news is that the principles are the same so you should feel safe using them with the knowledge you've gained.

When you play with composables, don't be afraid to dive deep and research which modifiers you can use on which components. You might be pleasantly surprised. :]

In the next chapter, you'll learn one of the **most important things** about Jetpack Compose: how to **manage states**. When you complete that chapter, **Jet Notes** will be one step closer to being a fully functional app.

Chapter 7: Managing State in Compose

By Denis Buketa

Great job on completing the first two chapters of this section. Now you know the basic principles of composing a UI and making it beautiful.

In this chapter, you'll change your focus from the UI of **JetNotes** to making it functional. To make any app functional, you need to know how to **manage state**, which is the topic of this chapter.

In this chapter, you'll learn:

- What **state** is.

- What **unidirectional data flow** is.

- How to think about **state** and **events** when creating **stateless** composables.

- How to use ViewModel and LiveData from **Android Architecture Components** to manage state in Compose.

- How to add functionality to the **Notes** screen.

Get ready to dive in by taking a deeper look at what state is and why it's critical for your app.

Understanding state

Before you can understand the **state management** theory, you need to define what **state** is.

At its core, every app works with specific values that can **change**. For example, **JetNotes** manages notes, and users can make changes to the list of notes. They can:

- Add new notes.

- Delete current notes.

- Change a note.

- Complete a note.

State is any **value** that **can change over time**. Those values can include anything from an entry in a database to a property of a class. And as the state changes, you need to **update the UI** to reflect those changes.

UI update loop

When you think about how users interact with Android apps, you can say that it's like having a conversation. Users communicate through events like clicking, dragging and speaking while the app responds by displaying the app's state.

Events are inputs generated outside the app, while the **state** is the result of the app's reaction to an event. In between, you have the **logic to update the state**.

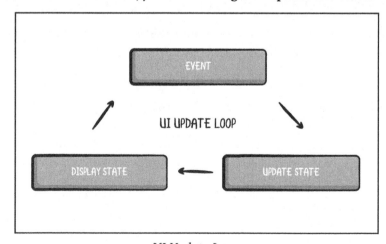

UI Update Loop

These three concepts form the **UI update loop**:

- **Event**: Input generated by the user or another part of the program.

- **Update state**: An event handler that reacts to the event and updates the state.

- **Display state**: The UI updates and displays the new state.

This is how all Android apps work. Understanding this concept is key to understanding how Compose manages state.

Handling state with Android UI Toolkit

Before going further, remind yourself how the current Android UI Toolkit manages state.

In Chapter 1, "Developing UI in Android", you had the chance to explore the data flow between the UI and the business logic for a basic Android component — a Spinner.

There, you saw that it's difficult to build a UI that represents the model — or a state, in this case — if the UI also owns and manages state.

That kind of design has some problems, including:

- **Testing**: It's difficult to test views like Activity or Fragment if the state of the UI is mixed in with them.

- **Partial state updates**: If the screen has a lot of events, it's easy to forget to update a part of the state, which can result in an incorrect UI.

- **Partial UI updates**: Whenever the state changes, you have to update the UI manually. The more things you have to update, the easier it is to forget something, once again resulting in an incorrect UI.

- **Code complexity**: When using this pattern, it's difficult to extract some of the logic. In the long run, the code tends to become difficult to read and understand.

- **No single source of truth**: Because both the UI and the model own the state, you have to make sure that they're in sync.

- **Update responsibility**: You don't always know if you're the one changing the View state, or if the event came from the user.

Keep this in mind as you learn about **unidirectional data flow** and how it can help.

Handling state with unidirectional data flow

In the previous Spinner example, the data flow had multiple directions it could come from and multiple directions it could go to, depending on trigger events and UI updates it reflected. This means it's hard to keep everything in sync and its hard to know where the change is coming from at all times.

Unidirectional data flow on the other hand is a concept where both the state changes and UI updates have only one direction, as the name states. This means that state change events can only come from one source, usually from user interactions, and UI updates can come only from the state manager, the event handler or the model, however you want to refer to it.

Unidirectional data flow isn't a new concept in programming. It's well-established that it's a good idea to **decouple** components that **display state** in the UI from the parts of the app that **store and change state**.

Compose was built with unidirectional data flow in mind.

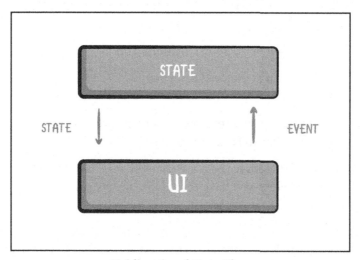

Unidirectional Data Flow

The key concept here is that **state flows down** and **events flow up**, as the image above shows.

Another key concept is that the UI **observes the state**. Every time there's new state, the UI displays it.

Here's how the UI update loop for an app that uses unidirectional data flow looks:

- **Event**: A **UI component** generates input and **passes it up**.

- **Update state**: An event handler **may or may not change** the state. For some UI components, the new state is already in the correct format, so it doesn't need to change.

- **Display state**: The UI **observes the state**. Upon creation, the new state is **passed down** to the UI that displays it.

Even though Compose didn't have a built-in `Spinner` at the time of this writing, you can reimagine how you used one in Chapter 1, "Developing UI in Android" with the unidirectional data flow in mind.

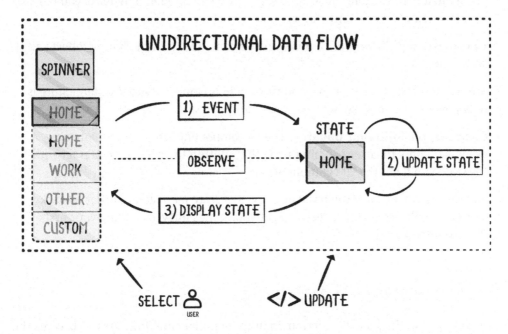

Unidirectional Data Flow

In the figure, you can see two distinct parts of the unidirectional data flow:

1. The **UI**, represented by the spinner.

2. The **state**, represented by `State` properties.

The `Spinner` observes the state and can generate events. An event handler may or may not update the state when the new event comes. When the state changes, the `Spinner` is aware of and displays that change.

Just as when you worked with it in the previous example, the user can interact with the `Spinner` — the main difference now is how you interact with it in the code. In code, you don't interact directly with the `Spinner`; you only update the state. Since the `Spinner` observes that state, the UI updates correctly when the state changes.

Following this pattern when using Jetpack Compose has several advantages:

- **Testability**: Since the UI is decoupled from the state, you can test each component in isolation.

- **State encapsulation**: Because state can only be updated in one place, you're less likely to create inconsistent states.

- **UI consistency**: Since your UI observes the state, the UI immediately reflects all state updates.

- **Single source of truth**: The UI and the model no longer share the state. State is only present in one place, which is now the single source of truth.

- **Clear responsibility for updates**: The UI component can only generate new events and only the user can interact with it. Within the code, you interact with the state itself, not the UI component.

Good! Now that you know the basic principles of state management that Jetpack Compose is built upon, you're ready to get your hands dirty, by adding your first feature to **JetNotes**. :]

Compose & ViewModel

As mentioned in the previous section, in unidirectional data flow, the UI observes the state. The Android framework offers some great **Android Architecture Components** that make it easy for you to follow that approach, including the `ViewModel` and `LiveData`.

A `ViewModel` lets you extract the **state** from the UI and define **events** that the UI can call to update that state. `LiveData` allows you to create **observable state holders** that provide a way for anyone to observe changes to the state.

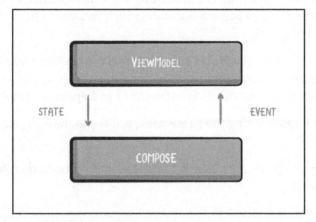

Unidirectional Data Flow With Architecture Components

You'll use the architecture shown in the figure above for your app.

The `ViewModel` will represent the **state**, while your composables will represent the **UI**. In your `ViewModels`, you'll use `LiveData` to hold state.

In your composables, you'll observe that state and propagate events from child composables to the `ViewModel`.

Enough theory, it's time to put this into practice! :]

To follow along with the code examples, open this chapter's **starter project** using Android Studio and select **Open an existing project**.

Next, navigate to **07-managing-state-in-compose/projects** and select the **starter** folder as the project root. Once the project opens, let it build and sync and you'll be ready to go!

Note that if you skip ahead to the **final project**, you'll be able to see the **Notes** screen and the list of notes in it. :]

Creating the Notes screen

So far, **JetNotes** has no screens. The only thing you can do with it at the moment is pull out the app drawer and inspect one note, which you use to track your progress. This is about to change. :]

Your next step is to create the **Notes** screen. To make it easier for you to work on this screen, the database already contains some notes and colors. If you're interested in the code behind them, check out `initDatabase()` in **RepositoryImpl.kt**.

Before you start implementing the `ViewModel`, you'll add the entry point for the **Notes** screen.

In the **screens** package, create a new Kotlin file named **NotesScreen.kt** and add the following code to it:

```
@Composable
fun NotesScreen(viewModel: MainViewModel) {

}
```

This creates your root composable function for **Notes**. Notice that `NotesScreen()` takes `MainViewModel` as a parameter. You need this because you'll observe states from the `MainViewModel` in `NotesScreen()`. You also need a reference to `MainViewModel` so you can pass events up to it from the UI.

For this to build successfully, you have to add these necessary imports:

```
import androidx.compose.runtime.Composable
import
com.raywenderlich.android.jetnotes.viewmodel.MainViewModel
```

Before adding any more code to **NotesScreen.kt**, you need make to this screen the default screen that appears when you open the app. To do this, go to **MainActivity.kt** and replace the code inside `JetNotesTheme()` with `NotesScreen(viewModel)`, like this:

```
JetNotesTheme {
  NotesScreen(viewModel = viewModel)
}
```

This ensures that **Notes** opens whenever you run the app. By removing the old code, you temporarily removed the app drawer from the app — but don't worry, you'll add it back soon.

Now, add the import for the `NotesScreen`.

```
import com.raywenderlich.android.jetnotes.ui.screens.NotesScreen
```

Finally, build and run the app. You'll see an empty screen, like this:

Empty Notes Screens

OK, your canvas is ready!

In the next section, your task will be to connect `NotesScreen()` with `MainViewModel`.

Implementing unidirectional data flow

Now that you have an entry point to **Notes**, you need to implement `MainViewModel` so it supports unidirectional data flow.

Remember, there are two key concepts in play: **states** and **events**.

First, try your hand at breaking down which states are present here. The **Notes** screen displays a list of notes, which is the state of that screen. Each note contains a few states, which are all encapsulated in `NoteModel`.

Now, try to expose that state in your `MainViewModel`.

Open **MainViewModel.kt** and add the following code to the class:

```
val notesNotInTrash: LiveData<List<NoteModel>> by lazy {
    repository.getAllNotesNotInTrash()
}
```

`Repository`, which came pre-prepared in the starter project, exposes `getAllNotesNotInTrash()`, which returns the `LiveData` of the list of `NoteModel`s. With this, you can easily expose the state of the notes you want to display on the **Notes** screen.

Now, you need to add few imports:

```
import androidx.lifecycle.LiveData
import com.raywenderlich.android.jetnotes.domain.model.NoteModel
```

This was pretty simple. Next, you need to break down which events to pass from `NotesScreen` to `MainViewModel`. Looking at the design tells you that there are three events to handle. Users can:

- Click on a specific note.

- Click on a floating action button (FAB) to create a new note.

- Check off a note.

To handle these events, add the following to the bottom of `MainViewModel`:

```
fun onCreateNewNoteClick() {
    // TODO - Open SaveNoteScreen
}

fun onNoteClick(note: NoteModel) {
    // TODO - Open SaveNoteScreen in Edit mode
}

fun onNoteCheckedChange(note: NoteModel) {
    viewModelScope.launch(Dispatchers.Default) {
        repository.insertNote(note)
    }
}
```

Here, you added three functions that represent three possible events that the view can pass.

- **onCreateNoteClick()**: You call this function when the user clicks on a FAB. Right now, its body is empty, but you'll complete it when you work on the **Save Note** screen.

- **onNoteClick()**: This reacts when the user clicks on any note. To know which note the user selected, it uses `NoteModel` as a parameter. Once again, its body will remain empty until after you complete the **Save Note** screen.

- **onNoteCheckedChange()**: You call this when the user clicks on a checkbox in any note. It tells the repository to update the specific note in the database.

Finally, to make Android Studio happy, add these imports as well:

```
import androidx.lifecycle.viewModelScope
import kotlinx.coroutines.Dispatchers
import kotlinx.coroutines.launch
```

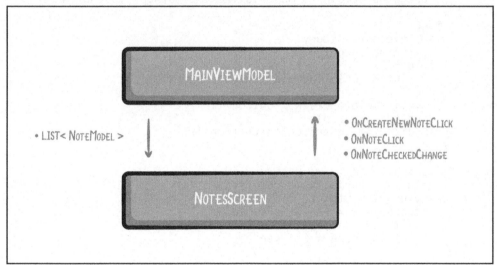

Unidirectional Data Flow — Notes Screen

Great job! You're now ready to use the `MainViewModel` in `NotesScreen`.

Creating the app bar

Before connecting the `NotesScreen` to the `MainViewModel`, you need to implement the UI components that make up the **Notes** screen.

In your **Notes** screen, you'll need to add an app bar. But wait a second — check the design and you'll see that you need that app bar in *all* your screens. Therefore, it would be handy to implement it as a separate component and reuse it whenever you need it.

In **ui.components**, create a new Kotlin file named **TopAppBar.kt** and add the following code to it:

```kotlin
@Composable
fun TopAppBar(
  title: String,
  icon: ImageVector,
  onIconClick: () -> Unit,
) {
  Row(
    modifier = Modifier
      .fillMaxWidth()
      .height(56.dp)
      .background(color = MaterialTheme.colors.primarySurface)
  ) {
    Image(
      imageVector = icon,
      contentDescription = "Top App Bar Icon",
      colorFilter = ColorFilter
        .tint(MaterialTheme.colors.onPrimary),
      modifier = Modifier
        .clickable(onClick = onIconClick)
        .padding(16.dp)
        .align(Alignment.CenterVertically)
    )
    Text(
      text = title,
      color = MaterialTheme.colors.onPrimary,
      style = TextStyle(
        fontWeight = FontWeight.Medium,
        fontSize = 20.sp,
        letterSpacing = 0.15.sp
      ),
      modifier = Modifier
        .fillMaxWidth()
        .align(Alignment.CenterVertically)
        .padding(start = 16.dp, end = 16.dp)
    )
  }
}
```

This code creates an app bar composable that you can reuse on multiple screens. It's a pretty straightforward composable. You used a Row to align an icon and a text field next to each other. You should be familiar with all the modifiers and specific properties that you use here — you saw them in the previous chapter.

You also exposed a couple of parameters to let you customize the screen. title allows you to change the screen title, while icon lets you set any icon for the app bar. Finally, since the icon is clickable, you exposed onIconClick so the parent composable can react when the user clicks the icon.

The important concept here is `onIconClick`. You already saw this concept in Chapter 5, "Combining Composables". By exposing that specific parameter, you allow the **click event** to be **passed up** when the user interacts with this composable.

Pay attention to this concept going forward. You'll see it a lot in this chapter.

For the code above to work, you need to add some imports as well:

```
import androidx.compose.foundation.Image
import androidx.compose.foundation.background
import androidx.compose.foundation.clickable
import androidx.compose.foundation.layout.Row
import androidx.compose.foundation.layout.fillMaxWidth
import androidx.compose.foundation.layout.height
import androidx.compose.foundation.layout.padding
import androidx.compose.material.MaterialTheme
import androidx.compose.material.Text
import androidx.compose.material.primarySurface
import androidx.compose.runtime.Composable
import androidx.compose.ui.Alignment
import androidx.compose.ui.Modifier
import androidx.compose.ui.graphics.ColorFilter
import androidx.compose.ui.graphics.vector.ImageVector
import androidx.compose.ui.text.TextStyle
import androidx.compose.ui.text.font.FontWeight
import androidx.compose.ui.unit.dp
import androidx.compose.ui.unit.sp
```

Now, it's time to wrap up the `TopAppBar()`. Add the following code to the bottom of **TopAppBar.kt**:

```
@Preview
@Composable
private fun TopAppBarPreview() {
  JetNotesTheme {
    TopAppBar(
      title = "JetNotes",
      icon = Icons.Filled.List,
      onIconClick = {}
    )
  }
}
```

Here, you added the preview composable so you can check `TopAppBar()` in the preview panel. You also took an extra step and used `JetNotesTheme` as a wrapper to make `TopAppBar()` use the colors you defined in your theme. However, the preview would work without that, too.

Don't forget to include these imports as well:

```
import androidx.compose.material.icons.Icons
import androidx.compose.material.icons.filled.List
import androidx.compose.ui.tooling.preview.Preview
import com.raywenderlich.android.jetnotes.theme.JetNotesTheme
```

Build the project and check the preview panel. You'll see something like this:

TopAppBar Composable — Preview

Great! You've now built an app bar composable that you can reuse in any screen you want. :]

The next thing you'll do is adapt Note() so you can use it for the **Notes** screen.

Stateless composables

In MainViewModel, you exposed the list of NoteModels as a state, but your Note() still isn't ready to render a specific NoteModel.

If you check Note(), which you completed in the previous chapter, you see that its values are all hard-coded. You'll change that in this section.

Before writing any code, take a moment to think about which state you need to render a note and which events each note should expose.

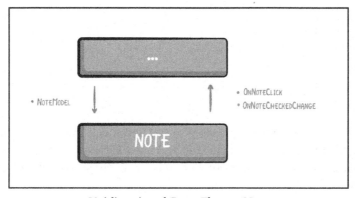

Unidirectional Data Flow — Note

As you saw before, `NotesScreen()` needs to be able to pass three events up to `MainViewModel` and two of those events are a note's responsibility.

Also, if you want to render the correct information in `Note()`, you need the data from a `NoteModel`. `NoteModel` is a state that a parent composable will pass down to `Note()`.

Now, you're ready to open **Note.kt** and add the following parameters to `Note()`:

```
@Composable
fun Note(
  note: NoteModel,
  onNoteClick: (NoteModel) -> Unit = {},
  onNoteCheckedChange: (NoteModel) -> Unit = {}
) {
    // ...
}
```

The parameters in the code above represent state and events that will be passed up and down between `Note()` and its parent composable.

An important principle is hidden in these parameters: **state hoisting**. If your composable has state, you can use state hoisting to make it **stateless**. State hoisting is a programming pattern where you **move state to the caller of a composable** by replacing internal state in a composable with **a parameter** and **events**.

For composables, this often means introducing two parameters to the composable:

• **value: T**: The current value to display.

• **onValueChange: (T) -> Unit**: An event that requests a change to a value, where T is the proposed new value.

The value T represents a generic type, that depends on the data and the UI you're showing. If you look at the parameters of `Note` again, you see that you follow the same approach for your state and events. In that case, your T is actually a `NoteModel`.

By applying **state hoisting** to a composable, you make it stateless — which means it can't change any state itself. Stateless composables are easier to test, tend to have fewer bugs and offer more opportunities for reuse.

A **stateful** composable would be a composable that has a dependency on the final class, which can directly change a specific state. In this example, a **stateful** composable would be any parent composable that both has a dependency on `MainViewModel` and can call `MainViewModel.onNoteCheckedChange()`. Why that specific function? Because it changes the state in the `MainViewModel`.

Finally, import `NoteModel`:

```
import com.raywenderlich.android.jetnotes.domain.model.NoteModel
```

Now that you understand stateless composables, your next step is to add the logic to render the `NoteModel` state.

Rendering NoteModel's state

To render the `NoteModel` in `Note()`, you need to replace your current, hard-coded values with the values from `NoteModel`.

Your first task is to update the code to use a color from `NoteModel` when you invoke a `NoteColor`.

```
NoteColor(
   modifier = Modifier
     .align(Alignment.CenterVertically)
     .padding(start = 16.dp, end = 16.dp),
   color = Color.fromHex(note.color.hex),
   size = 40.dp,
   border = 1.dp
)
```

This is pretty straightforward. You use the utility function that parses the string color value from `NoteModel.color.hex` to `Color`. Before it will work, you need to add an import to a utility function:

```
import com.raywenderlich.android.jetnotes.util.fromHex
```

Now, you're going to make sure that you show the correct title and content text. `Column` like this:

```
Column(
   modifier = Modifier
     .weight(1f)
     .align(Alignment.CenterVertically)
) {
   Text(
     text = note.title, // here
     ...
   )
   Text(
     text = note.content, // here
     ...
   )
}
```

This is also easy to understand. All you did was to replace the hard-coded values you used for the title and the content with `NoteModel.title` and `NoteModel.content`.

Now, the last thing to handle regarding state is the checkbox composable. Update the code that handles the checkbox, like this:

```
if (note.isCheckedOff != null) {
  Checkbox(
    checked = note.isCheckedOff,
    onCheckedChange = {},
    modifier = Modifier
      .padding(16.dp)
      .align(Alignment.CenterVertically)
  )
}
```

Here, you first check if `NoteModel.isCheckedOff` is null. If it is, that means that the note isn't set up for the user to check it off, so it shouldn't show the checkbox.

If `NoteModel.isCheckedOff` *isn't null*, you invoke `Checkbox()` and pass that state as a parameter called `checked`. By doing that, you make sure that the checkbox always has the right state.

Great job! `Note()` now can successfully render the state that is **passed down** to it.

Your next step is to add the code that will **pass events up**.

Passing up Note events

Remember, the first of the two events that a note can pass up to a parent is when a user clicks the note. You'll handle that first, by updating the Row modifier to allow that:

```
Row(
  modifier = Modifier
    .padding(8.dp)
    .shadow(1.dp, backgroundShape)
    .fillMaxWidth()
    .heightIn(min = 64.dp)
    .background(Color.White, backgroundShape)
    .clickable(onClick = { onNoteClick(note) }) // here
) {
  ...
}
```

Here, you made the Row clickable. As the user clicks on the Row, it triggers the internal onClick() handler from the modifier. That handler then notifies the parent, using onNoteClick(note). Doing so, it passes the NoteModel state of the clicked note up to the parent.

Finally, you need to add one import:

```
import androidx.compose.foundation.clickable
```

Well done! Now, you'll do the same thing for the second event. Update the Checkbox() by adding the following code to its onCheckedChange():

```
Checkbox(
  checked = note.isCheckedOff,
  onCheckedChange = { isChecked -> // here
    val newNote = note.copy(isCheckedOff = isChecked)
    onNoteCheckedChange(newNote)
  },
  modifier = Modifier
    .padding(16.dp)
    .align(Alignment.CenterVertically)
)
```

This a bit more complicated, but nothing you can't handle. :]

Whenever the user clicks the checkbox, it invokes onCheckedChange(), where isChecked contains the new value. You added the code that creates a new NoteModel with the new isCheckedOff state.

After that, you call onNoteCheckedChange(newNote) and pass an event up to the parent with the new NoteModel.

Finally, you shouldn't forget to update the preview composable to use the new parameters you added to Note:

```
@Preview
@Composable
private fun NotePreview() {
  Note(note = NoteModel(1, "Note 1", "Content 1", null))
}
```

Build the project and you'll see something like this in the preview:

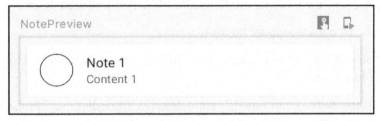

Notes Composable — Preview

Unidirectional data flow with stateless composables

Hoisting the state out of Note() has some advantages: It's now easier to reason about the composable, reuse it in different situations and to test it. Plus, now that you've decoupled Note() from how you store the state, if you modify or replace MainViewModel, you don't have to change how you implement Note().

State hoisting allows you to extend **unidirectional data flow** to **stateless** composables. The unidirectional data flow diagram for these composables maintains state going down and events going up as more composables interact with the state.

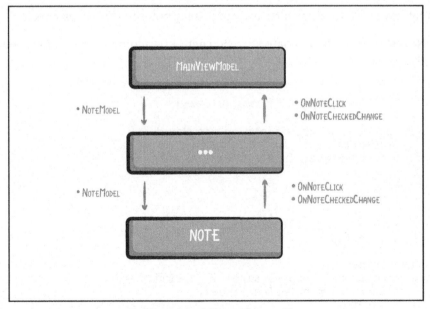

Unidirectional Data Flow — Note

It's important to understand that a stateless composable can still interact with state that changes over time by using unidirectional data flow and state hoisting.

Check out the UI update loop for `Note()`:

- **Event**: You call `onNoteCheckedChange()` in response to the user clicking a checkbox in a note.

- **Update State**: `Note()` can't modify state directly. The caller may choose to modify state(s) in response to `onNoteCheckedChange()`. Up the chain, a parent composable will call `onNoteCheckedChange()` on `MainViewModel`. This, in turn, causes the `notesNotInTrash` to update and the event updating it will originate from where you called `onNoteCheckedChanged()`.

- **Display State**: When `notesNotInTrash` changes, you call `NotesScreen()` again with the updated state. That state will propagate down to a specific note. As you saw in previous chapters, calling composables in response to state changes is called **recomposition**.

You've now laid all the groundwork, and you're ready to let your users see their notes!

Displaying notes in the Notes screen

Now that `Note` is stateless, you're ready to display notes in the **Notes** screen.

Open **NotesScreen.kt** and update `NotesScreen()` by adding the following code to the body:

```
@Composable
fun NotesScreen(viewModel: MainViewModel) {

  val notes: List<NoteModel> by viewModel
    .notesNotInTrash
    .observeAsState(listOf())

  Column {
    TopAppBar(
      title = "JetNotes",
      icon = Icons.Filled.List,
      onIconClick = {}
    )
    LazyColumn {
      items(count = notes.size) { noteIndex ->
        val note = notes[noteIndex]
        Note(
          note = note,
```

```
        onNoteClick = {
          viewModel.onNoteClick(it)
        },
        onNoteCheckedChange = {
          viewModel.onNoteCheckedChange(it)
        }
      )
    }
   }
  }
 }
}
```

OK, there are a couple of things to unpack here. The most interesting line is the first one, where you access the note's state from `MainViewModel`. You can break it apart like this:

- **val notes: List**: Declares a variable `notes` with the type `List<NoteModel>`.

- **viewModel.notesNotInTrash**: Returns an object with the type `LiveData<NoteModel>`.

- **.observeAsState(listOf())**: Converts `LiveData<NoteModel>` into a `State<NoteModel>` so that Compose can react to value changes. You pass `listOf()` as an initial value to avoid possible null results before `LiveData` initializes. If you didn't pass the initial value, `notes` would be `List<NoteModel>?`, which is nullable.

- **by**: This keyword is the property delegate syntax in Kotlin. It automatically unwraps the `State<List<NoteModel>>` from `observeAsState` into a regular `List<NoteModel>`.

Composable functions get **subscribed** to a `State` any time you read the value property during its execution. Reading the `notes`' value when passing it to `LazyColumn` subscribed it to `State<List<NoteModel>>`. Any changes to that state will schedule a recomposition of `NotesScreen()`.

The rest of the code handles emitting UI. You used a `Column` and put a `TopAppBar` and a `LazyColumn` into it.

Notice that in `LazyColumn()`, you used `Note()`, which you adapted in the previous section. You pass `NoteModel` to pass down state. Finally, to allow each `Note()` to pass up events, you passed calls to `viewModel.onNoteClick()` and `viewModel.onNoteCheckedChange()`.

Before building, you need to add these imports.

```
import androidx.compose.foundation.layout.Column
import androidx.compose.foundation.lazy.LazyColumn
import androidx.compose.material.icons.Icons
import androidx.compose.material.icons.filled.List
import androidx.compose.runtime.getValue
import androidx.compose.runtime.livedata.observeAsState
import com.raywenderlich.android.jetnotes.domain.model.NoteModel
import com.raywenderlich.android.jetnotes.ui.components.Note
import
com.raywenderlich.android.jetnotes.ui.components.TopAppBar
```

Now, build the project and run the app. You'll see something like this:

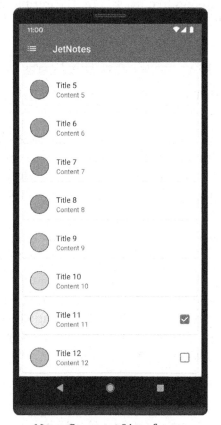

Notes Screen — List of notes

You can see the Notes that were created for you in the starter project. Scroll down to the last two notes and click a checkbox. You'll notice that state updates whenever you check off a note.

Extracting a stateless composable

Look at NotesScreen() code and you'll see it has a dependency on the final class, MainViewModel, which directly changes notesNotInTrash's state. That makes it a stateful composable.

You can also see that the code that changes state is related to the list of notes. Both calls to MainViewModel are inside LazyColumn().

Do you notice something? You could extract that code and make a stateless composable — which is what you'll do next.

Add the following code to the bottom of **NotesScreen.kt**:

```kotlin
@Composable
private fun NotesList(
  notes: List<NoteModel>,
  onNoteCheckedChange: (NoteModel) -> Unit,
  onNoteClick: (NoteModel) -> Unit
) {
  LazyColumn {
    items(count = notes.size) { noteIndex ->
      val note = notes[noteIndex]
      Note(
        note = note,
        onNoteClick = onNoteClick,
        onNoteCheckedChange = onNoteCheckedChange
      )
    }
  }
}

@Preview
@Composable
private fun NotesListPreview() {
  NotesList(
    notes = listOf(
      NoteModel(1, "Note 1", "Content 1", null),
      NoteModel(2, "Note 2", "Content 2", false),
      NoteModel(3, "Note 3", "Content 3", true)
    ),
    onNoteCheckedChange = {},
    onNoteClick = {}
  )
}
```

Don't forget to add the `Preview` import as well:

```
import androidx.compose.ui.tooling.preview.Preview
```

Whenever you extract a stateless composable, you should keep two things in mind:

- The **state** you're passing down.

- The **events** you're passing up.

`NotesList()` has a parameter of type `List<NoteModel>`, which represents state for `NotesList()`. You need a list of notes in order to **pass down** the `NoteModels` to each `Note()`.

As you learned above, every note needs to pass two events: a click on a note and a click on a checkbox. `NoteList` exposes the same events because it displays the list of notes. So, when you check the remaining parameters in `NotesList`, you see that you added `onNoteCheckedChange: (NoteModel) -> Unit` and `onNoteClick: (NoteModel) -> Unit`, just as in `Note()`.

Once again, you applied the principle of state hoisting. Check the code inside `NotesList()` and you'll notice that this composable can't change any state. It can only pass state down or pass specific events up. It's decoupled from how its state, `List<NoteModel>`, is stored. By applying state hoisting, you made this composable stateless.

Finally, replace `LazyColumn` inside `NotesScreen` with `NotesList`:

```
Column {
  TopAppBar(
    title = "JetNotes",
    icon = Icons.Filled.List,
    onIconClick = {}
  )
  NotesList( // here
    notes = notes,
    onNoteCheckedChange = { viewModel.onNoteCheckedChange(it) },
    onNoteClick = { viewModel.onNoteClick(it) }
  )
}
```

This code is pretty straightforward, just be sure to notice that you passed down the same arguments as before. For state, you passed `notes` and you also passed two calls to `MainViewModel`.

Now, build and run. In the app, you'll see the same screen as before, but you'll see your `NotesList` in the preview panel.

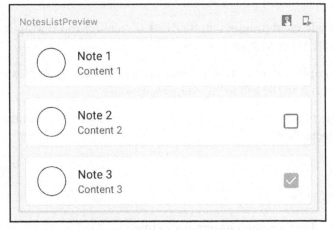

NotesList Composable — Preview

Well done! Before you wrap up this chapter, take a moment to review how you're passing state and events in the **Notes** screen.

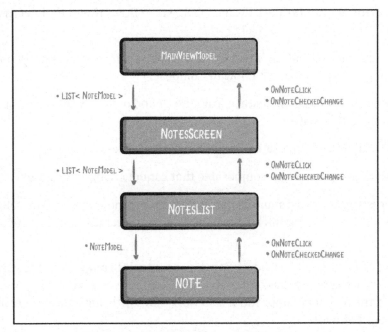

Unidirectional Data Flow — Notes Screen

This is the main concept behind **state management** in Compose. Always keep in mind that you **pass down** state and **pass up** events. Using **state hoisting** to create **stateless** composables makes that really easy.

Wow! You've made great progress on the **Notes** screen. :] You'll wrap it up in Chapter 8, "Applying Material Design to Compose".

Great job on completing this chapter! State management is a complex topic, and you'll see more of it in the following chapters as well.

You can find the final code for this chapter by navigating to **07-managing-state-in-compose/projects/final**.

Key points

- **State** is any **value** that **can change over time**.
- The **UI update loop** is made of three key concepts: **event**, **update state** and **display state**.
- **Unidirectional data flow** is a design where **state flows down and events flow up**.
- You can use the Android Architecture Components, ViewModel and LiveData, to implement unidirectional data flow in Compose.
- A ViewModel lets you extract **state** from the UI and define **events** that the UI can call to update that state.
- LiveData allows you to create **observable state holders**.
- A **stateless** composable is a composable that cannot change any state itself.
- **State hoisting** is a programming pattern where you move state to the caller of a composable by replacing internal state in that composable with a parameter and events.

In the next chapter, you'll see how you can use **material components** to easily build UI. You'll replace some of the composables that currently use basic composables and you'll build the rest of the app. You'll also work more with state since there are two more screens to build!

Chapter 8: Applying Material Design to Compose

By Denis Buketa

Well done! You've arrived at the last chapter in this section. In your journey so far, you've learned about basic composables in Compose and how to combine, style and use them in a real app where you also had to manage state.

In this chapter, you'll:

- Learn how to use **Material Design composables**, which Jetpack Compose provides for you.

- Go over **state management** in more depth.

- Complete the **Save Note** screen.

- Learn about **Material theming**.

- Change **JetNotes** to support a **dark theme**.

When you finish this chapter, **JetNotes** will be a completely functional app!

Opening the Notes screen

Before you can start working on the **Save Note** screen, you need a way to open it. By looking at the design, you can see that you've planned two ways to do that:

1. By clicking a floating action button (FAB), which will open the **Save Note** screen in **Create** mode, where the user create a new note.

2. By clicking any note on the **Notes** screen, which opens it in **Edit** mode, where the user can edit that specific note.

You'll start with the first case. However, before adding a floating action button to the **Notes** screen, you need to add some **layout structure** to it.

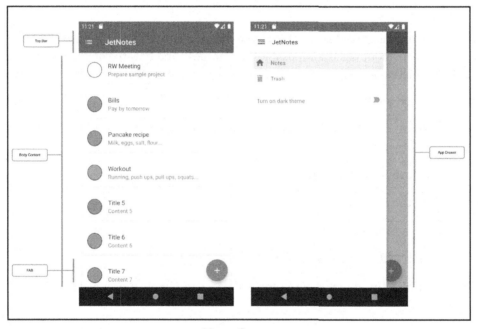

Notes Screen

Take a moment to look at the different parts of the screen. You have the:

- Top bar

- Body content

- Floating action button

- App drawer

This is a common layout structure for Android apps. Most apps today follow a similar design. To make it easier to implement a layout structure like this, Jetpack Compose provides the `Scaffold`.

Before going into any details, you'll add a `Scaffold` to the **Notes** screen.

Adding Scaffold

To follow along with the code examples, open this chapter's **starter project** in Android Studio and select **Open an existing project**.

Next, navigate to **08-applying-material-design-to-compose/projects** and select the **starter** folder as the project root. Once the project opens, let it build and sync and you're ready to go!

Note that you can see the completed **JetNotes** app by skipping ahead to the **final project**.

For now, open **NotesScreen.kt** and replace `Column()` with `Scaffold()`:

```
@Composable
fun NotesScreen(viewModel: MainViewModel) {

    // Observing notes state from MainViewModel
    ...

    Scaffold(
      topBar = {
        TopAppBar(
          title = "JetNotes",
          icon = Icons.Filled.List,
          onIconClick = {}
        )
      },
      content = {
        if (notes.isNotEmpty()) {
          NotesList(
            notes = notes,
            onNoteCheckedChange = {
              viewModel.onNoteCheckedChange(it)
            },
            onNoteClick = { viewModel.onNoteClick(it) }
          )
        }
      }
    )
}
```

Here's a breakdown of what you just did, You removed the `Column()` and its children, which you used to stack a `TopAppBar` and a `NotesList` on top of each other, and you replaced it with `Scaffold()`.

Now, you need to add an import for `Scaffold`.

```
import androidx.compose.material.Scaffold
```

Build and run. You'll notice that the behavior is the same as before:

Notes Screen

`Scaffold` implements the basic **Material Design** visual layout structure. It provides an API to combine several Material composables to construct your screen by ensuring they have a proper layout strategy and by collecting necessary data so the components will work together correctly.

This is the `Scaffold()` signature from the Jetpack Compose documentation:

```
@Composable
fun Scaffold(
  modifier: Modifier = Modifier,
  scaffoldState: ScaffoldState = rememberScaffoldState(),
```

```
    topBar: @Composable () -> Unit = {},
    bottomBar: @Composable () -> Unit = {},
    snackbarHost: @Composable (SnackbarHostState) -> Unit =
{ SnackbarHost(it) },
    floatingActionButton: @Composable () -> Unit = {},
    floatingActionButtonPosition: FabPosition = FabPosition.End,
    isFloatingActionButtonDocked: Boolean = false,
    drawerContent: @Composable (ColumnScope.() -> Unit)? = null,
    drawerGesturesEnabled: Boolean = true,
    drawerShape: Shape = MaterialTheme.shapes.large,
    drawerElevation: Dp = DrawerDefaults.Elevation,
    drawerBackgroundColor: Color = MaterialTheme.colors.surface,
    drawerContentColor: Color =
contentColorFor(drawerBackgroundColor),
    drawerScrimColor: Color = DrawerDefaults.scrimColor,
    backgroundColor: Color = MaterialTheme.colors.background,
    contentColor: Color = contentColorFor(backgroundColor),
    content: @Composable (PaddingValues) -> Unit
)
```

Notice how it provides an API for the **top bar**, **bottom bar**, **floating action button**, **drawer** and **content**. You can pick and choose from these options, using only what you need.

In **NotesScreen.kt**, you only used topBar and content. Scaffold() will make sure that the content you provided for the topBar is at the top of the screen and the content you provided for the content is below the topBar content. That's why the screen looked the same when you replaced Column() with Scaffold().

Resurrecting the app drawer

In the previous chapter, you temporarily removed the app drawer from the **Notes** screen. Now, it's time to put it back, slightly improved.

As you just learned, Scaffold() allows you to add app drawer content. It also lets the user pull the drawer out by dragging it from the left side of the screen.

Add AppDrawer back to the **Notes** screen by updating the code:

```
@Composable
fun NotesScreen(viewModel: MainViewModel) {

  // Observing notes state from MainViewModel
  ...

  // here - Drawer state
  val scaffoldState: ScaffoldState = rememberScaffoldState()
```

```
    // here - Coroutine scope used for opening/closing the drawer
    val coroutineScope = rememberCoroutineScope()

    Scaffold(
      topBar = {
        TopAppBar(
          title = "JetNotes",
          icon = Icons.Filled.List,
          onIconClick = {
            // here - Drawer open
            coroutineScope.launch {
              scaffoldState.drawerState.open()
            }
          }
        )
      },
      scaffoldState = scaffoldState, // here - Scaffold state
      drawerContent = { // here - Drawer UI
        AppDrawer(
          currentScreen = Screen.Notes,
          closeDrawerAction = {
            // here - Drawer close
            coroutineScope.launch {
              scaffoldState.drawerState.close()
            }
          }
        )
      },
      ...
    )
}
```

First, you passed an AppDrawer() for the drawerContent parameter.

By passing Screen.Notes to currentScreen, you made sure the notes item is selected when the user opens the app drawer. For the second parameter, you passed an action that manages the scaffoldState.

Above Scaffold() call, you used rememberCoroutineScope() to retrieve a CoroutineScope. This function return a CoroutineScope bound to this point in the composition using the optional CoroutineContext provided by getContext(). getContext() will only be called once and the same CoroutineScope instance will be returned across recompositions. This scope will be cancelled when this call leaves the composition.

You should use this scope to launch jobs in response to callback events such as clicks or other user interaction where the response to that event needs to unfold over time and be cancelled if the composable managing that process leaves the composition.

Notice that you used a coroutine to call `scaffoldState.drawerState.open()`. If you check `DrawerState` documentation, you can see that `open()` and `close()` are **suspendable** functions.

They open/close the drawer with animation and **suspend** until the drawer is fully opened/closed or animation has been canceled. Because of that, you have to call those methods within a coroutine.

Look at the line above `rememberCoroutineScope()`. There, you added `val scaffoldState: ScaffoldState = rememberScaffoldState()`. This is a new concept for you, which you'll learn more about next. The knowledge from the previous chapter will help you understand it better. :]

Don't forget to add all the necessary imports:

```
import androidx.compose.material.ScaffoldState
import androidx.compose.material.rememberScaffoldState
import com.raywenderlich.android.jetnotes.routing.Screen
import
com.raywenderlich.android.jetnotes.ui.components.AppDrawer
import androidx.compose.runtime.rememberCoroutineScope
import kotlinx.coroutines.launch
```

Now that you've added the drawer, you can finally see if it works like before. Build and run your app.

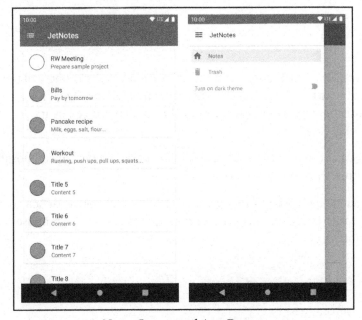

Notes Screen and App Drawer

Again, you can open the app drawer by either clicking the icon in the top bar or dragging right from the left side of the screen.

Try pulling out the app drawer and then changing the device's orientation. You'll see that when the app recreates the activity, the app drawer will still be open, meaning `remember()` successfully preserved the state. But how exactly does that work?

Memory in composable functions

`Scaffold()` can manage two composables that have state: app drawer and snackbar. Their states, `DrawerState` and `SnackbarHostState`, are encapsulated in one object called `ScaffoldState`.

If you use one of these composables with `Scaffold`, you need to make sure that their state updates accordingly and is preserved during recomposition.

Compose lets you **store values in the composition tree**. Another way of saying this is that composable functions can access what happened the last time they were called. This is where `remember()` helps you.

Using remember

Here's how `remember()` looks in code:

```
@Composable
inline fun <T> remember(calculation: @DisallowComposableCalls ()
-> T): T
```

There are a couple of different variations of `remember()`. This one will remember the value that `calculation()` produces, which is evaluated during composition. During the recomposition, `remember()` will return the value produced by its `composition()`.

Also notice `@DisallowComposableCalls`, to avoid remembering composable functions within the remember call.

When you added `AppDrawer()` to `Scaffold()`, you used `rememberScaffoldState()` to create a `ScaffoldState`. This is its signature in the Jetpack Compose documentation:

```
@Composable
fun rememberScaffoldState(
  drawerState: DrawerState = rememberDrawerState(
    DrawerValue.Closed
```

```
    ),
  snackbarHostState: SnackbarHostState = remember {
    SnackbarHostState()
  }
): ScaffoldState
```

Notice how here, remember() creates and **remembers** a SnackbarHostState. For DrawerState, you use rememberDrawerState(), which will create and **remember** a DrawerState.

Look at that function's implementation:

```
@Composable
fun rememberDrawerState(
    initialValue: DrawerValue,
    confirmStateChange: (DrawerValue) -> Boolean = { true }
): DrawerState {
  return rememberSaveable(saver =
DrawerState.Saver(confirmStateChange)) {
        DrawerState(initialValue, confirmStateChange)
  }
}
```

Here, you can see that rememberSaveable() is being used, which behaves similarly to remember() except that the stored value will survive the activity or process recreation by using the saved instance state mechanism.

When it comes to the DrawerState, rememberScaffoldState() relies on rememberSaveable() to preserve the state during the recomposition and Activity recreation. In this example, there are two times the state will change: when the user opens the app drawer and when they close it.

You added two actions, and you made sure the ScaffoldState updates when the user clicks an icon or when AppDrawer() passes up the **close drawer** event.

For SnackbarState, rememberScaffoldState() relies on remember() to preserve the if the snackbar is visible or not during the recomposition. However, you won't worry about that for this app because it doesn't use a snackbar.

Finally, you passed scaffoldState to Scaffold(). That lets Scaffold() display the correct state when it changes. You're reading a lot about state and Scaffold() and how it preserves its state, but it's easier to just visualize what happens in the Jetpack Compose tree.

Remember's effect on the composition tree

Here's how the composition tree looks for NotesScreen().

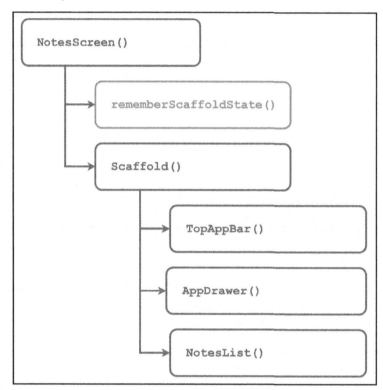

Notes Screen - Composition Tree

In Chapter 5, "Combining Composables", you learned that there can be other types of nodes in the composition tree beside UI elements. This is one example. Calling remember() will result in an additional node in the tree that stores a specific value.

This also means that values remembered in composition are forgotten as soon as their calling composable is removed from the tree. They will be re-initialized if the calling composable moves in the tree. For example, that could happen if you move items in a LazyColumn or a LazyColumnFor.

This was a nice digression to state management. But now it's time to come back to **Material Design composables**. :]

Continue to the next section, where you'll add a FloatingActionButton to the **Notes** screen.

Adding the FAB

A **floating action button** represents the primary action of a screen. In the **Notes** screen, the primary action is the action to create a new note.

In the previous section, you learned that Scaffold() already provides an API to add the FAB to the layout. To implement it, update Scaffold() in **NotesScreen.kt**:

```
@Composable
fun NotesScreen(viewModel: MainViewModel) {

  // Observing notes state from MainViewModel
  ...

  val scaffoldState: ScaffoldState = rememberScaffoldState()

  Scaffold(
    ...,
    floatingActionButtonPosition = FabPosition.End,
    floatingActionButton = {
      FloatingActionButton(
        onClick = { viewModel.onCreateNewNoteClick() },
        contentColor = MaterialTheme.colors.background,
        content = {
          Icon(
            imageVector = Icons.Filled.Add,
            contentDescription = "Add Note Button"
          )
        }
      )
    },
    ...
  )
}
```

Here, you used FloatingActionButton() and passed it as the floatingActionButton parameter. You then passed FabPosition.End as the floatingActionButtonPosition parameter, which positions the FAB in the bottom-right corner.

FloatingActionButton() exposes a few more parameters, but you only used what you need. Clicking the button executes viewModel.onCreateNewNoteClick(). With this, you're passing an event up to the ViewModel, which can then decide what to do with it.

For the content, you passed an icon that renders as a plus sign. To make the content of the icon the same color as the background, you passed MaterialTheme.colors.background as the contentColor.

Android Studio will complain if you don't add these imports as well:

```
import androidx.compose.material.*
import androidx.compose.material.icons.filled.Add
```

Some of the imports might be condensed into the `import androidx.compose.material.*` statement, so make sure to clean up your imports and remove any redundant statements.

Build and run the app and you'll now see the FAB in the **Notes** screen.

Notes Screen with Floating Action Button

Click it, but nothing will happen. So far, `viewModel.onCreateNewNoteClick()` doesn't do anything.

You'll change that once you implement an entry point to the **Save Note** screen.

Adding an entry point

In the previous section, you added the FAB that allows you to open the **Save Note** screen in the Create mode.

Before you can do that, however, you need to add an entry point composable for it. You'll do this in three steps:

1. You'll setup `MainActivityScreen()` to show different screens based on the `JetNotesRouter` state.

2. You'll connect the composable to `MainActivity` as its content.

3. You'll call the `JetNotesRouter` to change the state, when the user taps on the `FloatingActionButton`.

Open **SaveNoteScreen.kt** and add the following composable at the top of the file:

```
@Composable
fun SaveNoteScreen(viewModel: MainViewModel) {

}
```

Don't forget to include an import for `MainViewModel`:

```
import
com.raywenderlich.android.jetnotes.viewmodel.MainViewModel
```

With this, you created a composable function that represents the root of the **Save Note** screen.

Using JetNotesRouter to change screens

In the previous chapter, you added the code that opens the **Notes** screen whenever you start `MainActivity`. It's time to add logic to change screens with `JetNotesRouter`.

Open **MainActivity.kt** and add the following composable to the bottom of the file, outside `MainActivity`:

```
@Composable
@ExperimentalMaterialApi
private fun MainActivityScreen(viewModel: MainViewModel) {
  Surface {
    when (JetNotesRouter.currentScreen) {
      is Screen.Notes -> NotesScreen(viewModel)
```

```
    is Screen.SaveNote -> SaveNoteScreen(viewModel)
    is Screen.Trash -> TrashScreen(viewModel)
  }
 }
}
```

`MainActivityScreen` subscribes to `Screen` when it's invoked. That state is held in
the `JetNotesRouter`. Whenever the state changes, `MainActivityScreen` will
recompose and call the correct root composable for each screen.

Here, you used `Surface()`, one of the most basic composables. It's responsible for
things like clipping the children to a specific shape, adding a background to the app
and configuring the color of the text. It's often used as a root composable for the
app's content.

For the code above to work, you need to add following imports as well:

```
import androidx.compose.material.Surface
import androidx.compose.runtime.Composable
import com.raywenderlich.android.jetnotes.routing.JetNotesRouter
import com.raywenderlich.android.jetnotes.routing.Screen
import
com.raywenderlich.android.jetnotes.ui.screens.SaveNoteScreen
import com.raywenderlich.android.jetnotes.ui.screens.TrashScreen
```

You might ask yourself why did you have to add `@ExperimentalMaterialApi`. Some
of the composables that you are going to build in this section will use an
experimental API. To save you some time so that you don't have to go through each
composable and add this annotation in the future, you'll add it now. Don't worry,
you'll be aware of when you use something from the experimental material API.

Connecting your composable to MainActivity

Next, you'll connect this composable to `MainActivity`. Update `setContent()` in the
`MainActivity`:

```
class MainActivity : AppCompatActivity() {

  ...

  @ExperimentalMaterialApi
  override fun onCreate(savedInstanceState: Bundle?) {
    super.onCreate(savedInstanceState)

    setContent {
      JetNotesTheme {
        MainActivityScreen(viewModel = viewModel) // here
```

```
      }
    }
  }
}
```

Here, you made `MainActivityScreen()` the root composable for the app. You also wrapped it in `JetNotesTheme()` to apply the theme colors you defined in **Theme.kt**.

You now have a way to change screens in the app! The last thing to do before you can open the **Save Note** screen is to call `JetNotesRouter` from `MainViewModel`.

Calling JetNotesRouter

Open **MainViewModel.kt** and update `onCreateNewNoteClick()`:

```
class MainViewModel(private val repository: Repository) :
ViewModel() {

  ...

  fun onCreateNewNoteClick() {
    JetNotesRouter.navigateTo(Screen.SaveNote)
  }

  ...
}
```

For this to work, you also need to add `JetNotesRouter` and `Screen` imports.

```
import com.raywenderlich.android.jetnotes.routing.JetNotesRouter
import com.raywenderlich.android.jetnotes.routing.Screen
```

Nice! You've now connected your `MainViewModel` with the `JetNotesRouter`. Since you're passing the FAB click event from the `SaveNotesScreen()` to the `MainViewModel`, you can react to it by updating the `Screen` state in the `JetNotesRouter`.

By updating that state, you trigger a recomposition of `MainActivityScreen()`. This removes `NotesScreen` from the composition tree and adds `SaveNotesScreen`, instead.

Excellent! Build and run your app. Click the FAB in the **Notes** screen and see what happens.

You'll see that the **Save Note** screen opens... but it's empty. Don't worry, you'll add content to that screen in the following sections.

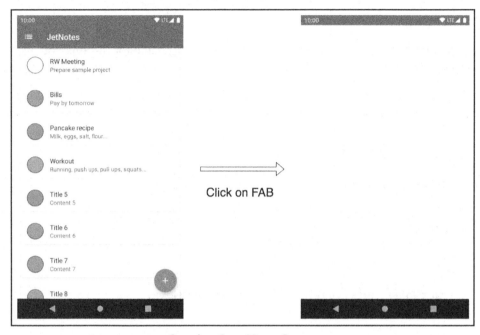

Opening Save Notes Screen

Another issue is that you can't go back to the **Notes** screen. Clicking the **Back** button just closes **JetNotes**.

Your first step to fix both these issues is to add a top bar.

Adding the top bar

Until now, you've focused on adding code to open the **Save Note** screen. But now that you can open it, the **Save Note** screen is empty. In this section, you'll add composables to it. :]

You'll start with the top bar. Before diving straight into the code, look at the design. Again, you'll see that the screen has a familiar layout structure.

You can divide the **Save Note** screen into two parts: the top bar and the body content. Because of that, you can again use Scaffold() as your root composable.

Open **SaveNoteScreen.kt**, then update SaveNoteScreen():

```
@Composable
fun SaveNoteScreen(viewModel: MainViewModel) {
  Scaffold(
    topBar = {},
    content = {}
  )
}
```

With this, you added placeholders for your top bar and body content.

Don't forget to add the Scaffold() import, too:

```
import androidx.compose.material.Scaffold
```

Now, you can start working on the actual composables for the top bar.

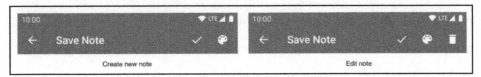

Save Note Screen: Top Bar

Adding SaveNoteTopAppBar

In the **Save Note** screen, the top bar needs to support two different modes:

1. **Create mode**: This lets the user create a new note. There are two actions in the top bar that deal with this case: one to complete the note creation and one to open a color picker.

2. **Edit mode**: The user selects this to edit an existing note. This mode has three actions, one to save changes, one to open the color picker and one to delete the existing note.

Now that you've defined what you need, think about the top bar in terms of state and events. What state should be passed to the top bar and which events should you expose for the parent composable?

In total, there's one state that you should pass down to the top bar composable and four events that the top bar composable should expose. Next, you'll define SaveNoteTopAppBar() to allow that.

Add the following code below `SaveNoteScreen()`:

```
@Composable
private fun SaveNoteTopAppBar(
  isEditingMode: Boolean,
  onBackClick: () -> Unit,
  onSaveNoteClick: () -> Unit,
  onOpenColorPickerClick: () -> Unit,
  onDeleteNoteClick: () -> Unit
) {

}
```

Here are the important things to note in this code:

- **isEditingMode**: Represents whether the top bar is in Edit mode.

- **onBackClick**: Exposes an event when the user returns to the **Notes** screen.

- **onSaveNoteClick**: Exposes an event when the user saves a new or existing note.

- **onOpenColorPickerClick**: Exposes an event when the user opens the color picker.

- **onDeleteNoteClick**: Exposes an event when the user deletes the existing note.

Displaying the top bar

Now that you've prepared the root composable for the top bar, you'll add the composable that emits the top bar in the UI.

Add the following code to `SaveNoteTopAppBar()`:

```
TopAppBar(
  title = {
    Text(
      text = "Save Note",
      color = MaterialTheme.colors.onPrimary
    )
  }
)
```

Here, you used a Material Design composable: `TopAppBar`. This particular definition of `TopAppBar` has slots for the `title`, `navigationIcon` and `actions` — exactly what you need for the **Save Note** screen. You'll add each of these components, but for now, you added the `title`.

You represented the title with a simple Text(), where you defined the screen title and text color. Next you have to define the navigationIcon that will represent the back button. Do that by adding the navigationIcon parameter to TopAppBar():

```
navigationIcon = {
  IconButton(onClick = onBackClick) {
    Icon(
      imageVector = Icons.Default.ArrowBack,
      contentDescription = "Save Note Button",
      tint = MaterialTheme.colors.onPrimary
    )
  }
}
```

For the navigationIcon, you passed IconButton() and defined the onClick action and the correct asset. This icon will display as a back arrow. This is pretty straightforward. Next add the actions:

```
actions = {
  // Save note action icon
  IconButton(onClick = onSaveNoteClick) {
    Icon(
      imageVector = Icons.Default.Check,
      tint = MaterialTheme.colors.onPrimary,
      contentDescription = "Save Note"
    )
  }

  // Open color picker action icon
  IconButton(onClick = onOpenColorPickerClick) {
    Icon(
      painter = painterResource(
        id = R.drawable.ic_baseline_color_lens_24
      ),
      contentDescription = "Open Color Picker Button",
      tint = MaterialTheme.colors.onPrimary
    )
  }
}
```

These two actions are represented by two IconButtons. The buttons will trigger onSaveNoteClick and onOpenColorPickerClick actions respectively. The final action you need to add is the delete action. Do that by adding the following code to actions:

```
// Delete action icon (show only in editing mode)
if (isEditingMode) {
  IconButton(onClick = onDeleteNoteClick) {
    Icon(
```

```
      imageVector = Icons.Default.Delete,
      contentDescription = "Delete Note Button",
      tint = MaterialTheme.colors.onPrimary
    )
  }
}
```

For the last action, you defined that the app should only add `IconButton()` if the top bar is in Edit mode.

Even though you didn't specify the layout structure for the `IconButtons`, they're still organized in a Row. That's because the `TopAppBar` defines `actions` like this: `actions: RowScope.() -> Unit = {}`. You define content that you passed for `actions` with a `RowScope`.

As usual, you need to add a couple of imports as well:

```
import androidx.compose.material.*
import androidx.compose.material.IconButton
import androidx.compose.material.MaterialTheme
import androidx.compose.material.TopAppBar
import androidx.compose.material.icons.Icons
import androidx.compose.material.icons.filled.ArrowBack
import androidx.compose.material.icons.filled.Check
import androidx.compose.material.icons.filled.Delete
import androidx.compose.ui.res.vectorResource
import com.raywenderlich.android.jetnotes.R
```

Now, add the preview composable for `SaveNoteTopAppBar`:

```
@Preview
@Composable
fun SaveNoteTopAppBarPreview() {
  SaveNoteTopAppBar(
    isEditingMode = true,
    onBackClick = {},
    onSaveNoteClick = {},
    onOpenColorPickerClick = {},
    onDeleteNoteClick = {}
  )
}
```

Build your project and, in the preview panel, you'll see something like this:

SaveNoteTopAppBar Composable (Editing Mode) — Preview

You can also play a little bit and pass `false` for `isEditingMode`. If you refresh your preview then, you'll see how your top bar looks when it's not in editing mode.

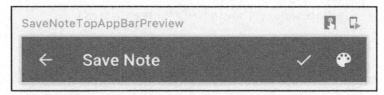

SaveNoteTopAppBar Composable (New Note Mode) — Preview

Awesome! Want to see your top bar in action? In the next section, you'll add SaveNoteTopAppBar() to the **Save Note** screen. :]

Displaying the SaveNoteTopAppBar composable

Now that you've created the SaveNoteTopAppBar(), you can display it in the **Save Note** screen. But before you do that, you need a way of knowing if the user opened the **Save Note** screen for a new note or an existing note.

Open **MainViewModel.kt** and add the following code below notesNotInTrash:

```
private var _noteEntry = MutableLiveData(NoteModel())
val noteEntry: LiveData<NoteModel> = _noteEntry
```

With this, you added a state for a note entry that the user opened to edit in the **Save Note** screen. Both models will use this state, and you'll differentiate the two modes by using NoteModel's ID.

Now, update `SaveNoteScreen()`:

```
@Composable
fun SaveNoteScreen(viewModel: MainViewModel) {

  val noteEntry: NoteModel by viewModel.noteEntry
    .observeAsState(NoteModel())

  Scaffold(
    topBar = {
      val isEditingMode: Boolean = noteEntry.id != NEW_NOTE_ID
      SaveNoteTopAppBar(
        isEditingMode = isEditingMode,
        onBackClick = {
          JetNotesRouter.navigateTo(Screen.Notes)
        },
        onSaveNoteClick = { },
        onOpenColorPickerClick = { },
        onDeleteNoteClick = { }
      )
    },
    content = {}
  )
}
```

Here, you added the code to observe `viewModel.noteEntry`'s state. Whenever that state changes, `SaveNoteScreen()` will go through a recomposition.

In `Scaffold()`, you passed `SaveNoteTopAppBar()` for the `topBar` slot.

With `noteEntry.id`, you check if the screen is in Editing mode. If `NoteModel.id` equals `NEW_NOTE_ID`, the screen is in Create mode. Otherwise, it's in Editing mode.

For now, you just passed empty actions for the other events. You'll add them later.

Next, add the necessary imports:

```
import androidx.compose.runtime.getValue
import androidx.compose.runtime.livedata.observeAsState
import
com.raywenderlich.android.jetnotes.domain.model.NEW_NOTE_ID
import com.raywenderlich.android.jetnotes.domain.model.NoteModel
import com.raywenderlich.android.jetnotes.routing.JetNotesRouter
import com.raywenderlich.android.jetnotes.routing.Screen
```

Finally, build and run the app.

Adding the Top Bar to the Save Note Screen

Now, when you open the **Save Note** screen, you see the top bar. You can also go back to the **Notes** screen by clicking the **Back** button in the top bar.

Opening the Save Note screen in Editing mode

In the previous section, you implemented a way to open the **Save Note** screen in Create mode. Now, you'll add the logic that allows the user to edit an existing note.

Open **MainViewModel.kt** and update onCreateNewNoteClick() and onNoteClick() like this:

```kotlin
fun onCreateNewNoteClick() {
    _noteEntry.value = NoteModel()
    JetNotesRouter.navigateTo(Screen.SaveNote)
}

fun onNoteClick(note: NoteModel) {
    _noteEntry.value = note
```

```
    JetNotesRouter.navigateTo(Screen.SaveNote)
}
```

This is pretty simple. In the previous section, you defined that `SaveNoteScreen()` will subscribe to `viewModel.noteEntry`'s state when it executes.

Here, you simply update that state with the correct `NoteModel`, depending on how the user opens the **Save Note** screen. If the user selected a note, you update the state with the selected note before opening the **Save Note** screen. If the user clicked the FAB, you update the state with an empty `NoteModel`.

By doing that, when `SaveNoteScreen()` executes for the first time, `viewModel.noteEntry` will already contain the `NoteModel` state.

Build and run, then click any note in the **Notes** screen.

Save Note Screen in Edit Mode

Note that there are now three actions in the top bar, which means it's in Editing mode. That's because `isEditingMode` is set to `true` because `NoteModel.id` is not equal to `NEW_NOTE_ID`.

But there's still content missing, so let's implement that next.

Creating a content composable

You need to be able to edit notes in the **Save Note** screen, so your next step is to create a content composable to let you do that.

Refer to the design and you'll see that the user can use a color picker to select a color for the note. However, right now they can't see which color they picked. So your first task will be to implement the component that shows which color you picked from the color picker.

Displaying the selected color

To do this, go to **SaveNoteScreen.kt** and add the following composable below `SaveNoteTopAppBar()`:

```
@Composable
private fun PickedColor(color: ColorModel) {
  Row(
    Modifier
      .padding(8.dp)
      .padding(top = 16.dp)
  ) {
    Text(
      text = "Picked color",
      modifier = Modifier
        .weight(1f)
        .align(Alignment.CenterVertically)
    )
    NoteColor(
      color = Color.fromHex(color.hex),
      size = 40.dp,
      border = 1.dp,
      modifier = Modifier.padding(4.dp)
    )
  }
}
```

This is a pretty simple composable, and you're already familiar with its components. You've even built some of the theme yourself — like `NoteColor()`. :]

You used a `Row` to organize two elements, `Text()` and `NoteColor()`, next to each other. With modifiers, you added some padding and instructed `Text()` to use all the available width.

`PickedColor()` doesn't expose any events since its only job is to show which color the user picked, so it takes a `ColorModel` as the state to render.

Now, add the preview composable as well by adding the following code below
`SaveNoteTopAppBarPreview()`:

```
@Preview
@Composable
fun PickedColorPreview() {
   PickedColor(ColorModel.DEFAULT)
}
```

Great! Now, build your project and check the preview panel. You'll see something like
this:

PickedColorComponent Composable — Preview

Well done! You've completed one of your three tasks. Now, it's time to work on a
component that allows you to make any note checkable.

Letting users check off a note

In some cases, your users might want to check off a note — when they've completed a
task, for example. By default, there's no option to indicate that a note has been
completed. Users need to mark notes as checkable if they want that feature. Your
next step is to give them that possibility.

In **SaveNoteScreen.kt**, add the following composable below `SaveNoteTopAppBar()`:

```
@Composable
private fun NoteCheckOption(
   isChecked: Boolean,
   onCheckedChange: (Boolean) -> Unit
) {
   Row(
     Modifier
        .padding(8.dp)
        .padding(top = 16.dp)
   ) {
     Text(
        text = "Can note be checked off?",
        modifier = Modifier.weight(1f)
     )
     Switch(
        checked = isChecked,
```

```
          onCheckedChange = onCheckedChange,
          modifier = Modifier.padding(start = 8.dp)
      )
    }
  }
```

Just like `PickedColor()`, this composable's layout structure is pretty simple. You use a `Row()` to align a `Text()` with a `Switch()`.

`Switch()` is one of the **Material Design composables** in Jetpack Compose. It's familiar because it behaves the same as its counterpart in the current Android UI toolkit. You also used it earlier, when you implemented the app drawer.

When it comes to state and events, `NoteCheckOption()` takes a `Boolean` value for its state and exposes `onCheckedChange: (Boolean) -> Unit` as an event.

The parent passes down `isChecked`'s state so `Switch()` knows how to render itself. And whenever the user interacts with `Switch()`, an event with the new value will be sent up to the parent composable.

For this to work, you need to add one additional import:

```
import androidx.compose.material.Switch
```

Don't forget to give it a preview composable by adding the following code below `SaveNoteTopAppBarPreview()`:

```
@Preview
@Composable
fun NoteCheckOptionPreview() {
  NoteCheckOption(false) {}
}
```

Here, you pass `false` for the `isChecked` state and an empty action for `onCheckedChange`.

Build your project and you'll see your composable in the preview panel.

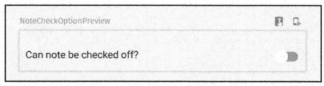

CanBeCheckedOffComponent Composable — Preview

Great job! There's just one more composable to add before assembling the content of the **Save Note** screen. :]

Adding a title and content

So far, you've added composables to represent the note's color and whether the user can check the note off when they complete a task. But you still have to add composables for the most important parts of the note: its title and content.

In **SaveNoteScreen.kt**, add the following code below `SaveNoteTopAppBar()`:

```
@Composable
private fun ContentTextField(
  modifier: Modifier = Modifier,
  label: String,
  text: String,
  onTextChange: (String) -> Unit
) {
  TextField(
    value = text,
    onValueChange = onTextChange,
    label = { Text(label) },
    modifier = modifier
      .fillMaxWidth()
      .padding(horizontal = 8.dp),
    colors = TextFieldDefaults.textFieldColors(
      backgroundColor = MaterialTheme.colors.surface
    )
  )
}
```

You'll use this composable for the text fields where the user enters the note's title and content. Here, you use the Material Design composable, `TextField()`.

`TextField()` lets you easily implement components to take the user's input. For state, the parent composable will pass `text` and `ContentTextField()` will pass up the change in the text as an event using `onTextChange: (String) -> Unit`. You also exposed a `label` to communicate what the text field is for. And you exposed a `modifier`, as good practice, allowing you to pass in custom modifiers at the call site.

Next, add a preview composable below `SaveNoteTopAppBarPreview()`:

```
@Preview
@Composable
fun ContentTextFieldPreview() {
  ContentTextField(
    label = "Title",
    text = "",
    onTextChange = {}
  )
}
```

Now, build your project and check the preview panel. There, you'll see
`ContentTextFieldPreview()`:

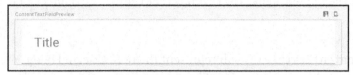

ContentTextField Composable — Preview

Excellent work! You now have all the pieces to create the content of the **Save Note**
screen.

Building the Save Note content

The next thing you'll do is put together all the composables that you created to make
the **Save Note** screen content. In **SaveNoteScreen.kt**, add `SaveNoteContent()`
below `SaveNoteTopAppBar()`:

```
@Composable
private fun SaveNoteContent(
  note: NoteModel,
  onNoteChange: (NoteModel) -> Unit
) {
  Column(modifier = Modifier.fillMaxSize()) {

  }
}
```

This composable will represent the entire logic of creating and editing notes. You'll
show the data from the `note` in input fields and other elements, and you'll use
`onNoteChange()` to notify the parent when you want to save or update a note.

Now add the input fields to the `Column()`:

```
ContentTextField(
  label = "Title",
  text = note.title,
  onTextChange = { newTitle ->
    onNoteChange.invoke(note.copy(title = newTitle))
  }
)

ContentTextField(
  modifier = Modifier
    .heightIn(max = 240.dp)
    .padding(top = 16.dp),
  label = "Body",
```

```
    text = note.content,
    onTextChange = { newContent ->
      onNoteChange.invoke(note.copy(content = newContent))
    }
)
```

These two `ContentTextFields` will represent the note title and body. You also added a bit of styling and respective `onTextChange` handlers to the input. Through them, you update the internal state of the `note` and let the parent know about the update.

Finally, add the `NoteCheckOption()` and the `PickedColor()` to represent more details of the `note`:

```
val canBeCheckedOff: Boolean = note.isCheckedOff != null

NoteCheckOption(
  isChecked = canBeCheckedOff,
  onCheckedChange = { canBeCheckedOffNewValue ->
    val isCheckedOff: Boolean? = if (canBeCheckedOffNewValue)
false else null

    onNoteChange.invoke(note.copy(isCheckedOff = isCheckedOff))
  }
)

PickedColor(color = note.color)
```

From the design, you see that you want to organize the components in a column where the first two components are responsible for taking the user's input for a note's title and content. Below those two components is a `NoteCheckOption()` so that the user can make the note checkable. The last composable in is `PickedColor()` that shows which color the user picked for the note.

Next, add the following import:

```
import androidx.compose.material.*
```

It would be awesome to preview the `SaveNoteContent()` as well. Add the following code below `SaveNoteTopAppBarPreview()`:

```
@Preview
@Composable
fun SaveNoteContentPreview() {
  SaveNoteContent(
    note = NoteModel(title = "Title", content = "content"),
    onNoteChange = {}
  )
}
```

Build the project and, in the preview panel, you'll see how `SaveNoteContent` looks:

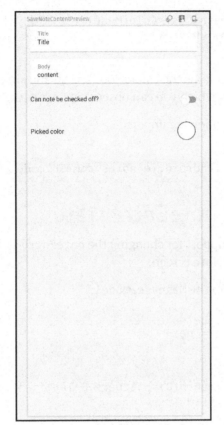

Content Composable — Preview

Wrapping up the Save Note screen

Great job so far! You have just one more step before you're done with the UI for the **Save Note** screen. You'll now focus on `MainViewModel`, which you need to complete the **Save Note** screen.

Adding ViewModel support

In `MainViewModel`, you already added the code to expose the `noteEntry` state, but you still need to add one more state. In the **Save Note** screen, the user can choose a color for a note. To display the list of colors the user can choose, you need to provide them to `SaveNoteScreen()`.

Open **MainViewModel.kt** and add the following code below `noteEntry`:

```
val colors: LiveData<List<ColorModel>> by lazy {
  repository.getAllColors()
}
```

The database already contains the colors you'll need. You simply exposed them here by adding the `LiveData`, which you can observe in `SaveNoteScreen()`.

Don't forget to add the following import:

```
import
com.raywenderlich.android.jetnotes.domain.model.ColorModel
```

Changing the noteEntry state

Next, you need to add support for changing the `noteEntry` state when the user interacts with the **Save Note** screen.

Add the following code to the `MainViewModel`:

```
fun onNoteEntryChange(note: NoteModel) {
  _noteEntry.value = note
}

fun saveNote(note: NoteModel) {
  viewModelScope.launch(Dispatchers.Default) {
    repository.insertNote(note)

    withContext(Dispatchers.Main) {
      JetNotesRouter.navigateTo(Screen.Notes)

      _noteEntry.value = NoteModel()
    }
  }
}

fun moveNoteToTrash(note: NoteModel) {
  viewModelScope.launch(Dispatchers.Default) {
    repository.moveNoteToTrash(note.id)

    withContext(Dispatchers.Main) {
      JetNotesRouter.navigateTo(Screen.Notes)
    }
  }
}
```

Time to break down each method:

With `onNoteEntryChange()`, you update the `noteEntry` state. You'll call this method each time the user makes a change in the **Save Note** screen.

`saveNote()` is responsible for updating the note in the database. If the user is creating a new note, you'll add a new entry in the database. If the user is editing an existing note, you'll update it instead.

You use a coroutine to update the database in the background. This method also closes the **Save Note** screen and returns the user to the **Notes** screen. Note that you had to switch to the main thread to update the state in `JetNotesRouter`. You can only update `State` from the main thread.

`moveNoteToTrash()` behaves similarly to `saveNote()`. It moves the note to the trash and returns the user to the **Notes** screen.

Connecting the SaveNoteScreen to the MainViewModel

Now that `MainViewModel` is ready, you can complete the UI part of the **Save Note** screen.

Open **SaveNoteScreen.kt** and update `Scaffold()` in `SaveNoteScreen()`:

```
Scaffold(
  topBar = {
    val isEditingMode: Boolean = noteEntry.id != NEW_NOTE_ID
    SaveNoteTopAppBar(
      isEditingMode = isEditingMode,
      onBackClick = {
        JetNotesRouter.navigateTo(Screen.Notes)
      },
      onSaveNoteClick = { // here
        viewModel.saveNote(noteEntry)
      },
      onOpenColorPickerClick = { },
      onDeleteNoteClick = { // here
        viewModel.moveNoteToTrash(noteEntry)
      }
    )
  },
  content = { // here
    SaveNoteContent(
      note = noteEntry,
      onNoteChange = { updateNoteEntry ->
        viewModel.onNoteEntryChange(updateNoteEntry)
```

```
        }
      )
    }
  )
```

All that you did here is you filled the content with SaveNoteContent(). That composable will show all the note's details and data, while letting you change it to update a note, or fill it in to create a new one.

Great! Build and run your app.

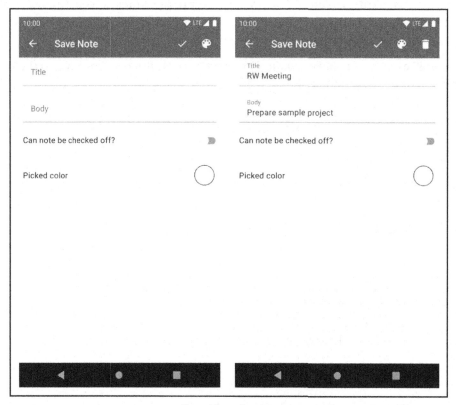

Save Note Screen

You can open the **Save Note** screen in Create mode to create a new note or you can click any note in the note list to open the screen in Editing mode.

Make a change in the title or body and click on the check icon in the top bar. You'll see that your change will save.

You can also move the note to the trash by clicking the trash icon.

Changing the note's color

There is still one thing missing: You still can't change the color of the notes. To fix that, update SaveNoteScreen() like this:

```
@Composable
@ExperimentalMaterialApi // here (BottomDrawer)
fun SaveNoteScreen(viewModel: MainViewModel) {

  ...

  // here
  val colors: List<ColorModel> by viewModel.colors
    .observeAsState(listOf())

  // here
  val bottomDrawerState: BottomDrawerState =
    rememberBottomDrawerState(BottomDrawerValue.Closed)

  val coroutineScope = rememberCoroutineScope()

  Scaffold(
    topBar = {
      val isEditingMode: Boolean = noteEntry.id != NEW_NOTE_ID
      SaveNoteTopAppBar(
        ...,
        onOpenColorPickerClick = { // here
          coroutineScope.launch { bottomDrawerState.open() }
        },
        ...
      )
    },
    content = {
      BottomDrawer( // here
        drawerState = bottomDrawerState,
        drawerContent = {
          ColorPicker(
            colors = colors,
            onColorSelect = { color ->
              val newNoteEntry = noteEntry.copy(color = color)
              viewModel.onNoteEntryChange(newNoteEntry)
            }
          )
        },
        content = {
          SaveNoteContent(
            note = noteEntry,
            onNoteChange = { updateNoteEntry ->
              viewModel.onNoteEntryChange(updateNoteEntry)
            }
          )
```

```
            }
          )
        }
      )
    }
```

First, check what you defined above `Scaffold()`: You subscribed `SaveNoteScreen()` to `viewModel.colors`'s state. That lets you pass that state to `ColorPicker()`.

Next, you created a `bottomDrawerState` of type `BottomDrawerState`. You need this for the new Material Design composable you used in `Scaffold()`. You also used it to open the bottom drawer when the user clicks on a color picker button in the top bar.

In `Scaffold()`, you wrapped `SaveNoteContent()` in a `BottomDrawer()`. `BottomDrawer()` is a Material Design composable that allows you to specify a modal drawer that's anchored to the bottom of the screen. In the time of writing, this was part of an experimental material API. Because of that you had to add `@ExperimentalMaterialApi` annotation to `SaveNoteScreen()`.

Notice that you passed `ColorPicker()` for the `drawerContent` and `SaveNoteContent()` for the content. The principle of state management for this drawer is similar to what you implemented for the `AppDrawer()` in `NotesScreen()`.

Build and run the app. Open **Save Note** and swipe up from the bottom of the screen or click on the color picker icon in the top bar.

Color Picker on Save Note Screen

You can now change the color of any existing note or set a color for a new note. Next, you'll add a feature to confirm that the user really wants to discard a note.

Confirming a delete action

While the **Save Note** screen is now functionally complete, it's always nice to pay attention to the details.

Right now, when the user clicks the trash icon in the top bar, the note will immediately move to the trash. However, it's a good practice to ask the user to confirm an action like that first.

In **SaveNoteScreen.kt**, add the following line before `Scaffold()`:

```
val moveNoteToTrashDialogShownState: MutableState<Boolean> =
rememberSaveable {
  mutableStateOf(false)
}
```

This state represents whether the dialog is visible.

Next, update the `SaveNoteTopAppBar()`, by changing the `onDeleteNoteClick` to the following:

```
SaveNoteTopAppBar(
  ...,
  onDeleteNoteClick = {
    moveNoteToTrashDialogShownState.value = true
  }
)
```

Now, when the user clicks the trash icon in the top bar, you'll just update moveNoteToTrashDialogShownState's value property to `true` to display the dialog. This piece of state will persist through configuration changes, using the savedInstanceState.

Finally, add the following code to the bottom of the content for `Scaffolds()`'s bodyContent:

```
Scaffold(
  topBar = { ... },
  content = {
    BottomDrawer(...)

    if (moveNoteToTrashDialogShownState.value) {
      AlertDialog(
        onDismissRequest = {
```

```
          moveNoteToTrashDialogShownState.value = false
        },
        title = {
          Text("Move note to the trash?")
        },
        text = {
          Text(
            "Are you sure you want to " +
              "move this note to the trash?"
          )
        },
        confirmButton = {
          TextButton(onClick = {
            viewModel.moveNoteToTrash(noteEntry)
          }) {
            Text("Confirm")
          }
        },
        dismissButton = {
          TextButton(onClick = {
            moveNoteToTrashDialogShownState.value = false
          }) {
            Text("Dismiss")
          }
        }
      )
    }
  }
}
)
```

Here, you used the Material Design's `AlertDialog()`. It exposes parameters like `onDismissRequest`, `confirmButton` and `dismissButton`, which you can use to customize buttons and actions. It behaves like the standard `AlertDialog`, where you give the user an option to do agree to your request, or cancel or dismiss the request

Before running the app, add following imports:

```
import androidx.compose.runtime.MutableState
import androidx.compose.runtime.mutableStateOf
import androidx.compose.runtime.saveable.rememberSaveable
```

Build and run the app. Open any note and move it to the trash to see your alert dialog.

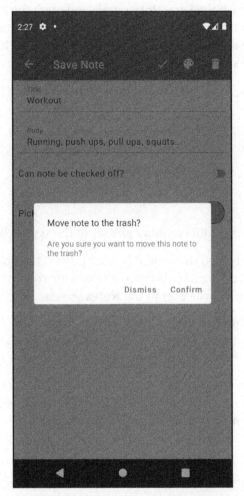

Alert Dialog in Save Note Screen

You can even change the device's orientation and the dialog will still display. This is a much better user experience.

Adding support for the Back button

Currently, when you open the **Save Note** screen and press the **Back** button, the app closes. Since you're not using activities or fragments that operate on back stacks and handle basic system navigation internally, you need to handle how your app behaves if the user presses the system back button.

In `SaveNoteScreen()`, add the following code above `Scaffold()`:

```
BackHandler(onBack = {
  if (bottomDrawerState.isOpen) {
    coroutineScope.launch { bottomDrawerState.close() }
  } else {
    JetNotesRouter.navigateTo(Screen.Notes)
  }
})
```

`BackHandler()` is an effect for handling presses of the system back button.

Specifically, here you defined that when the user presses the **Back** button in the **Save Note** screen when the color picker is open, it closes the color picker. If the color picker isn't open, it returns the user to the **Notes** screen.

Add one additional import as well:

```
import androidx.activity.compose.BackHandler
```

Now, build and run the app to verify everything works. There isn't a visual change in your app, but if you press the system back button now, you'll either close the bottom drawer on the **Save Note** screen, or go back to the **Notes** screen. :]

Using Material Design composables in the Notes screen

The Material Design composables that Jetpack Compose provides are all built with basic composables. When you built the **Notes** screen, you implemented the top app bar and note cards in the same way. But since Material Design composables offer additional support for theming, it's useful to replace the composables you built with Material Design's.

Open **NotesScreen.kt** and replace `TopAppBar()` in `Scaffold()` with Material
Design's `TopAppBar`:

```
Scaffold(
    topBar = {
        TopAppBar(
            title = {
                Text(
                    text = "JetNotes",
                    color = MaterialTheme.colors.onPrimary
                )
            },
            navigationIcon = {
                IconButton(onClick = {
                    coroutineScope.launch
{ scaffoldState.drawerState.open() }
                }) {
                    Icon(
                        imageVector = Icons.Filled.List,
                        contentDescription = "Drawer Button"
                    )
                }
            }
        )
    },
    ...
)
```

This is the same as the Material `TopAppBar` you used above.

Don't forget to replace the import for the old `TopAppBar` with the Material one:

```
import androidx.compose.material.TopAppBar
```

Using a Material composable for Note

There's one more thing you can replace with Material Design composables: your
`Note()`.

Open **Note.kt** and replace its entire contents with:

```
val background = if (isSelected)
    Color.LightGray
else
    MaterialTheme.colors.surface

Card(
    shape = RoundedCornerShape(4.dp),
    modifier = modifier
```

```
        .padding(8.dp)
        .fillMaxWidth(),
    backgroundColor = background
  ) {
    ListItem(
      text = { Text(text = note.title, maxLines = 1) },
      secondaryText = {
        Text(text = note.content, maxLines = 1)
      },
      icon = {
        NoteColor(
          color = Color.fromHex(note.color.hex),
          size = 40.dp,
          border = 1.dp
        )
      },
      trailing = {
        if (note.isCheckedOff != null) {
          Checkbox(
            checked = note.isCheckedOff,
            onCheckedChange = { isChecked ->
              val newNote = note.copy(isCheckedOff = isChecked)
              onNoteCheckedChange.invoke(newNote)
            },
            modifier = Modifier.padding(start = 8.dp)
          )
        }
      },
      modifier = Modifier.clickable {
        onNoteClick.invoke(note)
      }
    )
  }
}
```

Here, you used a Card() and a ListItem() to implement Note(). The Card() is a relatively simple composable. Cards are **surfaces** that display content and actions on a single topic. You can customize their shape, backgroundColor, contentColor, border and elevation.

The ListItem() is a Material Design implementation of list items. They represent items in a list, that have the distinct Material Design look and feel. You used its text for the title, secondaryText for content, icon for the NoteColor() and trailing for the Checkbox.

At the time of writing, `ListItem()` was a part of an experimental material API so add `@ExperimentalMaterialApi` annotation to `Note()`, as well as the `modifier` parameter:

```
@Composable
@ExperimentalMaterialApi // here
fun Note(
  modifier: Modifier = Modifier, // here
  note: NoteModel,
  onNoteClick: (NoteModel) -> Unit = {},
  onNoteCheckedChange: (NoteModel) -> Unit = {},
  isSelected: Boolean = false
) {
...
}
```

You are going to have to do that for all composables that explicitly or implicitly use `Note()`. Those are: `NotePreview()`, `NotesList()`, `NotesScreen` and `NotesListPreview()`.

You also need to add imports for the new composables that you used:

```
import androidx.compose.material.Card
import androidx.compose.material.ListItem
import androidx.compose.material.*
```

Build and run the app. You'll see that the **Notes** screen looks the same as before, but most of your composables are now Material Design composables. Nicely done!

Before wrapping up the chapter, there's one more thing to explore: **adding a theme**. You'll briefly learn about Material Design themes and how to support a dark theme for your app.

Theming in Compose

Every Android app has a specific color palette, typography and shapes. Jetpack Compose offers an implementation of the Material Design system that makes it easy to specify your app's thematic choices.

In JetNotes, you don't play much with typography and shapes, but the app uses a certain color palette throughout all its screens. **Theme.kt** contains the definitions of all JetNotes' colors:

```
private val LightThemeColors = lightColors(
  primary = rwGreen,
  primaryVariant = rwGreenDark,
  secondary = rwRed
)

private val DarkThemeColors = lightColors(
  primary = rwGreen,
  primaryVariant = rwGreenDark,
  secondary = rwRed
)


@Composable
fun JetNotesTheme(content: @Composable () -> Unit) {
  val isDarkThemeEnabled =
    isSystemInDarkTheme() ||
JetNotesThemeSettings.isDarkThemeEnabled

  val colors = if (isDarkThemeEnabled) DarkThemeColors else
LightThemeColors

  MaterialTheme(colors = colors, content = content)
}
```

There are two color definitions: `LightThemeColors` and `DarkThemeColors`. Currently, they share the same definition because the app doesn't support a dark theme — yet! :]

The core element to implement theming in Jetpack Compose is `MaterialTheme()`. `JetNotesTheme()` observes the state when the app should change to a dark theme. When you configure specific colors, you call `MaterialTheme()` and pass those colors to it, but you also pass the content that these colors apply to. Typography and shapes work the same way.

Then, you retrieve the parameters passed into this composable using `MaterialTheme()`. You've done this a few times when you were implement the app. This object exposes the properties of `colors`, `typography` and `shapes`.

Every Material component you used throughout the app has defined which properties to use by default. Since you used Material components and colors from `MaterialTheme()` when you built JetNotes, adding support for a dark theme is as easy as defining a dark color palette. :]

Open **Theme.kt** and replace `DarkThemeColors()` with this:

```
private val DarkThemeColors = darkColors(
  primary = Color(0xFF00A055),
  primaryVariant = Color(0xFF00F884),
  secondary = rwRed,
  onPrimary = Color.White,
)
```

Add the following imports:

```
import androidx.compose.material.darkColors
import androidx.compose.ui.graphics.Color
```

Build and run the app. Open the navigation drawer and turn on the dark theme.

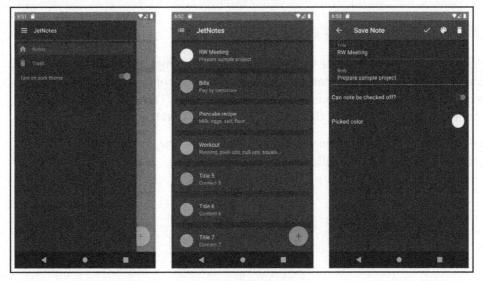

Dark Theme

Congratulations! You made it to the end of the second section! **JetNotes** is now a fully functional app. :]

Key points

- Jetpack Compose provides **composables** that make it easy to follow **Material Design**.

- With `remember()`, Compose lets you **store values in the composition tree**.

- Using the `OnBackPressedDispatcherOwner` and providing it through an **Ambient**, you gain access to system back button handling.

- Jetpack Compose offers a Material Design implementation that allows you to theme your app by specifying the **color palette**, **typography** and **shapes**.

- Using `MaterialTheme()`, you define a theme for your app, that customizes colors, typography and shapes.

- To define light and dark colors for different themes, you use `lightColors()` and `darkColors()`, respectively.

Where to go from here?

Hopefully, this was a fun ride for you. You've come a long way, from using just basic composables to managing states with Material Design composables. In the next section, you'll work on a more complex app, **JetReddit**! There, you'll learn more about how to build complex UI, how animations work and more.

But don't worry, with the knowledge you've gained so far, you won't have any problems taking on that challenge. :]

Section III: Building Complex Apps with Jetpack Compose

Now that you've built your app's basic UI, it's time to take it to another level. In this section, you'll apply custom, complex designs that help you stand out from thousands of similar apps! This usually involves building **complex custom components** and applying **animations** to represent state changes when your users interact with the UI.

Over the next five chapters, you'll dive deeper into the Jetpack Compose API to learn how to:

- Connect Compose UI to legacy Android code.

- React to Compose UI lifecycles.

- Animate different state changes and user interactions.

In the process, you'll build an awesome app that represents a real-world project and you'll apply some best practices to improve the **user experience**.

Chapter 9: Using ConstraintSets in Composables

By Tino Balint

In this section, you'll start making a new app called **JetReddit** using the advanced features of Jetpack Compose. JetReddit is a composable version of the Reddit app in raywenderlich.com style. :]

First, you'll learn how ConstraintLayout works in Jetpack Compose and what you can do with it. Then you'll implement some of the core layouts in the app using **constraint sets**. Let's get on it!

To follow this chapter, you need to know how ConstraintLayout works.

ConstraintLayout is, as its name says, a layout. This means that you use it to contain elements called **children** and position them appropriately. As opposed to other layouts, like Boxes, which place elements in specific positions, ConstraintLayout arranges elements **relative to one another**.

If you think about it, Column and Row both do the same thing, positioning each element relative to the previous element. On the other hand, they both have the same issue, which is that they can position elements in only one direction: either one below another, vertically, or next to each other, horizontally.

Understanding ConstraintLayout

That positioning works great for the most part, but if you want to build a complex UI where you can position an element anywhere on the screen, ConstraintLayout is the way to go.

ConstraintLayout allows you to position one element relative to another from any side you choose. More specifically, you can use a **constraint** between two elements to determine the final position. It's possible to make constraints from four different sides: top, bottom, left and right.

> **Note**: It's better to use start and end instead of left and right. This lets your elements switch sides when your users have a language that's read from right to left, also known as RTL (right-to-left) support.

ConstraintLayout Example

To make constraints easier to understand, look at the image below:

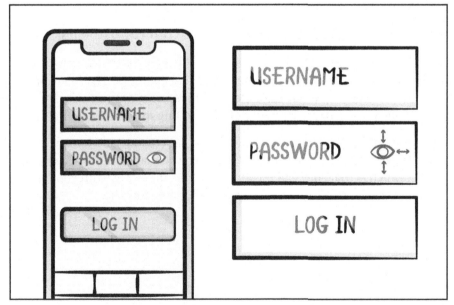

Constraint Layout Example

On the left side of the image, you see a basic login form with two inputs and a button. Inside the password input, you see a small eye icon that toggles whether or not the password displays in plain text, or if it's hidden.

On the right side of the image, you see the zoomed-in buttons corresponding to the login form. Around the eye icon, arrows show the constraint directions. When you position your element on the screen, you have to think from the perspective of that element relative to the other elements.

In simple words, you can say that the eye icon is in the vertical center of the password element. It's also constrained to the end of the password element, with a small space between the icon and the end of the box. When you set constraints, you follow this approach to model the positional information of the different elements.

Now, to implement that positioning. First, you make the constraint between the top of the icon and the top of the password element. Next, you make a constraint between the bottom of the icon and the bottom of the password element. Since one constraint pulls the icon to the top and the other one pulls to the bottom, the icon ends up in the vertical center.

Finally, you add a constraint between the end of the eye icon and the end of the password element. This positions the eye icon at the far-right side of the password element. To get the desired result, all you need to do is add a margin on the right side.

Now that you understand the essentials of working with `ConstraintLayout`, you're ready to learn about its composable version.

ConstraintLayout in Jetpack Compose

In Jetpack Compose, there's a composable with the same name called `ConstraintLayout`. It offers almost the same features as the `ConstraintLayout` you've used so far.

```
@Composable
fun ConstraintLayout(
    modifier: Modifier = Modifier,
    optimizationLevel: Int = Optimizer.OPTIMIZATION_STANDARD,
    crossinline content: @Composable ConstraintLayoutScope.() ->
Unit
)
```

This composable takes only three parameters:

- The `modifier` to expose styling options, which is pretty standard.

- `optimizationLevel` that sets the optimization level when managing constraints. The default option is `OPTIMIZATION_STANDARD` which optimizes direct constraints and barriers.

- `content`, which represents any number of composables that'll be its children.

Now, imagine that you have a scenario like in the image above, where you want to position the eye icon inside the password input element. Here's how you'd do that in Compose:

```
val (passwordInput, eyeIcon) = createRefs()

Icon(
    imageVector = ImageVector.vectorResource(id =
R.drawable.ic_eye),
    contentDescription = stringResource(id = R.string.eye),
    modifier = Modifier.constrainAs(eyeIcon) {
        top.linkTo(passwordInput.top)
        bottom.linkTo(passwordInput.bottom)
        end.linkTo(passwordInput.end)
    }.padding(end = 16.dp)
)
```

First, you create references for the elements inside the `ConstraintLayout`, which serve as an ID for each of your elements. Calling `createRefs()` creates those references for you. Next, you set the vector resource and call `constrainAs()`. `constrainAs()` sets the reference for the current element, then sets the constraints between it and other elements within a lambda function.

For this situation, you set the `eyeIcon` reference and make three constraints, as shown in the image. You make each of those constraints by calling `linkTo()`. You link the top of the eye icon to the top of the password input, the bottom of the eye icon to the bottom of the password input and the end of the eye icon to the end of the password input.

Finally, you set the padding at the end of the eye icon to get that small space shown in the image.

Keep in mind that this example works on the assumption that you've already constrained other elements, like the password input.

Now that you have some essential knowledge about working with the `ConstraintLayout()`, you're ready to start building your new app.

Implementing the app drawer layout

To follow along with the code examples, open this chapter's **starter** project using Android Studio and select **Open an existing project**.

Next, navigate to **09-using-constraint-layout-in-composables/projects** and select the starter folder as the project root. Once the project opens, let it build and sync and you'll be ready to go!

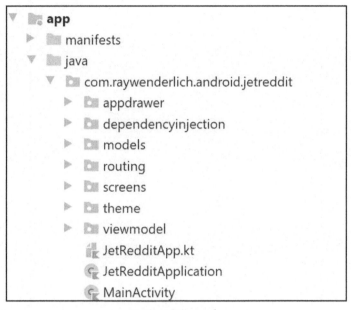

Project Hierarchy

There are several packages and classes already prepared for you, so you don't have to worry about handling navigation, dependency injection and theme switching. If this looks a bit overwhelming, don't worry, you only need to make changes to the **appdrawer** and **screens** packages.

To work with the ConstraintLayout, you need to add the following dependency in your module level **build.gradle** file:

```
implementation "androidx.constraintlayout:constraintlayout-
    compose:$current-version"
```

This dependency was already added for you in your starter project, but keep it in mind when you are making new projects as it has a different version as compared to other Jetpack Compose dependencies.

Once you're familiar with the file organization, build and run the app. You'll see this screen:

Starting Screen

Here, you see a top bar and a bottom bar with three different icons. Clicking on any of them will display an empty screen and the title in the top bar will change. Clicking on the **Account** icon in the top bar displays an empty app drawer.

Your first step in creating JetReddit is to build the **app drawer**. Your goal is to make a screen similar to the one in the official Reddit app, which looks like this:

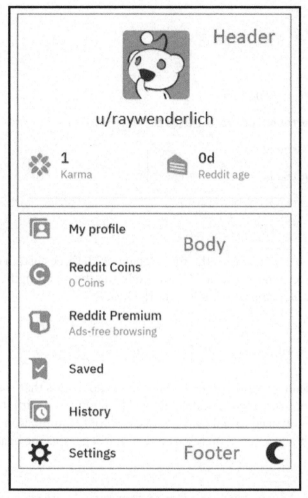

Reddit App Drawer

The screen is split into three different sections: header, body and footer. You'll implement each of them individually in the coming sections.

Before starting, check the root layout implementation for the app drawer by opening **appdrawer/AppDrawer.kt** and taking a look at `AppDrawer()`:

```
@Composable
fun AppDrawer(
  modifier: Modifier = Modifier,
  closeDrawerAction: () -> Unit
) {
  Column(
    modifier = modifier
      .fillMaxSize()
      .background(color = MaterialTheme.colors.surface)
  ) {
    AppDrawerHeader()

    AppDrawerBody(closeDrawerAction)

    AppDrawerFooter(modifier)
  }
}
```

The composable has a `Column` as the root element with three custom composables as children that correspond to the header, the body and the footer in the previous screenshot. Your first step is to implement the header.

Creating the app drawer header

Examining the header section of the Reddit screenshot shows that you can break it down into smaller parts. First, you'll need to add a profile icon with the user name below it. Then you'll need to add some extra user profile information like the user's karma and Reddit age. Finally, there's a divider that separates the header from the body.

Implementing the user icon and name

You'll implement the user icon and user name first. You'll add them in a `Column`, because they need to be ordered vertically. Add the `Column` and the `Image` first:

```
@Composable
private fun AppDrawerHeader() {
  Column(
    modifier = Modifier.fillMaxWidth(),
    horizontalAlignment = Alignment.CenterHorizontally
  ) {
    Image(
```

```
        imageVector = Icons.Filled.AccountCircle,
        colorFilter = ColorFilter.tint(Color.LightGray),
        modifier = Modifier
            .padding(16.dp)
            .size(50.dp),
        contentScale = ContentScale.Fit,
        alignment = Alignment.Center,
        contentDescription = stringResource(id =
    R.string.account)
        )
    }
}
```

In this code, you added a `Column` that centers everything horizontally. You put the provided account image at the top below which you'll add a `Text` with the default user name and a `Divider` to separate the header from the body. Do that next:

```
@Composable
private fun AppDrawerHeader() {
  Column(
      modifier = Modifier.fillMaxWidth(),
      horizontalAlignment = Alignment.CenterHorizontally
  ) {
    ...
    Text(
        text = stringResource(R.string.default_username),
        color = MaterialTheme.colors.primaryVariant
    )
  } // end of Column

  Divider(
      color = MaterialTheme.colors.onSurface.copy(alpha = .2f),
      modifier = Modifier.padding(
        start = 16.dp,
        end = 16.dp,
        top = 16.dp
      )
  )
}
```

The `Text` is using the `default_username` resource and you added an `onSurface` color to the `Divider`, with a custom alpha value. The divider also has some extra padding to make it look nicer while it separates the header from the body of the drawer.

Build and run, then open the drawer.

App Drawer Header Without Profile Info

At this point you can see the whole header section, except for the profile info, which you'll implement next.

Adding the profile info

To get a better understanding of what you need to implement, look at the following image:

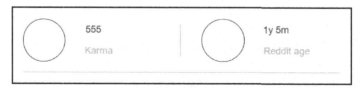

Profile Info

As you see, this image includes a lot of repeated elements. This is good because it means you can extract components and reuse them multiple times.

That's exactly what you'll do with the `Icon` and the two `Text` elements. You'll extract those components into a composable called `ProfileInfoItem`.

Extracting reusable components

Because these components require relative constraints, you'll use a
`ConstraintLayout`. Add the following code to `ProfileInfoItem()`:

```
@Composable
private fun ProfileInfoItem(
  ...
) {
  val colors = MaterialTheme.colors

  ConstraintLayout(modifier = modifier) {
    val (iconRef, amountRef, titleRef) = createRefs() //
references
    val itemModifier = Modifier

    Icon(
      contentDescription = stringResource(id = textResourceId),
      imageVector = iconAsset,
      tint = Color.Blue,
      modifier = itemModifier
        .constrainAs(iconRef) {
          centerVerticallyTo(parent)
          start.linkTo(parent.start)
        }.padding(start = 16.dp)
    )
  }
}
```

To begin building the reusable item, you need to create a `ConstraintLayout`,
children references and add an `Icon` as its child. Again, using `createRefs()` you can
create up to 16 component references and destructure them accordingly.

You then prepared the `itemModifier`, as it's good practice to differentiate between
parent and item modifiers.

Finally, using `constrainAs(iconRef)`, `centerVertically(parent)` and
`linkTo(parent.start)`, you tell the `Icon` where you want to position it. Specifically,
you want it to be centered vertically within the parent and at the very start of the
parent, with a small amount of padding.

Now, below the `Icon`, add the `Text` that'll represent the amount of karma points or
the Reddit age:

```
@Composable
private fun ProfileInfoItem(
  ...
) {
  val colors = MaterialTheme.colors
```

```
ConstraintLayout(modifier = modifier) {
  ...
  Text(
    text = stringResource(amountResourceId),
    color = colors.primaryVariant,
    fontSize = 10.sp,
    modifier = itemModifier
      .padding(start = 8.dp)
      .constrainAs(amountRef) {
        top.linkTo(iconRef.top)
        start.linkTo(iconRef.end)
        bottom.linkTo(titleRef.top)
      }
  )
  }
}
```

This should be familiar now, as you want this element to be relative to the `iconRef` and the `titleRef`. You constrain it as `amountRef`, linking it to the `top` and the end of the `iconRef`. You also link the `bottom` of the amount `Text` to the `top` of the title `Text`, which you'll add next.

```
@Composable
private fun ProfileInfoItem(
...
) {
  val colors = MaterialTheme.colors

  ConstraintLayout(modifier = modifier) {
    ...
    Text(
      text = stringResource(textResourceId),
      color = Color.Gray,
      fontSize = 10.sp,
      modifier = itemModifier
        .padding(start = 8.dp)
        .constrainAs(titleRef) {
          top.linkTo(amountRef.bottom)
          start.linkTo(iconRef.end)
          bottom.linkTo(iconRef.bottom)
        }
    )
  }
}
```

Pretty straightforward. You added another element, again being constrained to the `iconRef`, but this time at the `bottom` instead of the `top`. You also linked the `top` of the `titleRef` to the `bottom` of the `amountRef`.

It's important to know that you'll use `ProfileInfoItem()` inside `ProfileInfo()`, which has its own `ConstraintLayout` as a root. To avoid **constraint conflicts** between the parent and child composables, you have to pass the `modifier` from the parent as a parameter and set it to the child's `ConstraintLayout`.

Also, creating new references within this `ConstraintLayout` lets you avoid the previously mentioned conflicts when using multiple `ConstraintLayout` instances.

Build the app and take a look at the preview section to see the result.

Profile Info Item Preview

Don't worry if the colors are a bit off, they'll change to match the theme once you run the app.

Completing ProfileInfo

Now, you'll use your freshly made composable to complete `ProfileInfo()`. Replace the code of `ProfileInfo()` with the following implementation:

```
@Composable
fun ProfileInfo(modifier: Modifier = Modifier) {
  ConstraintLayout(
      modifier = modifier
          .fillMaxWidth()
          .padding(top = 16.dp)
  ) {
    val (karmaItem, divider, ageItem) = createRefs()
    val colors = MaterialTheme.colors

    ProfileInfoItem(
        Icons.Filled.Star,
        R.string.default_karma_amount,
        R.string.karma,
        modifier = modifier.constrainAs(karmaItem) {
          centerVerticallyTo(parent)
          start.linkTo(parent.start)
        }
    )

    Divider(
        modifier = modifier
```

```
                .width(1.dp)
                .constrainAs(divider) {
                    centerVerticallyTo(karmaItem)
                    centerHorizontallyTo(parent)
                    height = Dimension.fillToConstraints
                },
            color = colors.onSurface.copy(alpha = .2f)
        )

        ProfileInfoItem(
            Icons.Filled.ShoppingCart,
            R.string.default_reddit_age_amount,
            R.string.reddit_age,
            modifier = modifier.constrainAs(ageItem) {
                start.linkTo(divider.end)
                centerVerticallyTo(parent)
            }
        )
    }
}
}
```

Here, you added a `ConstraintLayout` as the root and created references for the three elements that it contains: karma, divider and age. You constrained the karma item at the start of the parent, centered vertically.

Next, you added a divider in the vertical center of the parent and the horizontal center of the first `ProfileInfoItem`.

Finally, you added another `ProfileInfoItem` containing the age information to the right of the divider and centered it vertically. This should be more and more familiar to you because constraints work just like they did in the XML version of the `ConstraintLayout`. The main difference is that you have to write them in code, but with the amazing Compose syntax, that's a piece of cake! :]

Now, add `ProfileInfo()` to `AppDrawerHeader()`:

```
@Composable
private fun AppDrawerHeader() {
  Column(
      modifier = Modifier.fillMaxWidth(),
      horizontalAlignment = Alignment.CenterHorizontally
  ) {
    Image(
        ...
    )

    Text(
        ...
    )
```

```
    ProfileInfo() // Add this
  }

  Divider(
    ...
  )
}
```

This shows the missing profile information in the header.

Build and run the app to see the result.

App Drawer Header With Profile Info

You can now see the profile info section, split into two parts by a divider.

With this, you've completed the header section and had the chance to familiarize yourself with working with ConstraintLayout.

All right, it's time to move on to the body!

Implementing the app drawer's body

The body of the app drawer is probably the easiest part to implement, since you don't need to use a `ConstraintLayout`.

The body section in the Reddit screenshot is your reference, but you'll implement a very simplified version of it. You only need to add two buttons here, one to open the profile and the other to view the saved screens.

The button composable, `ScreenNavigationButton`, has already been prepared for you in the starter code. This composable has an `icon`, a `label` and an `onClickAction`.

Next, add the following code to `AppDrawerBody()`:

```
@Composable
private fun AppDrawerBody(closeDrawerAction: () -> Unit) {
  Column {
    ScreenNavigationButton(
        icon = Icons.Filled.AccountBox,
        label = stringResource(R.string.my_profile),
        onClickAction = {
          closeDrawerAction()
        }
    )

    ScreenNavigationButton(
        icon = Icons.Filled.Home,
        label = stringResource(R.string.saved),
        onClickAction = {
          closeDrawerAction()
        }
    )
  }
}
```

Here, you added two `ScreenNavigationButtons` for the drawer's body. Currently, the action you pass to the buttons only closes the drawer because you haven't implemented those screens yet. You'll take care of that in the coming chapters.

Note that both buttons are set inside the `Column`. You did this so you can preview this composable, but it's not necessary since the root composable `AppDrawer` already uses a `Column`.

Remember that you passed `closeDrawerAction` as an argument in `AppDrawer()`:

```
fun AppDrawer(closeDrawerAction: () -> Unit, modifier: Modifier
= Modifier) {
```

```
    ...
    AppDrawerBody(closeDrawerAction)
    ...
}
```

Build and run the app, then open the app drawer once again.

App Drawer Body

You can now see the two buttons below the header section. When you click on either of them, the drawer closes.

Implementing the app drawer footer

Once again, check the Reddit screenshot, but this time, pay closer attention to the bottom of the screen. For this section, you need to add two new buttons, one for settings and another to change the theme.

Start by adding the initial `ConstraingLayout` setup to the `AppDrawerFooter()`:

```
@Composable
private fun AppDrawerFooter(modifier: Modifier = Modifier) {
  ConstraintLayout(
    modifier = modifier
      .fillMaxSize()
      .padding(
        start = 16.dp,
        bottom = 16.dp,
        end = 16.dp
      )
  ) {

    val colors = MaterialTheme.colors
    val (settingsImage, settingsText, darkModeButton) =
createRefs()
  }
}
```

Here you added the `ConstraintLayout`, styled it with modifiers and prepared all the references you'll need to position its children. Now add the settings `Icon` and its label:

```
@Composable
private fun AppDrawerFooter(modifier: Modifier = Modifier) {
  ConstraintLayout(
    ...
  ) {
    ...
    Icon(
      modifier = modifier.constrainAs(settingsImage) {
        start.linkTo(parent.start)
        bottom.linkTo(parent.bottom)
      },
      imageVector = Icons.Default.Settings,
      contentDescription = stringResource(id =
R.string.settings),
      tint = colors.primaryVariant
    )

    Text(
      fontSize = 10.sp,
      text = stringResource(R.string.settings),
```

```
            style = MaterialTheme.typography.body2,
            color = colors.primaryVariant,
            modifier = modifier
                .padding(start = 16.dp)
                .constrainAs(settingsText) {
                    start.linkTo(settingsImage.end)
                    centerVerticallyTo(settingsImage)
                }
        )
    }
}
```

These two elements are positioned at the bottom of the parent. The Icon sits at the start of the parent, while the label is linked to the end of the settingsImage. The rest of the code should be self-explanatory, as its mostly styling the Text and the Icon.

Now add the last element to the footer—the theme Icon:

```
@Composable
private fun AppDrawerFooter(modifier: Modifier = Modifier) {
  ConstraintLayout(
      ...
  ) {
      ...
    Icon(
        imageVector = ImageVector.vectorResource(id =
R.drawable.ic_moon),
        contentDescription = stringResource(id =
R.string.change_theme),
        modifier = modifier
            .clickable(onClick = { changeTheme() })
            .constrainAs(darkModeButton) {
                end.linkTo(parent.end)
                bottom.linkTo(settingsImage.bottom)
            },
        tint = colors.primaryVariant
    )
  }
}
```

The theme Icon follows the same principles, except that it's constrained to the bottom and end of the parent. Also, for the theme icon, you added an onClick action to change the theme by calling changeTheme(). This function is pre-built for you in the starter project.

Build and run the app, then open the drawer.

App Drawer Footer

There's now a footer inside the drawer with the settings and the theme icons. If you click on the theme icon, the app will change to the dark theme, which has all the colors already defined.

Advanced features of ConstraintLayout

ConstraintLayout makes building UI much easier than before. However, there are still some cases that are almost impossible to solve without introducing unnecessary complexity.

For example, consider the case from earlier in the chapter, when you made the profile info composable in the drawer. That setup had some elements at the left side of the screen and others close to the vertical line in the center.

Now, imagine that there was no vertical line. How would you position your elements to start from the center of the screen? One idea is to place an element in the center that's invisible and position your other elements relative to that object. The solution is a lot like that, only more optimized.

Guidelines

A **guideline** is an invisible object you use as a helper tool when you work with ConstraintLayout. You can create a guideline from any side of the screen and use one of two different ways to give it an offset:

- You can specify the fixed amount of dp you want the offset to be.

- You can give the **screen percentage** if you want the guideline to display in the same place, regardless of the screen size.

You use different functions to create guidelines, depending on where you want to place them. In your previous example, where you needed a guideline in the vertical center, you could use either of the following options:

```
createGuidelineFromStart(0.5f)
createGuidelineFromEnd(0.5f)
```

This creates a **vertical anchor** that's half a screen away from the start or half a screen away from the end. The anchor is a virtual helper that isn't displayed on the screen, but which allows you to make constraints to it. Here's an example of how to use one:

```
val verticalGuideline = createGuidelineFromStart(0.5f)
Icon(
    imageVector = iconAsset,
    contentDescription = stringResource(id =
R.string.some_string),
    modifier = Modifier
        .constrainAs(iconReference) {
            start.linkTo(verticalGuideline)
            top.linkTo(parent.top)
            bottom.linkTo(parent.bottom)
        }
)
```

Here, you create a vertical guideline at the center of the screen. Next, you add an icon that's centered vertically and starts from your guideline's position, the vertical center.

You can also use any of the following functions to create an anchor, depending on your need. For **vertical anchors** you can choose from:

- `createGuidelineFromStart()`
- `createGuidelineFromAbsoluteLeft()`
- `createGuidelineFromEnd()`
- `createGuidelineFromAbsoluteRight()`

For **horizontal anchors**, you have the following functions:

- `createGuidelineFromTop()`
- `createGuidelineFromBottom()`

You then use the vertical anchor to make vertical constraints and the horizontal anchor to make horizontal constraints.

Vertical constraints are:

- Start
- AbsoluteLeft
- End
- AbsoluteRight

Horizontal constraints are:

- Top
- Bottom

Note that all constraints and anchors with the **absolute** prefix represent the absolute left or right of the screen, regardless of the different layout directions, such as right-to-left.

If you want to learn more about guidelines, check out the official documentation: https://developer.android.com/reference/kotlin/androidx/compose/foundation/layout/ConstraintLayoutBaseScope.

Barriers

Now that you know how to position objects at specific places on the screen, it's time to think about some other problems you can solve.

Take a look at the image below to better understand the next problem:

Barrier

On the left side of the image, you see a button and two text fields: first and last name. In this scenario, you want to place the button to the left of the two text fields. In the first example, these texts have almost the same width, so the button will always be on the left, no matter which text you constrain to it.

In the second example, you have a long first name and a short last name. To have the button on the left side of both texts, you need to constrain it to the start of the first name, because that's the longer one.

In the last example, you have the opposite situation. To have the button on the left side of the two texts, you need to constrain it to the start of the last name.

From these examples, you can see that for this to work, the button should sometimes be constrained to the first name and sometimes to the last name, depending on which one is bigger.

To solve this problem, you add a **barrier** within the ConstraintLayout. A barrier is an element that can contain multiple constraint references.

Here's how you can use barriers to solve the problem from the previous example:

```
ConstraintLayout(modifier = Modifier.fillMaxSize()) {
  val (button, firstName, lastName) = createRefs()
  val startBarrier = createStartBarrier(firstName, lastName)

  Text(
    text = "long first name",
    modifier = Modifier.constrainAs(firstName) {
      end.linkTo(parent.end)
      top.linkTo(parent.top)
    }
  )
```

```
    Text(
      text = "last name",
      modifier = Modifier.constrainAs(lastName) {
        end.linkTo(parent.end)
        top.linkTo(firstName.bottom)
      }
    )

    Button(
      content = {},
      onClick = {},
      modifier = Modifier.constrainAs(button) {
        end.linkTo(startBarrier)
      }
    )
  }
```

First, you create constraint references for all three elements. Next, you create a **start barrier** by passing the references for the first and last name. You use the start barrier when you want to set a constraint to multiple elements from their left side.

Finally, you make a constraint from the end of the button to the start barrier. This will ensure that the button is always constrained to the element with the larger width, resolving the problem.

As with guidelines, you can create a barrier from any side by calling one of the following functions:

- createStartBarrier()

- createAbsoluteLeftBarrier()

- createEndBarrier()

- createAbsoluteRightBarrier()

- createTopBarrier()

- createBottomBarrier()

Chains

The final problem that you might face when using `ConstraintLayout` is when you have multiple elements that are constrained to each other. Here are the possible scenarios:

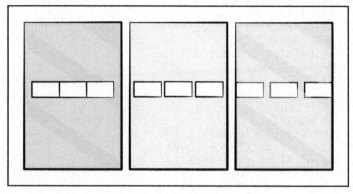

Chains

You can see three different screens, each containing three elements. In the first case, the elements are placed together in the middle, one next to the other. In the second case, they're spaced evenly from each other and the screen edges. In the last case, the elements are still evenly spaced, but they start at the edge of the screen.

With your current knowledge of constraints, if you had these three elements, you could constrain the elements to each other from both sides and to the parent at the edges. By doing this, you could achieve the first result, but not the other two.

Cases like these are solved with **chains**. A chain allows you to reference multiple elements that are constrained to each other, forming a chain as in the image above. Once you have a chain, you can specify the `ChainStyle` you want. There are three types of `ChainStyles`, which correspond to the scenarios described earlier:

- **Packed**: All the elements are packed in a group, as in the first example.

- **Spread**: All the elements are spread evenly from each other and the edges, as in the second example.

- **SpreadInside**: All the elements are spread evenly from each other but start at the edges, as in the third example.

Here is an example that uses `ChainStyle.SpreadInside`:

```
val (firstElement, secondElement, thirdElement) = createRefs()

Button(
  modifier = Modifier
  .constrainAs(firstElement) {
    start.linkTo(parent.start)
    end.linkTo(secondElement.start)
    top.linkTo(parent.top)
    bottom.linkTo(parent.bottom)
  }
)

Button(
  modifier = Modifier
  .constrainAs(secondElement) {
    start.linkTo(firstElement.end)
    end.linkTo(thirdElement.start)
    top.linkTo(parent.top)
    bottom.linkTo(parent.bottom)
  }
)

Button(
  modifier = Modifier
  .constrainAs(thirdElement) {
    start.linkTo(secondElement.end)
    end.linkTo(parent.end)
    top.linkTo(parent.top)
    bottom.linkTo(parent.bottom)
  }
)

createHorizontalChain(
    firstElement,
    secondElement,
    thirdElement,
    chainStyle = ChainStyle.SpreadInside
)
```

Note that applying a specific `ChainStyle` will only work if you create a chain between the elements. In the previous code, you do this by setting the constraint references between the three buttons. Also, keep in mind that you can create both vertical and horizontal chains.

Check out the official `ChainStyle` documentation for more information: https://developer.android.com/reference/kotlin/androidx/compose/foundation/layout/ChainStyle.

That was an overview of the most complex layout you can currently use in Android. By now, you should be able to make a screen of any complexity using what you've learned.

Keep this in mind because, in the next chapter, that's exactly what you'll be doing: making a complex UI to further implement the features in your JetReddit app.

You'll combine everything you learned so far and you'll use the component-based approach reuse as much code as possible. See you in the next chapter!

Key points

- `ConstraintLayout` positions its children **relative** to each other.
- Add `implementation androidx.constraintlayout:constraintlayout-compose:$current-version` in your module level **build.gradle** file to use `ConstraintLayout`.
- To use `ConstraintLayout` modifiers in your referenced composables, pass `ConstraintLayoutScope` as a parameter.
- It's better to use `start` and `end` constraints, rather than `left` and `right`.
- Use `createRefs()` to create constraint references for your composables.
- Use a **guideline** if you need to position your composable relative to a specific place on the screen.
- Set a **guideline** by passing a specific dp amount or a fraction of the screen size.
- Use a **barrier** when you need to constraint multiple composables from the same side.
- Use a **chain** when you need multiple elements constrained to each other.
- Use `ChainStyle` to specify the kind of chain to use.

Chapter 10: Building Complex UI in Jetpack Compose

By Tino Balint

Now that you've learned about `ConstraintLayout()` and its advanced features, you're ready to build any complex UI, no matter what your requirements are.

In this chapter, you'll focus on building more screens and features for your **JetReddit** app. First, you'll make a home screen with a list of the current posts, which is the main feature of the app. Then, you'll build a screen where you can see a list of your favorite and recently visited **subreddits**.

Building the home screen

To understand your task, take a look at the following example from the original Reddit app:

Reddit Home Screen

Here, you see a home screen with two posts. The screen consists of a header, content and post actions. There are two types of content, a text and an image. Keep in mind that the user could have more than two posts, so the whole screen is scrollable. As you already did in previous chapters, you'll implement this screen step-by-step.

Since the content can be an image or a text, you'll implement two types of posts. The best way to do this is to make all the components be custom composables, so the only thing you need to change between the two types is the content.

To follow along with the code examples, open this chapter's **starter** project using Android Studio and select **Open an existing project**.

Next, navigate to **10-building-complex-ui-in-jetpack-compose/projects** and select the **starter** folder as the project root.

Once the project opens, let it build and sync and you're ready to go!

You might already be familiar with the project hierarchy from the previous chapter, but in case you aren't, check out this image:

Project Hierarchy

There are several packages here, but you'll only change the code within **screens**, to implement new features of the app, and **components** for custom composables — for example, Post(), which those screens need.

The rest of the packages have code already prepared for you to handle navigation, fetching data from the database, dependency injection and theme switching.

Once you're familiar with the file organization, build and run the app. You'll see a screen like this:

Starting Screen

It's an empty home screen. It only contains the app drawer from the previous chapter.

You're ready to go now. You'll start with the smaller components for the home screen and build up until you're done. Your first task is to implement the post's header.

Adding a post header

Each post on the home screen has a header that contains the following information: the subreddit it belongs to, the name of the user who posted it, how old the post is and its title.

For your first step, open **Post.kt** inside **components** and replace `Header()` with the following implementation:

```
@Composable
fun Header(post: PostModel) {
    Row(modifier = Modifier.padding(start = 16.dp)) {
        Image(
            ImageBitmap.imageResource(id =
R.drawable.subreddit_placeholder),
            contentDescription = stringResource(id =
R.string.subreddits),
            Modifier
                .size(40.dp)
                .clip(CircleShape)
        )
        Spacer(modifier = Modifier.width(8.dp))
        Column(modifier = Modifier.weight(1f)) {
          Text(
                text = stringResource(R.string.subreddit_header,
post.subreddit),
                fontWeight = FontWeight.Medium,
                color = MaterialTheme.colors.primaryVariant
          )
          Text(
                text = stringResource(R.string.post_header,
post.username, post.postedTime),
                color = Color.Gray
          )
        }
        MoreActionsMenu()
    }

    Title(text = post.title)
}
```

Here's what you did with this code:

- First, you added a `Row()` where you placed the icon.

- Next, you added a `Column()` to position the two texts one below the other.

- At the end of the `Row()`, you added a **MoreActionsMenu** button, which was already prepared for you.

- Finally, you placed `Title()` outside the `Row()`. `Title()` is a `Text()` with custom styling already done for you.

To see your new header, build the project and open the split view to see the previews. Once the build finishes, look at the preview called `HeaderPreview`:

Header Preview

The header now has all the the elements it needs to have. Don't worry that the colors don't match your design, they'll change to fit the theme when you run the app.

The next component you'll write is the voting action button.

Building the voting action button

The voting action button has two images and a text, which makes it slightly different from other action buttons. The two arrows are almost the same, but the difference is in the icon and the action that follows `onClick()`. Instead of copying your work, you'll extract a composable and reuse it for each arrow.

Replace `ArrowButton()` code with the following:

```
@Composable
fun ArrowButton(onClickAction: () -> Unit, arrowResourceId: Int)
{
    IconButton(onClick = onClickAction, modifier =
Modifier.size(30.dp)) {
        Icon(
            imageVector = ImageVector.vectorResource(arrowResourceId),
            contentDescription = stringResource(id = R.string.upvote),
            modifier = Modifier.size(20.dp),
            tint = Color.Gray
        )
    }
}
```

Here, you added `IconButton()` with a modified color and size. You pass `onClick()` and the vector resource as parameters because you want to reuse this composable for both the up and down arrows.

To see your arrow button, build the project and look at the preview screen under
`ArrowButtonPreview()`:

Arrow Button Preview

You see a simple up arrow. Now, you'll use this composable to complete the voting
action button.

Replace `VotingAction()` code with:

```
@Composable
fun VotingAction(
  text: String,
  onUpVoteAction: () -> Unit,
  onDownVoteAction: () -> Unit
) {
  Row(verticalAlignment = Alignment.CenterVertically) {
    ArrowButton(onUpVoteAction,
R.drawable.ic_baseline_arrow_upward_24)
    Text(
      text = text,
      color = Color.Gray,
      fontWeight = FontWeight.Medium,
      fontSize = 12.sp
    )
    ArrowButton(onDownVoteAction,
R.drawable.ic_baseline_arrow_downward_24)
  }
}
```

You added a `Row()` with two `ArrowButtons` and a `Text()` in between. For each
`ArrowButton()` you passed a different `onClick()` and vector drawable. That lets you
set a different arrow image and the handler that defines what happens after clicking
the button.

Build the project and look at the preview section under `VotingActionPreview()`:

Voting Action Button Preview

You now see the two arrows, one for up-voting and one for down-voting. In the middle, you see the total number of votes.

The actions for commenting, sharing and awarding are very similar so they're pre-made for you. If you're interested in how they work, look at `PostAction()` in the starter project.

The last thing that's missing to complete `Post()` are its two content types. This time, you'll use a different approach: building the `Post()` before you finish the content.

Building the post

You might wonder how you'll build `Post()` without first implementing the content. To find out how — and why — make the following changes to `Post()`:

```
@Composable
fun Post(post: PostModel, content: @Composable () -> Unit = {})
{
  Card(shape = MaterialTheme.shapes.large) {
    Column(modifier = Modifier.padding(
        top = 8.dp,
        bottom = 8.dp)
    ) {
      Header(post)
      Spacer(modifier = Modifier.height(4.dp))
      content.invoke()
      Spacer(modifier = Modifier.height(8.dp))
      PostActions(post)
    }
  }
}
```

First, you added a `Card()` and a `Column()` to lay out the composable. Then, you added `Header()`, content and `PostActions()`.

It looks like you call content here even though you haven't implemented it yet. That's because, this time, you're using a composable as a function parameter, which you then invoke precisely where you need it.

content is present, but it's empty by default unless you provide it. You achieve this by providing {}, which returns empty content for the composable function.

Build the app and look at `PostPreview()` under the preview section:

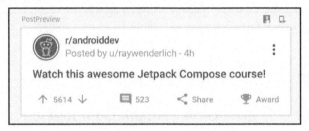

Post Preview

As you see, the post already contains the header and the actions. The only thing missing is the content. You'll address that part now.

Adding the content

Look at `TextPost()` and `ImagePost()`:

```
@Composable
fun TextPost(post: PostModel) {
  Post(post) {
    TextContent(post.text)
  }
}

@Composable
fun ImagePost(post: PostModel) {
  Post(post) {
    ImageContent(post.image ?: R.drawable.compose_course)
  }
}
```

The functions are already built for you because they only call `Post()` and pass one parameter: either `TextContent()` or `ImageContent()`, depending on what type of content you need to display. Feel free to check them out if you're curious about their implementation. :]

Next, find the following code at the bottom of the file:

```
@Preview
@Composable
fun ImagePostPreview() {
  Post(DEFAULT_POST) {
    ImageContent(DEFAULT_POST.image ?:
R.drawable.compose_course)
  }
}
```

Build the app and take a look at the preview section under `ImagePostPreview()`:

Image Post Preview

Your `Post()` is now complete with all its content and you're ready to finish the home screen.

Adding multiple posts

To finish the home screen, you need to add the ability to display multiple posts using Post(), which you just made. The posts should vary by type and content.

In this project, the **database**, **repository** and **viewmodel** layers are already prepared for you because you already covered them in Chapter 7, "Managing State in Compose".

Your task is to fetch the post data using the prepared classes and then render the content inside HomeScreen().

To start, open the **HomeScreen.kt** file and replace HomeScreen() code with the following:

```
@Composable
fun HomeScreen(viewModel: MainViewModel) {
  val posts: List<PostModel> by
viewModel.allPosts.observeAsState(listOf())

  LazyColumn(modifier = Modifier.background(color =
MaterialTheme.colors.secondary)) {
    items(posts) {
      if (it.type == PostType.TEXT) {
        TextPost(it)
      } else {
        ImagePost(it)
      }
      Spacer(modifier = Modifier.height(6.dp))
    }
  }
}
```

To complete this screen, you did the following:

- First, you fetched all the posts from the database, which are observed as a state to handle recomposition.

- Next, you added a LazyColumn() to make a scrollable list of the fetched posts.

- Finally, you rendered the post depending on its type and put a Spacer() at the bottom to separate the items, using items() from the LazyColumn.

Build and run the app, then take a look at the main screen when the app opens:

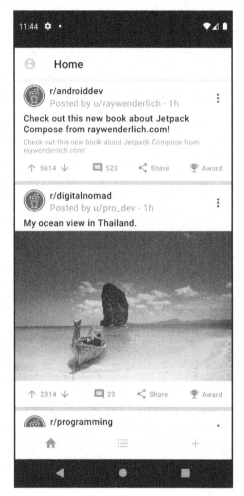

Home Screen

You now see a list of multiple posts with different content, which you can scroll through.

Now that you've finished the home screen, your next task is to make the Subreddits screen.

Building the Subreddits screen

First, take a look at the image below to understand what you'll build:

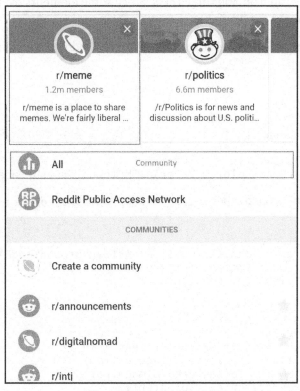

Subreddit Screen Example

The screen consists of two main parts: a horizontally scrollable list of subreddit items and a vertically scrollable Column() that contains both the subreddit list and a list of communities.

The two items that you'll build are marked in red. At the top, you see the **subreddit body**, which holds a subreddit item. Below it, you find the **community item**, which builds the list of communities.

Building the subreddit body

Look at the **subreddit body** from the example image once more. It consists of a background image, an icon and three texts. Since some elements overlap, you'll use ConstraintLayout() for flexibility.

Open **screens/SubredditsScreen.kt** and replace the code inside SubredditBody with the following:

```
@Composable
fun SubredditBody(subredditModel: SubredditModel, modifier:
Modifier = Modifier) {
  ConstraintLayout(
    modifier = modifier
      .fillMaxSize()
      .background(color = MaterialTheme.colors.surface)
  ) {
    val (backgroundImage, icon, name, members, description) =
createRefs() // 1

    SubredditImage( // 2
      modifier = modifier.constrainAs(backgroundImage) {
        centerHorizontallyTo(parent)
        top.linkTo(parent.top)
      }
    )

    SubredditIcon( // 3
      modifier = modifier.constrainAs(icon) {
        top.linkTo(backgroundImage.bottom)
        bottom.linkTo(backgroundImage.bottom)
        centerHorizontallyTo(parent)
      }.zIndex(1f)
    )

    SubredditName( // 4
      nameStringRes = subredditModel.nameStringRes,
      modifier = modifier.constrainAs(name) {
        top.linkTo(icon.bottom)
        centerHorizontallyTo(parent)
      }
    )

    SubredditMembers( // 5
      membersStringRes = subredditModel.membersStringRes,
      modifier = modifier.constrainAs(members) {
        top.linkTo(name.bottom)
        centerHorizontallyTo(parent)
      }
    )
```

```
    SubredditDescription( // 6
      descriptionStringRes =
  subredditModel.descriptionStringRes,
      modifier = modifier.constrainAs(description) {
        top.linkTo(members.bottom)
        centerHorizontallyTo(parent)
      }
    )
  }
}
```

There is a lot happening here, so here's a breakdown, one element at a time:

1. You first create necessary constraint references using `createRefs()`. They represent the five elements you'll show in a subreddit.

2. The first element is the image, which is centered horizontally and linked to the top of the parent. `SubredditImage()` is already built for you. Check out its definition to learn more.

3. Centered horizontally within the parent and vertically within the `backgroundImage` lies the `SubredditIcon()`. You also used `zIndex()` to raise the icon above the `backgroundImage`. In Jetpack Compose, the composables' order doesn't determine their order on the z axis — that depends on the composable's render speed, instead. That means that `SubredditImage()` might sometimes appear above `SubredditIcon()`.

   To avoid that, you used `zIndex()`, which lets you change the order to render composables that share the same parent. The greater the `zIndex()` value is, the later the app will draw the composable. The default value for `zIndex()` is **0**. By setting it to **1**, you ensured that the app will always draw `SubredditIcon()`.

4. You put the `SubredditName()` at the bottom of the `SubredditIcon()`, centered horizontally within the parent.

5. The `SubredditMembers()` follows the `SubredditName()`.

6. And finally, the `SubredditDescription()` follows `SubredditMembers()`.

To see the changes, build the app and look at the preview section under
`SubredditBodyPreview`:

Subreddit Body Preview

Adjusting the elements' height and shadowing

The elements' positions are correct, but their height is wrong and there are no visible
shadows at the edge.

Next, you'll fix the height and shadow problem. Replace the `Subreddit()` code with
the following:

```
@Composable
fun Subreddit(subredditModel: SubredditModel, modifier: Modifier
= Modifier) {
  Card(
```

```
    backgroundColor = MaterialTheme.colors.surface,
    shape = RoundedCornerShape(4.dp),
    modifier = modifier
      .size(120.dp)
      .padding(
        start = 2.dp,
        end = 2.dp,
        top = 4.dp,
        bottom = 4.dp
      )
  ) {
    SubredditBody(subredditModel)
  }
}
```

This code places `SubredditBody()` inside a `Card()` and sets that card's size, colors and padding.

Build the app and look at the preview section under `SubredditPreview()`:

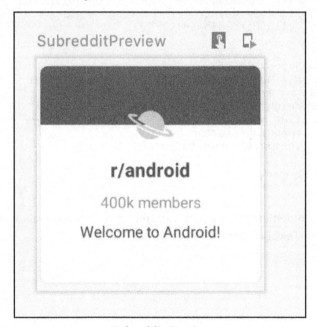

Subreddit Preview

The size of the composable is now correct and you can see the shadows at the border. Nice job! You've just finished another piece of the puzzle.

Next, you'll build the **community item**.

Building the community item

The community item is fairly simple; it only has an icon and a text. To build it, change Community() code to:

```
@Composable
fun Community(text: String, modifier: Modifier = Modifier,
onCommunityClicked: () -> Unit = {}) {
  Row(modifier = modifier
    .padding(start = 16.dp, top = 16.dp)
    .fillMaxWidth()
    .clickable { onCommunityClicked.invoke() }
  ) {
    Image(
        bitmap = ImageBitmap.imageResource(id =
R.drawable.subreddit_placeholder),
        contentDescription = stringResource(id =
R.string.community_icon),
        modifier = modifier
            .size(24.dp)
            .clip(CircleShape)
    )
    Text(
        fontSize = 10.sp,
        color = MaterialTheme.colors.primaryVariant,
        text = text,
        fontWeight = FontWeight.Bold,
        modifier = modifier
            .padding(start = 16.dp)
            .align(Alignment.CenterVertically)
    )
  }
}
```

As you see, this implementation is quite simple. It consists of a clickable Row() with an Image() and a Text() after it.

Build the app and look at the preview section under `CommunityPreview()`:

Community Preview

You see an icon and a community text, as you expect.

Adding a community list

Next, you'll build the list that contains all the main and added communities.

Add the following code inside `Communities()`:

```
@Composable
fun Communities(modifier: Modifier = Modifier) {
  mainCommunities.forEach {
    Community(text = stringResource(it))
  }

  Spacer(modifier = modifier.height(4.dp))

  BackgroundText(stringResource(R.string.communities))

  communities.forEach {
    Community(text = stringResource(it))
  }
}
```

There are two lists of `String` resources prepared for you: `mainComunities` and `communities`. In the first part of the screen, you added the main communities and in the second part, you added the rest.

Both lists are separated with a `Spacer()` and a `BackgroundText()`, which is pre-constructed for you. `BackgroundText()` is a `Text()` that contains a background color and fills the whole width of the screen.

Build the app and look at the preview section under `CommunitiesPreview()`:

Communities Preview

You see both lists of communities separated by the content generated by `BackgroundText()`. The colors will update when you run the app on a device.

Now that you have all the necessary components, you're ready to finish `SubredditsScreen()`.

Finishing the screen

The last part of the puzzle to build `SubredditsScreen()` is to combine everything you've built so far into a list that the user can scroll horizontally and vertically.

Start by replacing `SubredditsScreen` with the following:

```
@Composable
fun SubredditsScreen(modifier: Modifier = Modifier) {
  Column(modifier =
modifier.verticalScroll(rememberScrollState())) {
    Text(
      modifier = modifier.padding(16.dp),
      text =
```

```
    stringResource(R.string.recently_visited_subreddits),
        fontSize = 12.sp,
        style = MaterialTheme.typography.subtitle1
    )

    LazyRow(
      modifier = modifier.padding(end = 16.dp)
    ) {
        items(subreddits) { Subreddit(it) }
    }
    Communities(modifier)
  }
}
```

With the previous code, you added a scrollable `Column()` as the root so the user can scroll vertically.

Next, you added a `Column()` with a subtitle at the top. To create the list of horizontally scrolled subreddits, you used `LazyRow()` and passed an already-prepared list of `SubredditModels` to `items()`.

Finally, you added `Communities()` to display all the communities.

Build the app and run it on your device this time. Once you install the app, click the middle icon in the bottom bar.

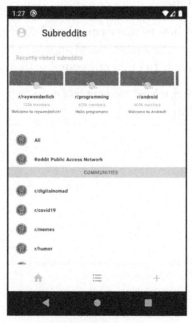

Subreddits Screen

314 Jetpack Compose by Tutorials

You see the list of subreddits at the top, which the user can scroll horizontally. Below that is the list of communities. The whole screen scrolls vertically — try it out!

Congratulations! You've built the main part of the JetReddit app and learned how to build complex elements. You can find the completed code for this chapter in **10-building-complex-ui-in-jetpack-compose/projects/final**.

Key points

- Build your app by first implementing the most basic components.

- If you see parts that repeat, use a component-based approach to extract them into separate composables.

- Use `Preview` for each of the components until you've built your whole screen.

- Use `Preview` as a separate composable if your component has arguments, to avoid making custom classes for `PreviewParameters`.

- Use `emptyContent()` to display empty content inside the composable.

- Use `zIndex()` if multiple composables overlap and you want to change their order of display in the z-orientation.

In this chapter, you learned how to make complex UI elements as well as the importance of following the component-based approach to break complex UI into simpler parts. You're now ready to build any complex UI in your own apps.

In the next chapter, you'll learn how to react to Compose's lifecycle and continue building your `JetReddit` app.

See you there!

Chapter 11: Reacting to Compose Lifecycle

By Tino Balint

In previous chapters, you focused on building the **JetReddit** app by adding advanced layouts and complex UI.

In this chapter, you'll learn how to react to the lifecycle of composable functions. This approach will allow you to execute your code at specific moments while your composable is active.

Jetpack Compose offers a list of events that can trigger at specific points in the the lifecycle, called **effects**. Throughout this chapter, you'll learn about the different kinds of effects and how to use them to implement your logic.

Events in Compose

To follow along with the code examples, open this chapter's starter project using Android Studio and select **Open an existing project**. Navigate to **11-reacting-to-compose-lifecycle/projects** and select the **starter** folder as the project root. Once the project opens, let it build and sync and you're ready to go!

You might already be familiar with the project hierarchy from the previous chapter, but in case you aren't, look at the following image:

Project Hierarchy

In this chapter, you'll only work with two of these packages: **screens**, to implement a new screen, and **routing**, to add a new routing option. The rest of the packages are already prepared to handle navigation, fetching data from the database, dependency injection and theme switching for you.

Once you're familiar with the file organization, build and run the app. You'll see:

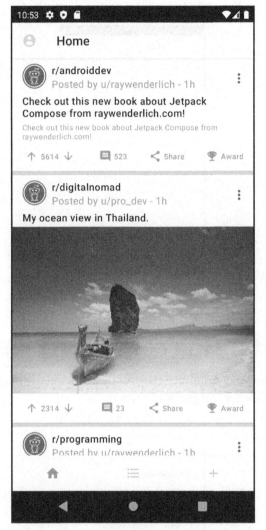

Home Screen

This is a fully implemented home screen. When you browse the app, you'll notice that two screens are pre-built and implemented for you: **My Profile**, in the app drawer, and **New Post**, the third option in the bottom navigation.

In this chapter, you'll implement the option to choose a community inside the **New Post** screen:

New Post Screen

Implementing the community chooser

Next, you'll implement a community chooser like the one the original Reddit app uses. Look at the following image for reference:

Reddit Community Chooser

The community chooser contains a toolbar, a search input field and a list of communities. To fetch the community list, you'll use a `ViewModel` that contains pre-built methods.

Open the **ChooseCommunityScreen.kt** file and look at the code. There are three composables: `ChooseCommunityScreen()` for the whole screen, `SearchedCommunities()` for the community list and `ChooseCommunityTopBar()`, for the pre-built top navigation bar.

Creating a list of communities

As you learned in the previous chapters, you'll build the smaller components first, starting with `SearchedCommunities()`. Start by changing `SearchedCommunities()` code to the following:

```
@Composable
fun SearchedCommunities(
    communities: List<String>,
    viewModel: MainViewModel?,
    modifier: Modifier = Modifier
) {
    communities.forEach {
        Community(
            text = it,
            modifier = modifier,
            onCommunityClicked = {
                viewModel?.selectedCommunity?.postValue(it)
                JetRedditRouter.goBack()
            }
        )
    }
}
```

In the composable parameters, you see a list of strings that represent community names, the `MainViewModel` to update the data and a default `Modifier`.

First, you iterate over the `communities` list and create a `Community()` for each element. You already made `Community()` in the previous chapter, so this is a perfect opportunity to reuse it.

Next, for each of the community elements, you pass its name and a `modifier`, then set the `onCommunityClicked` action. When the user clicks any of the communities, you notify the other composables about the selected value using `selectedCommunity`, which is stored inside the `viewModel`.

Finally, you close the screen after the user selects the community by calling `goBack()` on the `JetRedditRouter`.

To see the changes, add the preview code at the bottom of
ChooseCommunityScreen.kt:

```
@Preview
@Composable
fun SearchedCommunitiesPreview() {
  Column {
    SearchedCommunities(defaultCommunities, null, Modifier)
  }
}
```

Build the app and look at the preview section. You see a list of communities with
three elements:

Searched Communities Preview

Making the community list searchable

The next step is to add a `TextField()` to search the communities according to user
input. Replace `ChooseCommunityScreen()` with the code below:

```
@Composable
fun ChooseCommunityScreen(viewModel: MainViewModel, modifier:
Modifier = Modifier) {
  val scope = rememberCoroutineScope()
  val communities: List<String> by
viewModel.subreddits.observeAsState(emptyList())
  var searchedText by remember { mutableStateOf("") }
  var currentJob by remember { mutableStateOf<Job?>(null) }
  val activeColor = MaterialTheme.colors.onSurface

  LaunchedEffect(Unit) {
```

```
      viewModel.searchCommunities(searchedText)
    }

  Column {
    ChooseCommunityTopBar()
    TextField(
      value = searchedText,
      onValueChange = {
        searchedText = it
        currentJob?.cancel()
        currentJob = scope.async {
          delay(SEARCH_DELAY_MILLIS)
          viewModel.searchCommunities(searchedText)
        }
      },
      leadingIcon = {
        Icon(Icons.Default.Search, contentDescription =
stringResource(id = R.string.search))
      },
      label = { Text(stringResource(R.string.search)) },
      modifier = modifier
        .fillMaxWidth()
        .padding(horizontal = 8.dp),
      colors = TextFieldDefaults.outlinedTextFieldColors(
        focusedBorderColor = activeColor,
        focusedLabelColor = activeColor,
        cursorColor = activeColor,
        backgroundColor = MaterialTheme.colors.surface
      )
    )
    SearchedCommunities(communities, viewModel, modifier)
  }
}
```

Here, you first created a coroutineScope by calling rememberCoroutineScope().
rememberCoroutineScope() is a SuspendingEffect, which is a type of an effect in
Compose. It creates a CoroutineScope, which is bound to the composition.
CoroutineScope is only created once, and it stays the same even after
recomposition. Any Job belonging to this scope will be canceled when the scope
leaves the composition.

Then, you create three states: one for the list of communities, which is observed
from the database. The second for searchedText, which updates based on user
input. The third stores your search Job.

Next, you called LaunchedEffect(Unit) to search the communities when the
composition is first composed. Searching for an empty string will return all
communities from the database.

LaunchedEffect(key) runs the block of code whenever the composable enters recomposition, as long as the key you passed in changes between recompositions. Because you passed in Unit, which is a constant, it's only going to run once — the first time the element is shown.

Finally, you added a Column() with three composables: the pre-built ChooseCommunityTopBar(), TextField() to capture the user input and SearchedCommunities() to display the list of communities.

With each value change inside TextField(), this code cancels the previous Job and starts a new one inside the scope you already created.

Inside the code block of the coroutine, you added delay() with a 300-millisecond delay. This prevents a new community search from starting each time the user types a new character, unless more than 300 milliseconds pass between keystrokes. Updating searchedText cancels the previous Job and a new one launches with a new delay.

Build and run, then open the **New Post** screen by selecting the third option in the bottom navigation.

Click the **Choose a community** button to open the screen you just implemented:

Community Chooser

You see a list of communities and a search input field that you can use to filter the current list. If you type fast, the list won't update until you wait for more than 300 milliseconds.

Currently, you're fetching data from a local database, but when searches use a remote API, this implementation saves your network data and reduces the number of requests a server might receive.

If you want to go back without selecting a community, you can click the **Close** icon from the top app bar. But what happens when you click the built-in back button on your device? The app closes instead of navigating to the previous screen.

Next, you'll use effects to implement the back navigation.

Implementing the back button handler

In previous sections, you used built-in back button handlers. This time, you'll use effects to build your own.

To achieve back button handling in Compose, you need to use **dispatchers**, which allow you to register appropriate callbacks.

Open **BackButtonHandler.kt** inside **routing** and replace BackButtonHandler() with the following:

```
@Composable
fun BackButtonHandler(
  enabled: Boolean = true,
  onBackPressed: () -> Unit
) {
  val dispatcher = localBackPressedDispatcher.current ?: return
  val backCallback = remember {
    object : OnBackPressedCallback(enabled) {
      override fun handleOnBackPressed() {
        onBackPressed.invoke()
      }
    }
  }
  DisposableEffect(dispatcher) {
    dispatcher.addCallback(backCallback)
    onDispose {
      backCallback.remove()
    }
  }
}
```

`BackButtonHandler()` takes two parameters:

- **enabled**: Determines if back pressing is enabled.

- **onBackPressed()**: Invokes an action when the user presses a button.

First, you created a dispatcher property using `localBackPressedDispatcher`. `localBackPressedDispatcher` is a pre-built static `CompositionLocal` of type `OnBackPressedDispatcher` that allows you to add and remove callbacks for system back button clicks.

Next, you made a `backCallback` by overriding `OnBackPressedCallback`. This callback receives a parameter that indicates if it's enabled, then overrides `handleOnBackPressed()`, which triggers when the user presses the back button. Note that the callback consumes the composable parameters described earlier to set the enabled state and invoke the desired action.

Finally, you added `DisposableEffect()`, passing `dispatcher` as a parameter. You added a callback to `dispatcher`, then called `onDispose()` to remove that callback.

`DisposableEffect` is a side effect of the composition that accepts a parameter called `subject`. Every time `subject` changes, you need to dispose the effect and call it again. The effect is also disposed when you leave the composition. You handle this by calling `onDispose()` where you removed the dispatcher callback. This prevents leaks.

In your case, the effect is disposed and re-launched every time `dispatcher` changes, which is possible because `dispatcher` depends on the **lifecycle** of the app.

Adding an action to the back button

The next step is to build `BackButtonAction()` and provide the previous `CompositionLocal`. Replace `BackButtonAction()` with the following:

```
@Composable
fun BackButtonAction(onBackPressed: () -> Unit) {
  CompositionLocalProvider(
    localBackPressedDispatcher provides (
        LocalLifecycleOwner.current as ComponentActivity
        ).onBackPressedDispatcher
  ) {
    BackButtonHandler {
      onBackPressed.invoke()
    }
  }
}
```

BackButtonAction() takes one parameter, onBackPressed(), which is the action that needs to occur when the user presses the **Back** button.

You provided BackPressedDispatcher by passing LocalLifecycleOwner and calling current on it, which returns the current value of the lifecycle owner. You need to cast this value as ComponentActivity to retrieve the back press dispatcher for the current Activity by calling onBackPressedDispatcher.

Next, you used the previous BackButtonHandler() and invoked onBackPressed() as your action. You didn't pass the enabled parameter, which enables callbacks by default.

Calling the back button's action

Now that you've implemented BackButtonAction(), the only thing left to do is to call it from inside ChooseCommunityScreen().

To do this, add the following code at the bottom of ChooseCommunityScreen():

```
BackButtonAction {
    JetRedditRouter.goBack()
}
```

Here, you just added a BackButtonAction() and invoked goBack() on the router to go to the previous screen.

Build and run, then open the **Choose a community** screen. There are no new UI changes in the app, but you can now click either the close icon or the system back button to go to the previous screen.

At this stage, you've learned about two types of **effects** in Compose. Next, you'll cover even more effects.

Effects in Compose

To understand the topic of effects more clearly, you first need to learn how side effects work in Compose.

Side effects are operations that change the values of anything outside the scope of the function. An example of this is when a mutable object is passed to a function and changes some of that function's properties. Such changes can affect other parts of the code that use the same object, so you need to be careful when applying them.

The biggest problem with side effects is that you don't have control over when they actually occur. This is problematic in composables because the code inside them executes every time a recomposition takes place. Effects can help you by giving you control over when the code executes.

Here are more details about specific effects.

SideEffect

`SideEffect()` ensures that your event only executes when a composition is successful. If the composition fails, the event is discarded. In addition, only use it when you don't need to dispose the event, but want it to run with every recomposition.

Take a look at the snippet below:

```
@Composable
fun MainScreen(router: Router) {
  val drawerState = rememberDrawerState(DrawerValue.Closed)

  SideEffect {
    router.isRoutingEnabled = drawerState.Closed
  }
}
```

In this snippet, `SideEffect()` changes the state of the router. You disable the routing in the app when the drawer is closed: otherwise, you enable it. In this case, `router` is a `singleton` and you don't want to dispose it because other screens are using it for navigation.

The next effect, `LaunchedEffect()`, is similar to `rememberCoroutineScope()`, which you used earlier.

LaunchedEffect

`LaunchedEffect` launches a coroutine into the composition's `CoroutineScope`. Just like `rememberCoroutineScope()`, its coroutine is canceled when `LaunchedEffect` leaves the composition and will relaunch on recomposition.

See the example below to get a deeper insight:

```
@Composable
fun SpeakerList(searchText: String) {
  var communities by remember
{ mutableStateOf(emptyList<String>()) }
```

```
    LaunchedEffect(searchText) {
      communities = viewModel.searchCommunities(searchText)
    }

    Communities(communities)
  }
```

This snippet is similar to what you did when you implemented the search feature in ChooseCommunityScreen().

When you implemented ChooseCommunityScreen, searchText was a mutable state depending on the user input. This time, searchText is a function parameter and isn't saved as a mutable state. According to the Google guidelines, you should follow this approach to prevent performance issues.

LaunchedEffect initiates the first time it enters the composition and every time the parameter changes. It cancels all running Jobs during the parameter change or upon leaving the composition.

You now learned all effect types, but there are functions that might help you use those effects for more specific situations. These functions create different kinds of states that should be used inside effect composables. The first function on the list is rememberUpdatedState().

RememberUpdatedState

When using LaunchedEffect, it is initiated every time the passed parameter changes. If you want to use a constant parameter that never changes, your effect will never restart which is a problem if you have values that need to be updated.

In this case, you can use rememberUpdatedState on your value that needs to be updated. This creates a reference to that value and allows it to update when the composable is recomposed. The example when you would need this approach is a splash screen:

```
@Composable
fun LandingScreen(onSplashFinished: () -> NetworkData) {

  val currentOnSplashFinished by
rememberUpdatedState(onSplashFinished)

  LaunchedEffect(Unit) {
    delay(SplashWaitTimeMillis)
    currentOnSplashFinished()
  }
}
```

When the splash screen starts, you want to set a timeout for how long it should last and do some background work if you app requires it. When some of you background work is done, you might want to update the values in your composable which triggers the recomposition.

To update the value of your onSplashFinished lambda, you wrap it with rememberUpdatedState and then used inside the LaunchedEffect with Unit as a parameter. Since Unit is a constant value, the effect will never restart to ensure that your splash screen always has the same wait time, but your lambda will still be invoked with the latest value after the timeout is finished.

The next function that will help you when using effects is produceState.

ProduceState

Sometimes you want to do some work in the background and pass it down to the presentation layer. Remember that composable functions have States and any data used in composables needs to be converted into compose State in order to be used and survive the recomposition.

You can use produceState to write a function that fetches data and converts it directly into compose State. In the following code, you can see an example of loading books by author.

```
@Composable
fun loadBooks(author: String, booksRepository: BooksRepository):
State<Result<List<Book>>> {
   return produceState(initialValue = Result.Loading, author,
booksRepository) {

     val books = booksRepository.load(author)

     value = if (books == null) {
       Result.Error
     } else {
       Result.Success(books)
     }
   }
}
```

The function has two parameters, an author and booksRepository. ProduceState is called to create a coroutine and fetch the books and directly convert them to a composable State. If either of the two passed parameters change, the job will be canceled and relaunched with the new values.

This allows you to create a composable with the return type and call it from other composables like you would usually do in your `presenters` or `viewmodels`. Note that the name convention for composables with return type is to start with lowercase letter like other non-composable functions.

Migrate effects

If you used older version of Jetpack Compose, you might have have a few different effects that were not mentioned in this chapter. Those effects are now removed, but you can still achieve the same implementation using `LaunchedEffect`, `DisposableEffect` and `SideEffect`.

To migrate to the newer version, you can use this cookbook prepared for you:

```
// onActive without subject parameter
onActive {
  someFunction()
}
```

replace with:

```
LaunchedEffect(Unit) {
  someFunction()
}
```

You can replace `onActive()` without subject parameter by using `LaunchedEffect` with a constant value like `Unit` or `true`. This will ensure that the effect is used once, on the first composition.

Next, if you're using it like so:

```
// onActive with subject parameter
onActive(parameter) {
  someFunction()
}
```

replace it with:

```
LaunchedEffect(parameter) {
  someFunction()
}
```

If you use subject parameter with your `onActive()`, you can just replace it with `LaunchedEffect`.

Then if you're using something like:

```
// onActive with onDispose
onActive {
  val disposable = getData()

  onDispose {
    disposable.dispose()
  }
}
```

replace it with:

```
DisposableEffect(Unit) {
  val disposable = getData()

  onDispose {
    disposable.dispose()
  }
}
```

Like in the example without the subject parameter, you can replace onActive() with onDispose() inside by using DisposableEffect with a constant value like Unit or true.

Finally, if you're using:

```
// onCommit without subject parameter
onCommit {
  someFunction()
}
```

replace it with:

```
SideEffect {
  someFunction()
}
```

You can replace onCommit() without a subject parameter by using SideEffect with a constant value like Unit or true. This will ensure that the effect is used on the first composition, and again for every recomposition. To use onCommit() with the subject parameter or onDispose() inside, use the same code as for onActive().

Key points

- Use `rememberCoroutineScope()` when you are using coroutines and need to cancel and relaunch the coroutine after an event.

- Use `LaunchedEffect()` when you are using coroutines and need to cancel and relaunch the coroutine every time your parameter changes and it isn't stored in a mutable state.

- `DisposableEffect()` is useful when you aren't using coroutines and need to dispose and relaunch the event every time your parameter changes.

- `SideEffect()` triggers an event only when the composition is successful and you don't need to dispose the `subject`.

- Use `rememberUpdatedState()` when you want to launch your effect only once but still be able to update the values.

- Use `produceState()` to directly convert non-composable states into composable states.

- Names of the composables with a return type should start with the lowercase letter.

Where to go from here?

Congratulations! Now, you know how to react to Compose lifecycle, which is one of the most complex parts of Jetpack Compose. At this point, you've seen an overview of how to solve some of the most complex and important problems you encounter while working with Compose.

In the next chapter, you'll learn how to use animations to make your UI more beautiful. Animations are fun — and finally easy to do — so read on and enjoy!

Chapter 12: Animating Properties Using Compose

By Denis Buketa

Great job on completing the previous chapter. So far, in the third section of this book, you've learned how to use `ConstraintLayout`, build complex UI and react to Compose lifecycles. Those things are certainly fun, but what's even more fun? Playing with animations! And that's what you'll do now. :]

In this chapter, you'll learn how to:

- **Animate composable properties** using `animate*AsState()`.

- Use `updateTransition()` to **animate multiple properties** of your composables.

- **Animate composable content**.

- **Implement an animated button** to join a subreddit.

- **Implement an animated toast** that displays when the user joins a subreddit.

Before diving straight into the animation world, you'll create a composable representing a button that lets users join an imaginary subreddit.

You'll start by implementing a simple button, like the one shown below:

Simple Join Button

If a user hasn't joined the subreddit yet, they can do so by clicking the blue button with the **plus** icon. If the user is a member already, a white button with a blue check represents that state. Clicking the button again returns it to its previous state.

To follow along with the code examples, open this chapter's **starter project** in Android Studio and select **Open an existing project**.

Next, navigate to **12-animating-properties-using-compose/projects** and select the **starter** folder as the project root. Once the project opens, let it build and sync and you're ready to go!

Note that if you skip ahead to the final project, you'll find the completed button with all the animation logic implemented.

Now that you're all set, it's time to start coding.

Building JoinButton

In the **components** package, add a new file named **JoinButton.kt**, then open it and add the following code:

```
@Composable
fun JoinButton(onClick: (Boolean) -> Unit = {}) {

}

enum class JoinButtonState {
```

```
    IDLE,
    PRESSED
}

@Preview
@Composable
fun JoinButtonPreview() {
  JoinButton(onClick = {})
}
```

Not much to see here. You just created a root composable for your button and added a preview. Right now, there's nothing to preview because you haven't added any content yet.

You also added `JoinButtonState`, which represents the state of the button, The two options for the state are `IDLE` or `PRESSED`.

Next, add the following code to `JoinButton()`:

```
var buttonState: JoinButtonState
  by remember { mutableStateOf(JoinButtonState.IDLE) }

// Button shape
val shape = RoundedCornerShape(corner = CornerSize(12.dp))

// Button background
val buttonBackgroundColor: Color =
  if (buttonState == JoinButtonState.PRESSED)
    Color.White
  else
    Color.Blue

// Button icon
val iconAsset: ImageVector =
  if (buttonState == JoinButtonState.PRESSED)
    Icons.Default.Check
  else
    Icons.Default.Add
val iconTintColor: Color =
  if (buttonState == JoinButtonState.PRESSED)
    Color.Blue
  else
    Color.White

Box(
  modifier = Modifier
    .clip(shape)
    .border(width = 1.dp, color = Color.Blue, shape = shape)
    .background(color = buttonBackgroundColor)
    .size(width = 40.dp, height = 24.dp)
    .clickable(onClick = {
```

```
      buttonState =
        if (buttonState == JoinButtonState.IDLE) {
          onClick.invoke(true)
          JoinButtonState.PRESSED
        } else {
          onClick.invoke(false)
          JoinButtonState.IDLE
        }
    }),
  contentAlignment = Alignment.Center
) {
  Icon(
    imageVector = iconAsset,
    contentDescription = "Plus Icon",
    tint = iconTintColor,
    modifier = Modifier.size(16.dp)
  )
}
```

This might look like a lot of code, but you'll see that it's pretty simple. Here's a breakdown, starting from the top.

You first declared a `buttonState` with `remember()`. Ideally, you'd represent your state with `PostModel`, but this simplified approach is enough to demonstrate how animations work.

Next, you used `RoundedCornerShape()` to define the shape of the button.

You also defined the button's background color, which will change depending on the `buttonState`. When the button has `JoinButtonState.PRESSED`, it will be white. When it's `JoinButtonState.IDLE`, it will be blue.

Next, you defined the button's icon and icon color. When the button's state is `JoinButtonState.PRESSED`, you'll represent the icon with a white plus sign. If it's `JoinButtonState.IDLE`, you'll represent it with a blue check mark.

The last thing you added is the code that emits the button's UI. You used `Box()` to define the button shape and background and `Icon()` to define how the button's icon will look.

For that code to work, you need to add a few imports as well:

```
import androidx.compose.foundation.shape.CornerSize
import androidx.compose.foundation.shape.RoundedCornerShape
import androidx.compose.foundation.background
import androidx.compose.foundation.border
import androidx.compose.foundation.clickable
import androidx.compose.foundation.layout.Box
import androidx.compose.foundation.layout.size
```

```
import androidx.compose.material.Icon
import androidx.compose.material.icons.Icons
import androidx.compose.material.icons.filled.Add
import androidx.compose.material.icons.filled.Check
import androidx.compose.runtime.*
import androidx.compose.ui.Alignment
import androidx.compose.ui.Modifier
import androidx.compose.ui.draw.clip
import androidx.compose.ui.graphics.Color
import androidx.compose.ui.graphics.vector.ImageVector
import androidx.compose.ui.tooling.preview.Preview
import androidx.compose.ui.unit.dp
```

Great! Now, build the project and check the preview panel.

JoinButton — Idle State

Note that you can change buttonState's initial state to PRESSED, to preview the different settings for your button.

JoinButton — Pressed State

Awesome! Next, you'll add this button to Post().

Adding JoinButton to Post

Before animating JoinButton(), you'll add it to Post() so you can see it in the app.

Open **Post.kt** and edit Header() to look like this:

```
@Composable
fun Header(
  post: PostModel,
  onJoinButtonClick: (Boolean) -> Unit = {} // here
) {
  Row(
    modifier = Modifier.padding(start = 16.dp),
```

```
      verticalAlignment = Alignment.CenterVertically // here
  ) {
    Image(
      ImageBitmap.imageResource(id =
R.drawable.subreddit_placeholder),
      contentDescription = stringResource(id =
R.string.subreddits),
      Modifier
        .size(40.dp)
        .clip(CircleShape)
    )
    Spacer(modifier = Modifier.width(8.dp))
    Column(modifier = Modifier.weight(1f)) {
      Text(
        text = stringResource(
          R.string.subreddit_header,
          post.subreddit
        ),
        fontWeight = FontWeight.Medium,
        color = MaterialTheme.colors.primaryVariant
      )
      Text(
        text = stringResource(
          R.string.post_header,
          post.username,
          post.postedTime
        ),
        color = Color.Gray
      )
    }
    Spacer(modifier = Modifier.width(4.dp)) // here
    JoinButton(onJoinButtonClick) // here
    MoreActionsMenu()
  }

  Title(text = post.title)
}
```

In the code above, you added:

1. `verticalAlignment` to `Row()` to center the header content vertically.

2. `JoinButton()` and `Spacer()` to `Header()`.

3. `onJoinButtonClick` to `Header()`.

Excellent! Now, build and run the app. Check how your posts look:

Posts With the Join Button

Click one of the JoinButtons and you'll see how the icon and the background change instantly.

Animating the JoinButton background

So far, you've made the button background change from one color to another when the state changes. In this section, you'll animate that transition.

In **JoinButton.kt**, replace the current definition of buttonBackgroundColor with the following code:

```
// Button background
val buttonBackgroundColor: Color by animateColorAsState(
  if (buttonState == JoinButtonState.PRESSED)
    Color.White
  else
```

```
        Color.Blue
   )
```

Add one more import as well:

```
import androidx.compose.animation.animateColorAsState
```

Here, you wrapped the `if` clause that defined two different background colors with `animateColorAsState()`. By doing that, you implemented the animation between the two colors when the state changes.

With this simple change, you added your first animation. Can you even believe how easy that was? :]

Now, take a closer look at `animateColorAsState()`. It is just one of the `animate*AsState()` functions. In the Jetpack Compose documentation, you'll find a dozen different `animate*AsState()` signatures that allow you to animate a dozen different properties out of the box, including `Float`, `Color`, `Dp`, `Position`, `Size` and other. You can even define your own properties.

All those definitions have something in common: You use them for **fire-and-forget** animations. Once you create a fire-and-forget animation, the app will memorize its position, like other composables. To trigger the animation, or alter the course of the animation, you simply supply a different target to the composable.

The `animate*AsState()` functions are the simplest animation APIs in Compose for animating a single value. You only provide the end value (or target value), and the API starts animation from the current value to the specified value.

Now build and run the app. Click on any `JoinButton` in the app and notice how the background color changes.

Join Button's Background Animation

The figure shows how the button looks across several frames of the animation. Notice how the icon changes immediately after the click, while the background slowly transitions from one color to another. What's really impressive here is how easy it was to implement this animation, which makes your app even nicer!

Using transitions to animate JoinButton

In the previous section, you saw how to animate one property of your composables. Now, you'll add more content to `JoinButton()`. This will give you the opportunity to animate several properties at once.

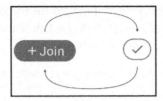

Join Button With More Content

The figure shows how you'll change `JoinButton`'s appearance in the `JoinButtonState.IDLE` state.

Before adding any code, analyze how you'll accomplish this animation. Which properties do you have to animate? To give the button its new look, you need to:

1. Animate the **background**, as you did in the previous example.

2. Change the icon. You'll change the asset the same way as before, but you'll improve that change by animating the **icon color**.

3. **Hide** and **show** the text depending on the state.

4. Animate the button's **width**.

So you need to animate **four** different properties. Keep that in mind when adding the following code.

Defining the transition

To animate these properties, you'll use `Transition`. `Transition` manages one or more animations as its children and runs them simultaneously between multiple states.

In **JoinButton.kt**, add the following code to `JoinButton()`, just below shape:

```
val transition = updateTransition(
  targetState = buttonState,
  label = "JoinButtonTransition"
)
```

Add this import as well:

```
import androidx.compose.animation.core.updateTransition
```

updateTransition creates and remembers an instance of Transition and updates its state. When targetState changes, Transition will run all of its child animations towards their target values specified for the new targetState. You'll add those target values next. You also passed in the label property, which let you inspect and debug those animations in Android Studio.

Next, you'll define child animations. Replace buttonBackgroundColor definition with the following code:

```
val duration = 600
val buttonBackgroundColor: Color
  by transition.animateColor(
    transitionSpec = { tween(duration) },
    label = "Button Background Color"
  ) { state ->
    when (state) {
      JoinButtonState.IDLE -> Color.Blue
      JoinButtonState.PRESSED -> Color.White
    }
  }
```

Add these imports as well:

```
import androidx.compose.animation.animateColor
import androidx.compose.animation.core.tween
```

Here, you defined the transition duration and first child animation in your transition. You used animateColor which is one of animate* extension functions that allow you to define a child animation in your transition. You specified the target values for each of the states. These animate* functions return an animation value that is updated every frame during the animation when the transition state is updated with updateTransition.

You also used tween(). With tween(), you created a TweenSpec configured with the given duration, delay and easing curve. Since you only specified a duration, the code uses 0 for delayMillis and FastOutSlowInEasing() for easing.

Easing is a way to adjust an animation's fraction. The fraction represents how far along the animation you are and its values are within the [0, 1] range, or [0, 100], representing the percent of the animation you finished.

Easing allows transitioning elements to speed up and slow down, rather than moving at a constant, linear, rate.

Next, add the remaining child animations. Below `buttonBackgroundColor`, add the following code:

```
val buttonWidth: Dp
  by transition.animateDp(
    transitionSpec = { tween(duration) },
    label = "Button Width"
) { state ->
    when (state) {
      JoinButtonState.IDLE -> 70.dp
      JoinButtonState.PRESSED -> 32.dp
    }
  }
val textMaxWidth: Dp
  by transition.animateDp(
    transitionSpec = { tween(duration) },
    label = "Text Max Width"
) { state ->
    when (state) {
      JoinButtonState.IDLE -> 40.dp
      JoinButtonState.PRESSED -> 0.dp
    }
  }
```

Don't forget to add these imports:

```
import androidx.compose.ui.unit.Dp
import androidx.compose.animation.core.animateDp
```

Finally, replace the current `iconTintColor` definition with this:

```
val iconTintColor: Color
  by transition.animateColor(
    transitionSpec = { tween(duration) },
    label = "Icon Tint Color"
) { state ->
    when (state) {
      JoinButtonState.IDLE -> Color.White
      JoinButtonState.PRESSED -> Color.Blue
    }
  }
```

Great! You've now prepared everything you need for your transition, but you still have to **connect** this code with the composables you want to animate.

Connecting the transition to the composables

Properties buttonBackgroundColor and iconTintColor are already in place so you don't have to change that.

Next, replace the Box() definition with the following:

```
Box(
  modifier = Modifier
    .clip(shape)
    .border(width = 1.dp, color = Color.Blue, shape = shape)
    .background(color = buttonBackgroundColor)
    .size(
      width = buttonWidth, // here
      height = 24.dp
    )
    .clickable(onClick = {
      buttonState =
        if (buttonState == JoinButtonState.IDLE) {
          onClick.invoke(true)
          JoinButtonState.PRESSED
        } else {
          onClick.invoke(false)
          JoinButtonState.IDLE
        }
    }),
  contentAlignment = Alignment.Center
) {
  Row(     // here
    verticalAlignment = Alignment.CenterVertically
  ) {
    Icon(
      imageVector = iconAsset,
      contentDescription = "Plus Icon",
      tint = iconTintColor,
      modifier = Modifier.size(16.dp)
    )
    Text(   // here
      text = "Join",
      color = Color.White,
      fontSize = 14.sp,
      maxLines = 1,
      modifier = Modifier.widthIn(
        min = 0.dp,
        max = textMaxWidth // here
      )
    )
  }
}
```

First, notice how you changed Box()'s content. You used a Row() to align an Icon() and a Text() beside one another. Second, notice how you didn't have to change how you access specific transition properties in Box()'s modifier and how you're using it for Icon() and Text(). Just like before, you used buttonBackgroundColor to access the button background or iconTintColor to access the icon tint color.

Add the following imports as well.

```
import androidx.compose.foundation.layout.Row
import androidx.compose.foundation.layout.widthIn
import androidx.compose.material.Text
import androidx.compose.ui.unit.sp
```

And that's it! This is now a complete button that will animate from one state to another. Build and run the app. You'll now see the new JoinButton in the posts.

Posts With the Completed Join Button

Click the button in any of the posts and see how it animates from one state to the other.

Join Button Animation

You see how the button's width and text change as well as the color animations in the button's background and icon.

Animating composable content

So far, you've seen how to animate the properties of your composables. In this section, you'll explore a different approach to creating animations by learning how to animate composable content.

> **Note**: At the time of writing, this animation API was in an **experimental** phase, so keep that in mind when you see `@ExperimentalAnimationApi` annotations in the code.

In this section, you'll implement a toast composable that appears when the user joins a subreddit. It will look like this:

Joined Toast

This toast will appear any time you join a new subreddit, by tapping the `JoinButton`. There are a few things you need to do, to implement such behavior, so let's start by creating the initial toast composable.

Adding JoinedToast

In **components**, create a new file named **JoinedToast.kt**. Then, add the following code to it:

```
@Composable
fun JoinedToast(visible: Boolean) {
  ToastContent()
}

@Composable
private fun ToastContent() {
  val shape = RoundedCornerShape(4.dp)
  Box(
    modifier = Modifier
      .clip(shape)
      .background(Color.White)
      .border(1.dp, Color.Black, shape)
      .height(40.dp)
      .padding(horizontal = 8.dp),
    contentAlignment = Alignment.Center
  ) {
    Row(verticalAlignment = Alignment.CenterVertically) {
      Icon(
        painter = painterResource(
          id = R.drawable.ic_planet
        ),
        contentDescription = "Subreddit Icon"
      )
      Spacer(modifier = Modifier.width(8.dp))
      Text(text = "You have joined this community!")
    }
  }
}

@Preview
@Composable
fun JoinedToastPreview() {
  JoinedToast(visible = true)
}
```

Here's what the code above does. You used a Box() to give your toast a specific background, shape, size and padding. In the Box(), you added a Row() to align an Icon(), Spacer() and Text().

For this to work, add the following imports as well:

```
import androidx.compose.foundation.background
import androidx.compose.foundation.border
import androidx.compose.foundation.layout.*
```

```
import androidx.compose.foundation.shape.RoundedCornerShape
import androidx.compose.material.Icon
import androidx.compose.material.Text
import androidx.compose.runtime.Composable
import androidx.compose.ui.Alignment
import androidx.compose.ui.Modifier
import androidx.compose.ui.draw.clip
import androidx.compose.ui.graphics.Color
import androidx.compose.ui.res.painterResource
import androidx.compose.ui.tooling.preview.Preview
import androidx.compose.ui.unit.dp
import com.raywenderlich.android.jetreddit.R
```

Build the project and check the preview panel to see your composable.

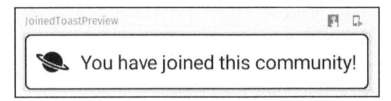

JoinedToast Composable — Preview

Awesome! Next, you'll animate the toast. :]

Animating JoinedToast

In **JoinedToast.kt**, replace the `JoinedToast()` code with the following:

```
@ExperimentalAnimationApi
@Composable
fun JoinedToast(visible: Boolean) {
  AnimatedVisibility(
      visible = visible,
      enter = slideInVertically(initialOffsetY = { +40 }) +
          fadeIn(),
      exit = slideOutVertically() + fadeOut()
  ) {
    ToastContent()
  }
}
```

Android Studio will complain if you don't add these imports as well.

```
import androidx.compose.animation.ExperimentalAnimationApi
import androidx.compose.animation.AnimatedVisibility
import androidx.compose.animation.fadeIn
import androidx.compose.animation.slideInVertically
import androidx.compose.animation.slideOutVertically
```

```
import androidx.compose.animation.fadeOut
```

As mentioned earlier, `@ExperimentalAnimationApi` is there because this is an experimental API — at least, at the time of writing.

Here, you wrapped `ToastContent()` with `AnimatedVisibility()`, which animates the appearance and disappearance of its content as the visible value changes.

This is `AnimatedVisibility()`'s signature, taken from the Jetpack Compose documentation:

```
@Composable
fun AnimatedVisibility(
    visible: Boolean,
    modifier: Modifier = Modifier,
    enter: EnterTransition = fadeIn() + expandIn(),
    exit: ExitTransition = shrinkOut() + fadeOut(),
    initiallyVisible: Boolean = visible,
    content: @Composable () -> Unit
): Unit
```

You can define different `EnterTransition` and `ExitTransition` in enter and exit for the appearance and disappearance animations. There are three types of `EnterTransition` and `ExitTransition`: **fade**, **expand/shrink** and **slide**. By using the + sign, you combine the enter and exit transitions. The combination's order doesn't matter since the transition animations start simultaneously.

Now, back to your code. You passed `visible` from `JoinedToast()` to `AnimatedVisibility()`. With that, you'll control when the animation triggers. When `visible` changes to `true`, it triggers the enter animation. Otherwise, it triggers the exit animation.

For the enter transition, you combined two transitions: `slideInVertically()` and `fadeIn()`. `slideInVertically()` slides the content vertically from a starting offset defined in `initialOffsetY` to 0. You control the direction of the slide by configuring `initialOffsetY`. A positive initial offset means the animation will slide up, whereas a negative value will slide the content down.

For the exit transition, you used `slideOutVertically()` and `fadeOut()`.

Bringing the JoinedToast home

Before you can see this animation in action, you need to add `JoinedToast()` to `HomeScreen()`. You also need to add `@ExperimentalAnimationApi` to any parent composable of `JoinedToast()`.

Start by adding `@ExperimentalAnimationApi` to `JoinedToastPreview()`:

```
@ExperimentalAnimationApi
@Preview
@Composable
fun JoinedToastPreview() {
  JoinedToast(visible = true)
}
```

Next, open **HomeScreen.kt** and update `HomeScreen()` like this:

```
@ExperimentalAnimationApi
@Composable
fun HomeScreen(viewModel: MainViewModel) {
  val posts: List<PostModel>
      by viewModel.allPosts.observeAsState(listOf())

  var isToastVisible by remember { mutableStateOf(false) }

  val onJoinClickAction: (Boolean) -> Unit = { joined ->
    isToastVisible = joined
    if (isToastVisible) {
      Timer().schedule(3000) {
        isToastVisible = false
      }
    }
  }

  Box(modifier = Modifier.fillMaxSize()) {
    LazyColumn(modifier = Modifier.background(color =
MaterialTheme.colors.secondary)) {
      items(posts) {
        if (it.type == PostType.TEXT) {
          TextPost(it, onJoinButtonClick = onJoinClickAction)
        } else {
          ImagePost(it, onJoinButtonClick = onJoinClickAction)
        }
        Spacer(modifier = Modifier.height(6.dp))
      }
    }

    Box(
      modifier = Modifier
        .align(Alignment.BottomCenter)
        .padding(bottom = 16.dp)
    ) {
      JoinedToast(visible = isToastVisible)
    }
  }
}
```

Add the following imports as well:

```
import androidx.compose.animation.ExperimentalAnimationApi
import androidx.compose.foundation.layout.Box
import androidx.compose.foundation.layout.fillMaxSize
import androidx.compose.foundation.layout.padding
import androidx.compose.ui.Alignment
import
com.raywenderlich.android.jetreddit.components.JoinedToast
import java.util.Timer
import kotlin.concurrent.schedule
```

You did a couple of things in the code above. You wrapped a LazyColumn() with a Box(), which allows you to fill the max size of the screen. You also added a second Box() and added JoinedToast() to its content. This second Box() lets you position JoinedToast() at the bottom. Then, you used remember() to define the visibility state of the toast.

Next, you defined the onJoinClickAction. Tapping any JoinButton triggers onJoinClickAction() and displays a toast. After three seconds, you hide the toast by changing isToastVisible to false.

Finally, you used onJoinClickAction as a parameter for the different posts. However, right now, the TextPost() and ImagePost() don't have an onJoinButtonClick parameter, so you'll see an error. You're going to fix that next.

Adding onJoinButtonClick to the Posts

Open **Post.kt** and replace TextPost(), ImagePost() and Post() with the following code:

```
@Composable
fun TextPost(
  post: PostModel,
  onJoinButtonClick: (Boolean) -> Unit = {}
) {
  Post(post, onJoinButtonClick) {
    TextContent(post.text)
  }
}

@Composable
fun ImagePost(
  post: PostModel,
  onJoinButtonClick: (Boolean) -> Unit = {}
) {
  Post(post, onJoinButtonClick) {
    ImageContent(post.image!!)
```

```
    }
  }

  @Composable
  fun Post(
    post: PostModel,
    onJoinButtonClick: (Boolean) -> Unit = {},
    content: @Composable () -> Unit = {}
  ) {
    Card(shape = MaterialTheme.shapes.large) {
      Column(
        modifier = Modifier.padding(
          top = 8.dp,
          bottom = 8.dp
        )
      ) {
        Header(post, onJoinButtonClick)
        Spacer(modifier = Modifier.height(4.dp))
        content.invoke()
        Spacer(modifier = Modifier.height(8.dp))
        PostActions(post)
      }
    }
  }
```

What's most important here is that you added onJoinButtonClick to the TextPost, ImagePost and Post signatures and passed it down to the Header(). Excellent work! The header already passes onJoinButtonClick to JoinButton() and handles everything, so you don't have to update those composables. However, because you're using an experimental animation API, you need to add appropriate annotations to your composables.

Adding experimental annotations

The annotation you have to add is @ExperimentalAnimationApi.

Open **JetRedditApp.kt** and add @ExperimentalAnimationApi to the following composables:

1. MainScreenContainer()

2. AppContent()

3. JetRedditApp()

You can follow Android Studio errors and use **quick actions** to easily add these imports. Otherwise, find these three functions and paste the following statement at the top of those functions: @ExperimentalAnimationApi.

Add this import as well:

```
import androidx.compose.animation.ExperimentalAnimationApi
```

Finally, open **MainActivity.kt** and add @ExperimentalAnimationApi to
onCreate(), like this:

```
@ExperimentalAnimationApi
override fun onCreate(savedInstanceState: Bundle?) {
  super.onCreate(savedInstanceState)
  setContent {
    JetRedditApp(viewModel)
  }
}
```

Don't forget to add an import for @ExperimentalAnimationApi as well:

```
import androidx.compose.animation.ExperimentalAnimationApi
```

Whew! Now, build and run the app. Click any JoinButton and observe the toast's
enter and exit animations.

Joined Toast

With that, you used three different APIs to animate your composables. Well done!

Key points

- You use `animate*AsState()` for **fire-and-forget** animations targeting **single properties** of your composables. This is very useful for animating size, color, alpha and similar simple properties.

- You use `Transition` and `updateTransition()` for **state-based** transitions.

- Use `Transitions` when you have to animate **multiple properties** of your composables, or when you have multiple states between which you can animate.

- Transitions are very good when showing content for the first time or leaving the screen, menu, option pickers and similar. They are also great when animating between multiple states when filling in forms, selecting options and pressing buttons!

- You use `AnimatedVisibility()` when you want to animate the appearance and disappearance of composable content.

- `AnimatedVisibility()` lets you combine different types of visibility animations and lets you define directions if you use predefined transition animations.

Hopefully, this was a fun ride for you. You had the chance to play with three different APIs to create some simple, yet beautiful animations. What follows is the last chapter of this book. You've come a long way indeed!

In the next chapter, you'll see how to combine the old `View` framework with Jetpack Compose and how both can coexist in the same codebase.

See you there! :]

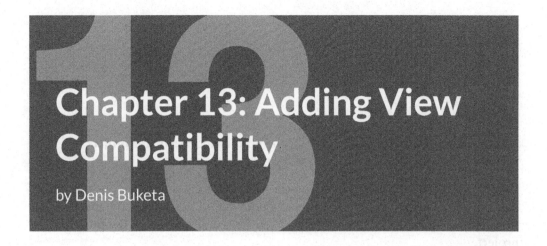

Chapter 13: Adding View Compatibility

by Denis Buketa

Congratulations on reaching the **last chapter** of this book!

So far, you've learned a lot about **Jetpack Compose**. In the book's first section, you learned about basic composables. In the second, you saw how to use Compose when building a real app. In the third section, you learned how to build a more complex UI and how to make simple but beautiful animations.

In this chapter, you'll finish your journey by learning the basic principles of **combining** Jetpack Compose and the old View framework, which can coexist in the same codebase. That knowledge will make it easier for you to gradually migrate your apps to Jetpack Compose.

Introducing the Chat screen and the Trending view

To follow along with the code examples, open this chapter's **starter project** in Android Studio and select **Open an existing project**.

Then, navigate to **13-adding-view-compatibility/projects** and select the **starter** folder as the project root. Once the project opens, let it build and sync and you're ready to go! You can see the completed project by skipping ahead to the **final project**.

Also make sure to clean the app's storage, before running the project.

For this chapter, we've added a few things to the **starter** project.

Home Screen Chat Button

These additions include a new **Chat** screen, which uses the old `View` framework. Access it by clicking the new **Chat icon** in the top bar of the **Home** screen, as you can see in the previous image.

If you tap that button, you'll open the following screen:

Chat Screen

In this chapter, you'll replace the **Start Chatting** button with a button made up of composable functions. To see the final implementation, check out **screens/ChatActivity.kt** and **res/layout/activity_chat.xml**. You'll also build a **Trending Today** component that will be the first item on the **Home** screen's list.

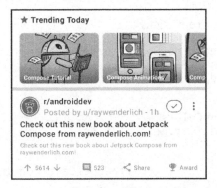

Trending View

You'll build the entire component using composables, except for one piece of functionality: **Trending topic**. This will use the View framework in **views/TrendingTopicView.kt** and **res/layout/view_trending_topic.xml**.

Next, you'll see how Jetpack Compose and the View framework work together.

Using composables with the View framework

Learning how to use composables with the old View framework will make it easier to migrate existing screens to Jetpack Compose. You'll start with small components and gradually migrate the whole screen.

Furthermore, some components are easier to make using Jetpack Compose. There's no reason *not* to use those components when the framework allows it. :]

In this section, you'll start by implementing the **Start Chatting** button using Jetpack Compose.

Implementing the Start Chatting button

Open **ChatActivity.kt** and add the following code below ChatActivity:

```
@ExperimentalMaterialApi
@Composable
private fun ComposeButton(onButtonClick: () -> Unit) {
  val buttonColors = buttonColors(
    backgroundColor = Color(0xFF006837),
    contentColor = Color.White
  )

  Button(
    onClick = onButtonClick,
    elevation = null,
    shape = RoundedCornerShape(corner = CornerSize(24.dp)),
    contentPadding = PaddingValues(
      start = 32.dp,
      end = 32.dp
    ),
    colors = buttonColors,
    modifier = Modifier.height(48.dp)
  ) {
    Text(
      text = "Start chatting".toUpperCase(Locale.US),
      fontSize = 16.sp,
      fontWeight = FontWeight.Medium
    )
  }
}

@ExperimentalMaterialApi
@Preview
@Composable
```

```
private fun ComposeButtonPreview() {
  ComposeButton { }
}
```

To break down the code, you added a root composable, `ComposeButton()`, for the button. You then exposed `onButtonClick` so it can react to clicks.

To emit the button UI, you used `Button()` from the `material` composables. You specified the background and content color with `buttonColors()` and passed in the `backgroundColor` and the `contentColor`. You also set the shape and styled the text to match the current implementation. At the time of writing, `Button()` was an experimental API so you added `ExperimentalMaterialApi`.

You also added `@Preview` to visualize how your button looks in Android Studio.

For this to work, you have to add the following imports as well:

```
import androidx.compose.foundation.layout.PaddingValues
import androidx.compose.foundation.layout.height
import androidx.compose.foundation.shape.CornerSize
import androidx.compose.foundation.shape.RoundedCornerShape
import androidx.compose.material.Button
import androidx.compose.material.ButtonDefaults.buttonColors
import androidx.compose.material.ExperimentalMaterialApi
import androidx.compose.material.Text
import androidx.compose.runtime.Composable
import androidx.compose.ui.Modifier
import androidx.compose.ui.graphics.Color
import androidx.compose.ui.text.font.FontWeight
import androidx.compose.ui.tooling.preview.Preview
import androidx.compose.ui.unit.dp
import androidx.compose.ui.unit.sp
import java.util.*
```

Build the project and check the preview panel. You'll see something like this:

ComposeButton Preview

Adding ComposeButton to ChatActivity

Next, you have to replace the old implementation with the composable button. Open
activity_chat.xml in the **layout** resource folder and replace the old
AppCompatButton with the following:

```
<androidx.compose.ui.platform.ComposeView
    android:id="@+id/composeButton"
    android:layout_width="wrap_content"
    android:layout_height="48dp"
    android:layout_marginTop="16dp"
    app:layout_constraintEnd_toEndOf="parent"
    app:layout_constraintStart_toStartOf="parent"
    app:layout_constraintTop_toBottomOf="@+id/subtitle" />
```

You also have to update ChatActivity. In **ChatActivity.kt**, replace onCreate() with
the following code:

```
@ExperimentalMaterialApi
override fun onCreate(savedInstanceState: Bundle?) {
  super.onCreate(savedInstanceState)
  binding = ActivityChatBinding.inflate(layoutInflater)
  val view = binding.root
  setContentView(view)

  binding.backButton.setOnClickListener {
    finish()
  }

  binding.composeButton.setContent {
    MaterialTheme {
      ComposeButton { showToast() }
    }
  }
}
```

Don't forget to add the following import for MaterialTheme:

```
import androidx.compose.material.MaterialTheme
```

The old button's implementation used AppCompatButton in **activity_chat.xml**. Here,
you replaced that with ComposeView, which is a View that can **host** Jetpack Compose
UI content. Compose needs a host Activity or Fragment to render UI.

setContent() supplies the **content composable function** for the view in
ChatActivity's onCreate().

ComposeView requires that the window it's attached to contains a
ViewTreeLifecycleOwner. This LifecycleOwner disposes the underlying
composition when the host lifecycle is destroyed. That allows you to attach and
detach the view repeatedly while preserving the composition.

Build and run the app. Open the Chat screen and check out your new button. The
button looks and acts the same as the old one did.

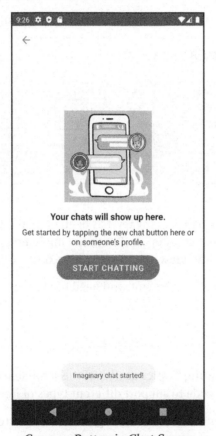

ComposeButton in Chat Screen

Great job! That was easy, wasn't it? With ComposeView, you can gradually migrate
any screen that uses the old View framework. Once you migrate the layout, you can
even remove the hosting Activity or Fragment and implement the whole screen
using just Jetpack Compose.

But the great thing is that you can mix and match the two frameworks however you
like it.

Using View with Jetpack Compose

Now, reverse the situation. Imagine that you decided to implement a screen or a component using Jetpack Compose, but for some reason — time restrictions, framework support, etc. — it would be easier to reuse a custom `View` you already implemented in that new screen. Well, Jetpack Compose allows you to do that! :]

In this section, you'll implement the component for **Trending Topics**.

Trending Topics

For this component, `TrendingTopicView` has been prepared for you. It represents one item in the scrollable list of topics. To see the implementation, check **TrendingTopicView.kt** and **view_trending_topic.xml**.

Before you implement that component, you need to make a few modifications to **HomeScreen.kt**.

Preparing the Home screen

Before you can add **Trending Topics** as part of the scrollable list in the Home screen, you need to prepare the code to support different types of items in the list.

Open **HomeScreen.kt** and add the following code at the bottom:

```
private data class HomeScreenItem(
  val type: HomeScreenItemType,
  val post: PostModel? = null
)

private enum class HomeScreenItemType {
  TRENDING,
  POST
}

private data class TrendingTopicModel(
```

```
    val text: String,
    @DrawableRes val imageRes: Int = 0
)
```

You added `HomeScreenItem`, which represents one item in the list, then defined its type with `HomeScreenItemType`. If the item's type is `POST`, the `post` parameter will contain data for the post. Otherwise, it will be `null`.

You also added `TrendingTopicModel`, which contains the data for one topic item that will be visible in the **Trending Topics** component.

To finish, add one additional import:

```
import androidx.annotation.DrawableRes
```

Adding TrendingTopic

Next, you'll create a composable to represent one topic item. Add the following code below `HomeScreen()`:

```
@Composable
private fun TrendingTopic(trendingTopic: TrendingTopicModel) {
  AndroidView({ context ->
    TrendingTopicView(context).apply {
      text = trendingTopic.text
      image = trendingTopic.imageRes
    }
  })
}

@Preview
@Composable
private fun TrendingTopicPreview() {
  TrendingTopic(trendingTopic = TrendingTopicModel(
    "Compose Animations",
    R.drawable.jetpack_compose_animations)
  )
}
```

To make Android Studio happy, add the following imports as well:

```
import androidx.compose.ui.tooling.preview.Preview
import androidx.compose.ui.viewinterop.AndroidView
import com.raywenderlich.android.jetreddit.R
import
com.raywenderlich.android.jetreddit.views.TrendingTopicView
```

Here, you added a root composable called `TrendingTopic` for one topic item. It takes `TrendingTopicModel` as an argument.

The star of the show is `AndroidView()`.

```
@Composable fun <T : View> AndroidView(
    factory: (Context) -> T,
    modifier: Modifier = Modifier,
    update: (T) -> Unit = NoOpUpdate
): Unit
```

`AndroidView()` composes an Android `View` obtained from `factory()`. The `factory` block will be called **exactly once** to obtain the `View` you need to compose. It's also **guaranteed to be invoked on the UI thread**. Therefore, in addition to creating the `factory`, the block can also perform one-off initializations and set `View`'s properties.

The app might run `update()` **multiple times** on the UI thread, as well, due to recomposition. It's the right place to set `View` properties that depend on the state. When the state changes, the block will re-execute to set the new properties. The block will also run **once**, right after `viewBlock()` completes.

In your code, you passed `trendingView` as `viewBlock()`. In `update()`, you left it as a `NoOpUpdate`, which is an empty lambda function, that doesn't update the IO.

You also added the preview composable so you can preview `TrendingTopic()` in the preview panel.

Build the project and check the preview panel and you'll see:

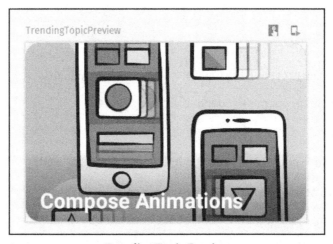

TrendingTopic Preview

Building a list of trending topics

Now that you have a composable that represents one trending topic, you'll work on a composable to represent the whole component with multiple trending topics.

Add the following code below `HomeScreen()`:

```
@Composable
private fun TrendingTopics(
  trendingTopics: List<TrendingTopicModel>,
  modifier: Modifier = Modifier
) {
  Card(
    shape = MaterialTheme.shapes.large,
    modifier = modifier
  ) {
    Column(modifier = Modifier.padding(vertical = 8.dp)) {
      // "Trending Today" heading
      Row(
        modifier = Modifier.padding(horizontal = 16.dp),
        verticalAlignment = Alignment.CenterVertically
      ) {
        Icon(
          modifier = Modifier.size(18.dp),
          imageVector = Icons.Filled.Star,
          tint = Color.Blue,
          contentDescription = "Star Icon"
        )
        Spacer(modifier = Modifier.width(4.dp))
        Text(
          text = "Trending Today",
          fontWeight = FontWeight.Bold,
          color = Color.Black
        )
      }

      Spacer(modifier = Modifier.height(8.dp))
    }
  }
}
```

This is a larger piece of code, but the structure of the components is very simple. You add a card that will hold the entire trending topic section. You add `Column()` as the root of `Card()`, as you'll have two elements ordered vertically. The first is `Row()` that holds the title and the star icon. Then second will be all the trending topic items.

Now add the last piece of code right after the last `Spacer()`, that represents the trending topic items:

```
LazyRow(
  contentPadding = PaddingValues(
    start = 16.dp,
    top = 8.dp,
    end = 16.dp
  ),
  content = {
    itemsIndexed(
      items = trendingTopics,
      itemContent = { index, trendingModel ->
        TrendingTopic(trendingModel)
        if (index != trendingTopics.lastIndex) {
          Spacer(modifier = Modifier.width(8.dp))
        }
      }
    )
  }
)
```

This code is pretty straightforward. For the trending topics content, you added `LazyRow()`. Within it, you built `TrendingTopic()` for each item in the list. You also added some padding to each item using `contentPadding`.

For this to work, you also have to add the following imports:

```
import androidx.compose.material.Card
import androidx.compose.material.Icon
import androidx.compose.material.Text
import androidx.compose.material.icons.Icons
import androidx.compose.foundation.layout.Column
import androidx.compose.foundation.layout.Row
import androidx.compose.foundation.layout.size
import androidx.compose.foundation.layout.width
import androidx.compose.foundation.layout.PaddingValues
import androidx.compose.foundation.lazy.LazyRow
import androidx.compose.foundation.lazy.itemsIndexed
import androidx.compose.material.icons.filled.Star
import androidx.compose.ui.graphics.Color
import androidx.compose.ui.text.font.FontWeight
```

Before adding the preview composable, first add the dummy data you'll use as an argument. Add the following above `HomeScreen()`:

```
private val trendingItems = listOf(
  TrendingTopicModel(
    "Compose Tutorial",
    R.drawable.jetpack_composer
  ),
  TrendingTopicModel(
    "Compose Animations",
    R.drawable.jetpack_compose_animations
  ),
  TrendingTopicModel(
    "Compose Migration",
    R.drawable.compose_migration_crop
  ),
  TrendingTopicModel(
    "DataStore Tutorial",
    R.drawable.data_storage
  ),
  TrendingTopicModel(
    "Android Animations",
    R.drawable.android_animations
  ),
  TrendingTopicModel(
    "Deep Links in Android",
    R.drawable.deeplinking
  )
)
```

This is just dummy data that represents fake trending topics. The images you used here were already prepared for you.

Now that you have the dummy data, add the preview composable above `TrendingTopicPreview()`:

```
@Preview
@Composable
private fun TrendingTopicsPreview() {
  TrendingTopics(trendingTopics = trendingItems)
}
```

Build the project and check the preview panel. You'll see this:

TrendingTopics Preview

Adding TrendingTopics to the Home screen

`TrendingTopics()` is now ready to use in the **Home** screen. Before integrating it into `HomeScreen()`, however, you have to add logic to map the trending items to `HomeScreenItems`.

In **HomeScreen.kt**, add the following code below `HomeScreen()`:

```
private fun mapHomeScreenItems(
    posts: List<PostModel>
): List<HomeScreenItem> {
  val homeScreenItems = mutableListOf<HomeScreenItem>()

  // Add Trending item
  homeScreenItems.add(
      HomeScreenItem(HomeScreenItemType.TRENDING)
  )

  // Add Post items
  posts.forEach { post ->
    homeScreenItems.add(
        HomeScreenItem(HomeScreenItemType.POST, post)
    )
  }

  return homeScreenItems
}
```

This function takes a list of `PostModels` and returns a list of `HomeScreenItems`, where the first item is of type `HomeScreenItemType.TRENDING`.

Now, add the code to invoke this method just above the Box() that defines HomeScreen()'s content:

```
fun HomeScreen(viewModel: MainViewModel) {
    ...

    // Add this line
    val homeScreenItems = mapHomeScreenItems(posts)

    Box(modifier = Modifier.fillMaxSize()) {
        LazyColumn(...)
        ...
    }
}
```

With this, you mapped the list of PostModels to a list of HomeScreenItems.

Finally, update the LazyColumn() in HomeScreen(), like this:

```
LazyColumn(
  modifier = Modifier
    .background(color = MaterialTheme.colors.secondary),
  content = {
    items(
      items = homeScreenItems,
      itemContent = { item ->
        if (item.type == HomeScreenItemType.TRENDING) {
          TrendingTopics(
            trendingTopics = trendingItems,
            modifier = Modifier.padding(
              top = 16.dp,
              bottom = 6.dp
            )
          )
        } else if (item.post != null) {
          val post = item.post
          if (post.type == PostType.TEXT) {
            TextPost(
              post = post,
              onJoinButtonClick = onJoinClickAction
            )
          } else {
            ImagePost(
              post = post,
              onJoinButtonClick = onJoinClickAction
            )
          }
          Spacer(modifier = Modifier.height(6.dp))
        }
      })
  }
)
```

Here, you added the logic that emits either `TrendingTopics()`, `TextPost()` or `ImagePost()`, depending on the `item.type` and `item.post` content.

Good job! :]

Build and run the app and check out your fancy trending topics component at the top of the Home screen.

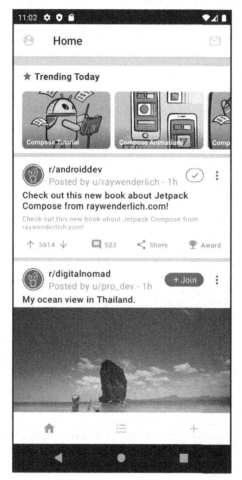

Trending Topics on the Home Screen

Excellent work! You just learned the basic principles of combining Jetpack Compose and the old `View` framework. This will allow you to migrate any app to Jetpack Compose with no trouble! :]

Key points

- Use `ComposeView` when you want to use a composable within the `View` framework. `ComposeView` is a `View` that can **host Jetpack Compose UI content**.

- Use `setContent()` to **supply the content composable function for the view**.

- `AndroidView()` lets you create a composable from the Android `View`.

- `AndroidView()` composes an Android `View` obtained from `factory()`. `factory()` will be called **exactly once** to obtain the `View` to compose. It's also **guaranteed** to be invoked on the UI thread.

- The `update()` block of the `AndroidView` can be run **multiple times (on the UI thread) due to recomposition**. It's the right place to set `View` properties that depend on state.

Where to go from here?

Congratulations, you just completed the last chapter of this book!

On this journey, you've learned many new concepts about **Jetpack Compose**. You can now implement a new app from scratch using Compose and migrate an existing app to this awesome framework.

Don't be afraid to dig more deeply into the subject. There's a lot to discover about **Jetpack Compose**. Check out the Jetpack Compose course: (https://www.raywenderlich.com/17332237-jetpack-compose) if you want to get a second example of building complex app using Compose, from the ground up.

Additionally, check out the Jetpack Compose Animations Tutorial: Getting Started article: (https://www.raywenderlich.com/13282144-jetpack-compose-animations-tutorial-getting-started), that dives even deeper into animations and shows you how to build cool custom components!

Wishing you all the best in your continued Jetpack Compose adventures!

Conclusion

Wow, we've taken a heck of a journey together! Throughout this book, you've jumped into a completely new framework and came out as an expert on Jetpack Compose. Even though it's still in development, Jetpack Compose is a powerful new UI toolkit, and after reading the book you know how to use a wide variety of tools that Compose exposes.

You learned about Compose's fundamental components and how they compare to the legacy UI toolkit in Android. Furthermore, you saw how easy it is to remember and handle the state in Compose, and how you can directly connect it to the rest of your app's architecture. Finally, you explored many options when it comes to styling your app including dark and light themes, modifiers and even Material Design and animations.

Using this knowledge will let you build beautiful apps with ease, as well as reuse your code across different projects. But it's not just that — writing UI code is *so much fun* in Jetpack Compose that you'll constantly be looking for nice new things to build, or new components to style.

However, since Jetpack Compose is still in development, there are always new versions to explore and new features to master on the horizon. It's impossible to teach everything there is to know about such an awesome framework, so we hope you'll practice it on your own projects.

If you want to explore more content about Jetpack Compose, we recommend watching our Jetpack Compose course (https://www.raywenderlich.com/17332237-jetpack-compose), which builds another cool app and explores all of these concepts using different components. Also, be sure to check out Jetpack Compose Animations Tutorial: Getting Started (https://www.raywenderlich.com/13282144-jetpack-compose-animations-tutorial-getting-started) to play around with more animations that you can build easily with Compose!

If you have any questions or comments as you work through this book, please visit our forums at http://forums.raywenderlich.com and look for the Jetpack Compose forum category.

Thank you again for purchasing this book. Your continued support is what makes the books, tutorials, videos and other things we do at raywenderlich.com possible. We truly appreciate it!

– The *Jetpack Compose by Tutorials* team

Made in the USA
Las Vegas, NV
31 August 2021